D0204933

Human Resources in
Japanese Industrial Development

Human Resources in
Japanese Industrial Development

by Solomon B. Levine and Hisashi Kawada

PRINCETON UNIVERSITY PRESS

PRINCETON, NEW JERSEY

Contents

Preface

THIS monograph deals with the process through which Japan generated human skills and talents required by modern economic activities since the beginning of Japanese industrialization more than a century ago. Because of the vast scope and complexity of the process, the authors decided to focus primarily on institutions established or utilized in major large-scale modern industries that have been leading sectors in Japan's achievement to become the second largest national economy of the world. We have examined these institutions against the background of Japan's overall economic and educational development. However, many other areas of the Japanese industrializing experience deserve treatment that we were unable to include in this study. In narrowing the scope of this work, we wished to concentrate on those large-scale industries that appear to represent the greatest departures and challenges for an agrarian society, such as Japan was in the 1870s, in developing human resources for industrialization. The reader will recognize that this is not the entire story and that a full analysis would include still other large-scale modern industries as well as agriculture and small-scale industrial and commercial sectors.

We have not gone deeply into the problems of human resource development that confront Japan at the present time. Rather, our chief concern was to present the historical context in which present-day problems have emerged. This is not to deny the importance of the latter, but it was our belief that an in-depth history of the institutions for generating industrial skills and talents is crucial to understanding the present situation.

We began this study about fifteen years ago as part of our ongoing joint work in analyzing the development of the Japanese industrial relations system in the post-World War II period. The opportunity to focus on the historical process of industrial skill generation was facilitated by assistance from the Inter-University Study of Labor Problems in Economic Development, which about that time was redesignated the Inter-University Study of Human Resources in National Development. We are most grateful for the guidance provided by the members of that project, which had embarked upon a wide variety of parallel and complementary studies in this field throughout the world. The help of the Inter-University Study permitted several collaborative research efforts for extended periods by the authors in Japan and the United States.

Similarly, we wish to express our gratitude to the Industrial Relations Exchange and Research Program conducted jointly by the Institute of Labor and Management Studies of Keio University in Tokyo and the Institute of Labor and Industrial Relations of the University of Illinois at Urbana-Champaign, under a generous grant from the Ford Foundation. The authors shared major responsibility for implementation of that program, including gathering and analyzing widely scattered materials for the present study, and in this connection are greatly indebted for the colleagueship of the late Professor Keizo Fujibayashi and Professor Bernard Karsh.

We wish particularly to thank various participants in the Keio-Illinois program for their assistance in preparing data for this work. They include Tsuneo Hasegawa, Dominick Horvath, Toshiaki Izeki, Chieko Kanno, Ryuji Komatsu, Yoshio Kunieda, Elizabeth J. Levine, Akira Matsumura, Chiyo Matsuura, Yoshihiro Mizuno, Yasumitsu Nihei, Ken Sakurai, Yoko Sano, Haruo Shimada, Kunio Shimada, Ari Uchida, and Masu Uekusa. We are especially indebted to Professor Charles A. Myers for his helpful comments on the drafts of the manuscript and his cheerful encouragement and enduring patience over the long period during which this study was in preparation. Also, we are grateful for valuable comments from Professors Frederick H. Harbison, Clark Kerr, and John T. Dunlop, as the other members of the Inter-University Study, and from Professors Haruo Shimada and Mikio Sumiya, who took time to review the manuscript. One of our greatest debts is to Catherine Ganshert, who labored over the typing and retyping of successive drafts of the study, with its enormous difficulties of Japanese names, places, and terms. In the text and footnote references to works in Japanese, we have followed the standard practices of citing names in Japanese order with surname first, italicizing Japanese terms, and using macrons to indicate long vowels except in familiar names and place names.

We dedicate this book to the memory of the late Frederick H. Harbison, whose leadership in the field of labor and human resources studies has been truly inspirational.

SOLOMON B. LEVINE

HISASHI KAWADA

April 23, 1979

Regrettably, Professor Kawada passed away while our study was being prepared for publication. It is my great privilege to have been so closely associated for more than 25 years with this wise, talented, and independent-minded individual. Professor Kawada was devoted to his many students and colleagues at home and abroad; and, with Mrs. Kawada, he spent his life promoting friendship among the peoples of this world.

S.B.L.

July 15, 1979

Human Resources in
Japanese Industrial Development

I.

Human Resources in Modern Economic Development

THIS study deals with institutions—in particular, educational and training institutions that generate the human resources required by modern economic enterprises. The study focuses on how these institutions emerged and evolved in Japan since that country began its transformation from a traditional agrarian society in the mid-nineteenth century to an advanced industrialized nation during the first half of the twentieth century. It fills a gap in the knowledge about the process by which an economically less developed country begins and sustains modern economic growth. Only in recent years has there been systematic treatment of the elements involved in such growth. Especially confounding is that part of the process whereby developing nations foster the human skills, knowledge, and abilities for launching and elaborating the new industrial undertakings.

The Japanese case is especially relevant for the insights to be gained not only because of Japan's unusually high rate of economic growth in recent years but also because Japan has been the only nation outside the Western world that succeeded in achieving a steady self-sustaining transformation beginning at least a hundred years ago.[1] Japan's modern economic development over

---

[1] Much has been written on various aspects of Japan's experience with economic growth. See in English the following studies: Marius B. Jansen, ed., *Changing Japanese Attitudes toward Modernization*, 1965; William W. Lockwood, ed., *The State and Economic Enterprise in Japan*, 1965; R. P. Dore, ed., *Aspects of Social Change in Modern Japan*, 1967; Robert B. Ward, ed., *Political Development in Modern Japan*, 1968; Donald Shively, ed., *Tradition and*

this period provides one of the most dramatic examples of human resource generation demanded by the process.

In general, the modernization of a "backward" economy requires increased proliferation, employment, and organization of previously unlearned and often highly sophisticated manual and mental skills throughout a developing nation's population in order to operate complex technologies and to staff large-scale enterprises efficiently. Acquisition of such skills depends upon a "strategy," conscious or unplanned, for tapping, changing, and enlarging the capacities of the nation's people and imparting to growing numbers of the population those types of knowledge of which there is little or no awareness or use within the society in the pre-modern era. Skill, capacity, and applied knowledge are the outputs sought in this strategy. Indeed, as others have pointed out:

> In the final analysis, the wealth of a country is based upon its power to develop and effectively utilize the innate capacities of its people. The economic development of nations, therefore, is ultimately the result of human effort. It takes skilled human agents to discover and exploit natural resources, to mobilize capital, to develop technology, to produce goods, to carry on trade, and to structure effective organizations for these purposes. Indeed, if a country is unable to develop its human resources, it cannot build anything else, whether it be a modern political system, a sense of national unity, or a prosperous country.[2]

Modernization in Japanese Culture, 1971 (all Princeton: Princeton University Press). See, also, Kazushi Ohkawa and Henry Rosovsky, *Japanese Economic Growth: Trend Acceleration in the Twentieth Century* (Palo Alto: Stanford University Press, 1971); and Hugh Patrick, ed., with the assistance of Larry Meissner, *Japanese Industrialization and Its Social Consequences* (Berkeley: University of California Press, 1976).

[2] Frederick H. Harbison and Charles A. Myers, *Manpower and Education: Country Studies in Economic Development* (New York: McGraw-Hill Book Co., 1965), p. ix. See also Frederick H. Harbison, *Human Resources as the Wealth of Nations* (New York: Oxford University Press, 1973).

Ample evidence now exists demonstrating the economic contribution of formally organized schooling (presumably transmitted into new capacities, knowledge, and skills that are put to use in modern productive processes) to the growth of economies.[3] Although it has proved difficult to measure precisely this contribution, either to the individual or society at large, there is little doubt of its eventual importance as a major source of increased national income in virtually every country that has developed a modern economy. For example, in the last three or four decades in the United States, additional investment in formal education alone is believed to have accounted for at least one-fifth of the rise in national income during that period. Over roughly the same time span, the contribution in Japan is calculated at about 25 percent.[4] If one could take account also of all the nonformal and informal ways in which new knowledge and skills are acquired and utilized and estimate their economic costs and benefits to society, in all likelihood the contribution of such human resource development would be even greater.

The relationship between education and economic growth no doubt deserves careful measurement. While education alone, even though necessary, is probably not a sufficient condition for growth, it may be "a more realistic and reliable indicator of modernization or development than any other single measurement."[5] Education, whether formal or not, certainly warrants as careful

[3] See, for example, Theodore W. Schultz, *The Economic Value of Education* (New York: Columbia University Press, 1963), especially its "Selected Bibliography," pp. 71-89; and Gary S. Becker, *Human Capital: A Theoretical and Empirical Analysis, with Special Reference to Education*, 2nd ed. (New York: Columbia University Press, 1975). For a critical review of the evidence, see Mark Blaug, "The Empirical Status of Human Capital Theory: A Slightly Jaundiced Survey," *The Journal of Economic Literature*, Vol. XIV, No. 3, September 1976, pp. 827-856.

[4] Ministry of Education, Government of Japan, *Japan's Growth and Education* (Tokyo, July 1963), pp. 143-148.

[5] Frederick Harbison and Charles A. Myers, *Education, Manpower, and Economic Growth: Strategies of Human Resource Development* (New York: McGraw-Hill Book Co., 1964), p. 14.

scrutiny as that given to material capital formation, population and labor supply, physical resources, structural change in the economy, industrial organization, international trade, monetary and fiscal management, consumption and savings, mobility of labor and capital, utilization of modern science and technology, and similar aspects that have been customarily dealt with in analyzing the processes of modern economic growth. This is not to claim that the sole function of educational and training institutions—in Japan or elsewhere—has been economic; education undoubtedly makes its contribution in the spheres of cultural, social, and political development as well.

"Strategy" in Human Resource Development

The process of modern economic development has required in all known cases the lifting of a nation's stocks of human resources from "lower" to "higher" levels as measured by the amount and types of education and training obtained by the population. What is not clearly understood is how an industrializing nation moves from the lower to higher levels. In general, however, a strategy usually involves a sequence of choices, although often difficult to identify and unconsciously determined. The choices in human resource development may be categorized among a number of dimensions: levels of education, duration of each level, quantities of enrollment at each level, quality of instruction and learning content, stress on subject matter (science, engineering, law, social sciences, arts, humanities, professional, technical, etc.), formal, nonformal, and informal programs, public and private auspices, rewards and penalties for obtaining schooling and applying learning and skills, and so forth.[6] Such an array of dimensions permits a wide variety of choices in the course of economic modernization; that is, strategies need not be uniform for all countries. Moreover, any given strategy adopted by a country at one

[6] *Ibid.*, pp. 173-174.

time may be altered over time. What is not known with any degree of certainty is whether modern economic growth is compatible with just a few or a much larger number of strategic approaches.

In our view, to focus on the choices made for human resource strategy requires more than a quantitative analysis of the enrollments in, expenditures on, and other measures of the size and output of the various types of education and schooling that come into existence in the process of modern economic growth.[7] It also calls for examining the nature of educational and training institutions—their objectives, organization, administration, and relationships to one another. Study of human resource strategy thus embraces dimensions that are best understood by probing the history of the institutions that are created and evolve. This study, therefore, emphasizes the qualitative rather than quantitative aspects from the historical point of view of determining how educational and training institutions became established and underwent change during the 100 years of Japan's industrialization.

Japan's Human Resource Strategy: Universal or Unique?

Recent studies have begun to clarify the historical development of formal education in the emergence of industrialized Japan.[8] As in other economically advanced nations, Japan's formal

---

[7] This is not to imply that we already know all that is to be quantitatively measured about human resources. See, especially, Frederick H. Harbison, Joan Maruhnic, and Jane Resnick, *Quantitative Analyses of Modernization and Development* (Princeton: Princeton University, Industrial Relations Section, 1970); and Charles N. Myers, *Education and National Development in Mexico* (Princeton: Princeton University, Industrial Relations Section, 1965), which analyzes regional differences in human resource development within one country rather than focusing on the national aggregate.

[8] For recent English language studies, see Ronald P. Dore, *Education in Tokugawa Japan* (Berkeley: University of California Press, 1965); Herbert Passin, *Society and Education in Japan* (New York: Columbia University, 1965); Ronald S. Anderson, *Japan: Three Epochs of Modern Education* (Washington, D.C.:

educational institutions expanded enormously and underwent a highly complex elaboration. By the early part of the present century, when Japan joined the ranks of the great world powers (at least in a military sense), the Japanese government had structured a formal school system that, except for subsequent expansion, remained essentially intact for the next four to five decades. Obviously, these institutions became a principal means for channeling labor force entrants toward new arrays of skills and talents required for the constantly changing occupations and functions in the long-run expansion and industrialization of the Japanese economy.

Far less explored in the Japanese case, or for that matter the case of most countries, is the part that nonformal and informal education and training institutions played in Japan's industrialization. As distinguished from formal education, nonformal and informal education are systems of instruction and learning that are established outside state-supported or officially recognized conventional schools. Nonformal programs are usually organized, while informal education is not. For example, there is a widespread impression that Japan utilized to an unusual degree a wide array of training-within-industry programs outside the formal school system for generating skills and talents for modern industry. Our study attempts to trace the evolution of such programs and to assess their role in human resource development alongside the formal educational establishment.

In taking account of formal, informal, and nonformal institutions, the Japanese experience of human resource development may be especially germane to present-day developing nations that are seeking a "model" of human resource strategy drawn from non-Western experience. Despite the firm hold of a distinc-

U.S. Department of Health, Education and Welfare, 1959), Bulletin 1959, No. 11; and Japanese National Commission for Unesco, *The Role of Education in the Social and Economic Development of Japan* (Tokyo, Japan: Ministry of Education, 1966); and Toshiomi Kaigo, *Japanese Education: Its Past and Present* (Tokyo: Kokusai Bunka Shinkōkai, 1968).

tive Eastern culture and feudalistic traditions (or perhaps in part because of them), Japan took less than fifty years to emerge as a predominantly industrial society, the first outside the West.[9] Except for the severe interruption caused by the events of World War II and its immediate aftermath, Japanese industrialization grew with increasing tempo and scope.[10] From the mid-1950s, Japan's rate of economic growth was one of the highest and most sustained in the history of nations, averaging until the 1970s close to a 10 percent gain per year in real national income. From 1954 to 1964 alone, the decade following the restoration of the Japanese economy to its prewar levels, total production per capita tripled, manufacturing output almost quadrupled, and real consumption per family grew about 50 percent.[11] Also, in this period, the agricultural labor force dropped from nearly one-half the total to barely one-fifth. These trends continued into the 1970s when, following a series of domestic and international difficulties, Japan's economic growth markedly slowed.

In terms of human resource strategy, the rapid transformation of the Japanese economy remains largely unexplained. It is known that, despite economic imbalances,[12] there has been

[9] Rosovsky identifies Japan's transition to modern economic growth as taking place between 1868 and 1885. See Henry Rosovsky, ed., *Industrialization in Two Systems* (New York: John Wiley and Sons, Inc., 1966), pp. 91-139.

[10] It is believed that Japan's average annual long-run rate of economic growth from 1868 to World War II was substantial—about 3 percent a year—and among the highest in the world in that period. Over these decades, moreover, the long-run rate tended to accelerate. See Ohkawa and Rosovsky (1971). As discussed in Chapter III, the growth rates estimated for the earlier decades have been seriously questioned as too large on the grounds that Japan "took off" from higher levels than originally assumed. See Lockwood (1965), Chapters 2, 6, and 8. If this is so, then the contribution of education to the growth in GNP may also have been less than believed for the early years of modern economic development, and may have only "paid off" later. For some additional doubts on this point, see Koji Taira, "Education and Literacy in Meiji Japan: An Introduction," *Explorations in Economic History*, Vol. 8, No. 4, July 1971, pp. 371-394.

[11] Lockwood (1965), p. 449.

[12] Japan's ranking as an "advanced" industrial nation is correct only in certain senses, such as total gross national product, degree of industrialization, rate of

remarkable evenness in increases of formal educational levels throughout Japan's growing population over the decades. Six years of primary schooling became virtually universal by the early 1900s. Close to 100-percent literacy was achieved in the 1920s. The spread of formal education undoubtedly created an ever-enlarging pool of potential talents to fill increasing numbers of jobs for industrial policy makers, managers, administrators, engineers, scientists, technicians, teachers, craftsmen, and other functionaries skilled in the operation of advanced techniques and technologies.[13] Indeed, as will be seen in Chapters II to IV, with the rapid expansion of formal schooling relatively early in the process of modern economic development, Japan seemingly became "overendowed" with educated human resources compared to other industrialized countries at similar developmental stages.

However, it seems paradoxical that, although there was an early rise in Japan of large-scale and technologically advanced enterprises (especially with the formation of government-owned corporations and private *zaibatsu* complexes) that required high skill levels and sophisticated divisions of labor, at the same time there was a proliferation of small, family-centered shops and residential factories that depended upon comparatively little capital but

---

urbanization, etc.; it has not fallen fully into this category by still other measures of economic development. See Leon Hollerman, *Japan's Dependence on the World Economy* (Princeton: Princeton University Press, 1967), Chapter 1.

[13] In Japan's white-collar employment, for example, nonmanual employees accounted for probably no more than 10 percent of the nonfarm labor force in the 1920s. By the end of World War II, the proportion had grown to almost one-fourth and in the mid-1970s was more than one-third. Since the 1920s, white-collar employment has been increasing at twice the rate of blue-collar. From 1930 to 1955, when the Japanese labor force was expanding by about one-third, the number of managers and professionals each doubled, civil servants tripled, and engineers, technicians, and clerical workers as a group quadrupled. See Solomon B. Levine, "Unionization of White-Collar Employees in Japan," in Adolf Sturmthal, ed., *White Collar Trade Unions* (Urbana, Illinois: University of Illinois Press, 1966), pp. 216-222; and Shun'ichiro Umetani, "Prospects for Japan's Labor Market from 1975 to 1985," *Japan Labor Bulletin*, Vol. 15, No. 1, January 1976, pp. 4-8.

large amounts of low-skilled labor. (Until recently, in fact, the latter persistently absorbed a majority of the nonagricultural labor force.)[14] While this "dualism" probably meant that even the less productive sectors benefited from increasingly educated work forces, on the other hand the Japanese labor force as a whole appears to have been "underutilized" in terms of its potential skill development capacity given the rise in educational levels.

We do not necessarily accept that contention. Rather, our hypothesis is that education, training, and allocation of human resources in the process of modern economic growth constitute a highly complex set of dynamic arrangements. These reflect a variety of political, social, cultural, technological, and economic influences that make it unlikely that education and skill at any given time will closely match economic achievement. Moreover, there is no necessarily close correlation between formal educational levels and skill arrays in the modern economy. Between the schools and jobs and occupations is likely to be a set of screening and training institutions, mostly informal or nonformal, which allocate labor force entrants and reentrants among the

[14] Although this "dualistic" structure long characterized the Japanese economy, in recent years there has been an acceleration of the transfer of human resources from the less to more modernized sectors of the industrial economy, so that the dualism appears to be in the process of dissolution, if not already dissolved. From 1956 to 1975, as the total labor force grew from about 43 to 53 million, or almost 26 percent, the total nonfarm labor force rose from 27 to 46 million, or more than 70 percent. From 1957 to 1972 alone the number of employees in private nonfarm enterprises each with 100 or more employees increased from 4.73 million to more than 10.9 million; those in private nonfarm enterprises each with 30 to 99 employees rose from about 2.77 to over 7.23 million; and those in private nonfarm firms each with fewer than 30 employees increased from about 8.39 to close to 12.50 million. The tertiary or service sector, which abounds with small shops and individuals on their own account, constituted nearly 35 percent of the total labor force in 1955 and more than 50 percent in 1975. See the Japan Institute of Labour, *Japan Labour Statistics* (Tokyo: The Japan Institute of Labour, 1974); Umetani (1976), p. 6; and *Japan Labor Bulletin*, Vol. 17, No. 5, May 1978, p. 5.

work positions in existence or becoming available. Labor market arrangements are not likely to be simple devices for matching supply and demand in general, but rather highly intricate labyrinths that in themselves condition particular supplies and particular demands. In examining labor market institutions that evolved in the course of Japan's industrialization, this study depicts the particular combination of formal, nonformal, and informal education and training of the work forces that came to man modern Japanese enterprises.

Japan's long-run strategy of developing human resources for economic modernization may indeed have tended to "overendow" potential skills, at least in certain sectors. On the basis of formal education alone, however, we believe that this question cannot be answered in quantitative terms alone. One has to probe much further into the whole array of training and educational institutions to approximate a conclusion in this respect.

Even then, examination of the experience of one country such as Japan with the process of human resource development raises the question of whether that country devised an entirely unique approach, which is thus not amenable to cross-national transfer. Obviously, a study of a single nation does not permit systematic comparisons to determine feasibility of transfer. However, a "country study" proceeds at least with certain points of comparison in mind, inferred from findings about other nations individually or taken together. For this purpose, our principal reference point is the general analysis provided by Harbison and Myers summarizing the relationships among manpower, education, and economic growth for 75 countries.[15] Drawing from their comparative data, Harbison and Myers suggest that there is a growing commonality among nations in terms of strategies of human re-

[15] Harbison and Myers, *Education, Manpower, and Economic Growth*. The measures used originally in this study were subsequently revised and refined in Harbison, Maruhnic, and Resnick (1970). For our purposes here, however, the original measures are adequate.

source development in rising from "lower" to "higher" levels of economic development. For example, all categories of formal schooling—primary, secondary, and tertiary—appear to expand their enrollment ratios for the age populations they are intended to serve; financial support of formal education as a percentage of national income steadily grows—at least up to a point; and emphases in secondary school curricula, in nonformal and informal training, and among fields of higher education increasingly shift toward science, engineering, technical, and other professional or subprofessional subject matter. These do not just happen, it is contended, but are the result of deliberate choices made by public and/or private leadership in the society through conscious investment decisions and purposeful manipulation of incentives and rewards.

On the other hand, as Harbison and Myers themselves recognize, it is also clear that, despite such universal tendencies, industrializing nations at the same general level of economic development vary widely not only in the proportion of stocks and rate of flows of the various categories of human resources but also in the kinds of institutional arrangements built to motivate, and regulate human resource development. While moving in the same direction, the enrollment ratios at the various school levels, the relative reliance upon prework and at-work training programs, the emphases upon fields of study and subject matter content, and the reward structures and incentive systems actually appear to display a considerable range of differences from country to country even with similar levels of economic achievement.[16]

These observations suggest that, while there may be a degree of crossnational commonality in the strategy of human resource

[16] It is recognized that these differences may arise in part from varying endowments in natural resources, supplies of capital, trade opportunities, and the like. However, such factors may be considered to decrease in importance as economic development advances.

development, it is likely to pertain only to a limited number of general tendencies. Behind them, we suspect, lies a host of particularistic variations, and it may only be happenstance that one country's strategy resembles another in detail and, then, perhaps only for a given period of time. One could argue that, precisely because there are always varying economic, political, cultural, and technological conditions, significant differences among nations will abound in the "infrastructure" of overall strategies that seem generally alike. Depending upon the scope and depth of the analysis one pursues, the conclusions regarding a given country could stress either the similar or the unique.

This problem of "universalism" versus "particularism" raises fundamental conceptual questions for social and economic processes, including the use of strategic models of human resource development. For human resources, these are likely to be related to whether a nation's initial manpower development strategy tends to persist over time, whether disparities in human resources emerge and continue within the nation, and whether the nation's value system especially with respect to education is more or less affected by growing industrialization. It is useful to touch upon these matters briefly here, for the conclusions of this study will return to them.

The initial strategy for human resource development in all likelihood will vary according to the type of elite leadership that emerges to initiate a nation's drive for industrialization. This strategy, however, may become strongly institutionalized and inflexible as vested political, ideological, and economic interests in the society gain power. If there is an early congealing of a particularized strategy, and yet human resources continue to grow and diversify, it would cast doubt on the proposition that industrialization induces common tendencies everywhere and, in light of the internal conditions of newly developing countries, upon the transferability of manpower strategy from one nation to another.

Similarly, within a modernizing nation, patterns of strategy may be multiple and disparate, especially if modern and pre-modern sectors co-exist in its economy. Persistent dualistic economic structures are common among developing nations that embark upon rapid economic growth and industrialization. Therefore, it is likely that among them disparities of human resource development—by economic sector or by geographical region—will also emerge. The implication is that the "balance" among education and training institutions developed for one segment of the society may not be fitting for others. For such a nation, it may be more realistic to think in terms of sets of strategies than of a single strategy. If this is the case, it would compound the problem of devising a universal model of manpower development.

Finally, considerable controversy exists over the question of value changes in a society as the result of economic growth and industrialization. A major hypothesis is that, if industrialization is to be carried forward at all, a nation must increasingly value science and technology in common with other advancing societies and abandon the particularistic values of premodern culture. This "logic of industrialism," it is alleged, stresses the dynamic and leads increasingly to the diversification, versatility, flexibility, and mobility of skills and functions.[17] By implication, the "imperatives" of industrialization would also make strategies of

[17] For an elaboration of this thesis, see Clark Kerr, John T. Dunlop, Frederick H. Harbison, and Charles A. Myers, *Industrialism and Industrial Man: The Problems of Labor and Management in Economic Growth* (Cambridge: Harvard University Press, 1960); and by the same authors, "Postscript to 'Industrialism and Industrial Man,'" *International Labor Relations Review*, Vol. 103, No. 6, 1971, pp. 519-540. The same authors summarize their central themes and insights, as modified by some 20 years of testing and reevaluation, in their *Industrialism and Industrial Man Reconsidered: Some Perspectives on a Study over Two Decades of the Problem of Labor and Management in Economic Growth*, Final Report of the Inter-University Study of Labor Problems in Economic Development (Princeton, New Jersey; 1975). In this, they recognize a stronger role for diversity among industrializing nations than originally implied.

human resource development among modernizing nations more and more alike because the value systems underlying them become virtually identical.

Whether the "logic of industrialism" is in fact so, however, awaits further empirical testing. For example, it can be observed that, as industrial technologies and processes become increasingly well-known, they cross national boundaries, presumably carrying with them required patterns of education, training, and skills. But it does not necessarily follow that foreign patterns of human resource strategy will be "internalized" in all respects by "importing" nations. The extent to which this happens would depend at least upon how selective the industrial importation is, whether it is modified, and how complex a technology is involved. These, in turn, would be affected by the level of industrial development already achieved in the world as a whole when the importation takes place. If the available technology at a given stage of world history is relatively simple and limited, it probably accommodates readily to the social structures, political institutions, cultural values, and economic potentials that the importing nation develops in response to its own particular circumstances and heritage.

It is thus possible to conceive that, rather than a single value system becoming common to industrializing nations, there will be different "mixes" of modern and premodern values all of which are compatible with economic growth and industrial modernization over long periods of time. Value "mixes," moreover, may move within a fairly wide range, so that, if value changes occur, they are likely to occur at different rates and in different directions from one industrializing setting to another.[18] Such ranges of value "mixes" would suggest that policy makers in developing countries have wider choices for their strategies of human resource development and may still achieve the goal of

[18] See Solomon B. Levine, "Our Future Industrial Society: A Global Vision," *Industrial and Labor Relations Review*, Vol. 14, No. 4, July 1961, pp. 548-555.

modern economic growth than the "logic of industrialism" implies. At least this appears to have been likely in the case of Japanese industrialization.

In view of the possible range for human resource strategy, this study consciously emphasizes the seemingly "unique" and particular in the Japanese historical experience. Further, it attempts to explore what led to the "unique" choices Japan made in terms of its own set of economic, social, political, and technological conditions at successive stages of economic development. Stressing the particulars, however, does not imply that universal elements were wholly absent in the Japanese strategy of human resource development, at least no more than in other socioeconomic affairs. We believe, nonetheless, that before such universals are finally determined, the alleged particularisms first require close examination.

This admitted bias, we contend, has useful implications for policy making purposes, for it may well behoove a developing nation to give careful attention to the variations in detail of strategy, including the reasons for them, in seeking guides for its own human resource development. Failure to do so could lead to social, political, and economic consequences hardly intended, and perhaps undesirable, in the attempt to solve the nation's human resource problems. At the most general level, certainly these differences and their consequences for a society are readily apparent in the contrasting approaches to economic development of the decentralized market-oriented countries and the centrally planned states.

Methodological Approach

To depict variety and particularism in Japan's strategy of human resource development, we have gone beyond an analytical study confined to the national level as a whole. Rather, our method of analysis was to pry beneath trends in national averages and to focus specifically upon the history of ten industries (and some of their industrial enterprises) that appear to have been especially critical for and central to Japan's drive for modern industrialization. The industries selected for close historical examination are key components of Japan's modern economy. They include shipbuilding, steelmaking, railways, telecommunications, banking, mining, textile manufacturing, electrical equipment, heavy machinery, and chemicals. Data for each industry were derived from historical accounts and company case studies previously undertaken by others, mainly Japanese scholars. In these historical reviews, covered in Chapters V to VIII, our emphasis is on the generation of industrial skills in the pre-World War II era, during the emergence of these industries as major sectors of Japan's modern economy. We assume that patterns of human resource development were largely shaped during that period, and, while significant changes have occurred in the past thirty years, as we note, the prewar experience largely set the institutional framework for skill generation and allocation in the postwar decades.

If Japan's manpower strategy has had variegated and particularistic features, we expected to find them amply represented in the ten industries examined—although many other additional cases, industrial and nonindustrial, no doubt could have been fruitfully studied.[19] Inspection of Japan's recent history clearly indicates that major innovative efforts in manpower development were undertaken in industries such as those chosen. For each of the ten industries a common set of questions was initially posed:

1. What types of institutions emerged specifically to develop needed skills and talents? Did the types change over time? What accounted for these changes? To what extent was there reliance

[19] Unfortunately, there are only scattered data and almost no systematic and comprehensive studies available regarding human skills development in Japan's agricultural and small industrial sectors. This is a major gap that should be filled in order to obtain a fuller evaluation of Japanese manpower strategy than we present in this volume.

upon training by foreign experts? Did any of this take place abroad?

2. What sources of labor supply were drawn upon for skills and training? To what extent were recruits channeled through formal education, self-development, nonformal and informal training, and within and outside industry programs? Did these sources and channels shift as industrialization grew? If they did, why did the changes take place?

3. What was the nature of the education and training for each skill category? Was the educational content broad and general or narrow and specific? Was it short or long-term, ad hoc or continual? Was it based upon imported or indigenous technology? Were changes made in the content, and when and why did they occur?

4. What were the motivating forces for attracting and holding work forces in the various skill categories? What rewards and incentives were provided? Was the reward and incentive system altered? To what extent were labor market mechanisms relied upon for allocating skills?

In interpreting the data to answer as many of these questions as we could, we also sought clues to (1) where and by whom the pertinent decisions were made; (2) whether such decisions were made and implemented in response to changes in the political, social, economic, and technological environment; and (3) how the decisions themselves affected the choices of manpower strategy in other economic sectors, especially small and medium-size industry and agriculture. By tracing the decisions for each of the key industries over time and comparing them from one industry to another, we attempted basically (1) to identify and explain those particularistic features in Japan's overall strategy for human resource development which seemed to become entrenched and widespread during the 100-year period, and (2) to point up any significant changes in overall strategy as Japan progressed from lower to higher levels of industrialization.

Because a high level of industrialization was not accomplished by Japan in one fell swoop, we further divided our analysis of the ten modern industries into roughly two groups: those established virtually at the outset of the modern period to launch the drive for modernization, and those developed at later stages to carry industrialization to further heights. The division of the industries into "early" and "late" categories was prompted by the proposition that in the initial phases of modern industrialism a nation's long-run strategy of human resource development may be largely determined for the succeeding periods. By comparing industries that arose at the different times, we wished to determine whether such a "congealing" of strategy took place and whether the range of strategy choices actually narrowed over time. Also, by comparing the experiences of the most modern industries with the nation as a whole, we attempted to ascertain the degree to which disparities between the modern and nonmodern sectors existed and whether they lessened, remained the same, or increased over time.

Lastly, our examination of the ten modern industries had the intention of gauging the extent to which Japan's value system with respect to education and training changed as industrialization progressed. If such changes occurred, we would expect to see them most fully reflected in the institutions chosen for attracting, holding, and transferring human resources required by the modern industries. By comparing these to the premodern society, we could begin to impute the nature of value changes that have come to permeate the entire nation and to ascertain if a value "mix" has persisted or modified.[20] We especially looked for evidence that technology carried its own universal imperatives for human resource development without regard for cultural accommodation. We suspected that, if Japan showed significant persistencies in utilizing particularistic strategies for human re-

[20] On the question of the exploitation of Japan's traditional value system to further Japanese industrialization, see Ichirō Nakayama, *Industrialization of Japan* (Tokyo: The Center for East Asian Cultural Studies, 1963).

source development at the industrial level, even though under-going increasing industrialization, this would indicate that the "logic of industrialism" as strictly hypothesized requires modification and refinement—at least in any given national case.

Organization of the Study

The chapters that follow in effect fall into two parts. Chapters II to IV provide the overall historical and statistical review of Japan's economic and human resource development, starting from the premodern period and extending to the present. In order to furnish a set of benchmarks for the successive periods of Japanese human resource development, the review begins with an analysis of the phases of the modern economic growth of Japan. It then describes the emergence and development of Japan's modern educational system and presents some statistical measurements of Japan's human resource development at the national level in comparison to the indices developed by Harbison and Myers in their study of 75 nations. As a transition to the industry-level studies, Chapter IV focuses on the general development of vocational training institutions, inside and outside modern industry, for industrial work.

The second part of the study traces human resource developments for each of the selected modern industries identified with the initial and later phases of Japan's industrialization: shipbuilding and steel; railways and telecommunications; and banking, mining, and textiles; electrical and heavy machinery and chemicals.

A concluding chapter interprets the major historical trends for the nation as a whole and the ten industries with regard to Japan's overall human resource strategy. It then develops implications of the Japanese "model" for present-day developing countries, and ends with a discussion of Japan's own prospects for future human resource development.

II.

Formal Education in the Development of Japan's Modern Economy

ALTHOUGH the relationship between a nation's modern economic growth and its formal education system is not precisely understood, there is little question that they go hand in hand and that one paves the way for the other. The purpose of this chapter is to trace the critical points of this relationship during the course of Japan's economic advance and industrialization that began more than a century ago.[1] While it is not possible here to detail

[1] Unless otherwise noted, material in this chapter is based primarily on the following English-language sources: William W. Lockwood, *The Economic Development of Japan: Growth and Structural Change, 1868-1939* (Princeton: Princeton University Press, 1954); William W. Lockwood, ed., *The State and Economic Enterprise in Modern Japan* (Princeton: Princeton University Press, 1965); G. C. Allen, *A Short Economic History of Japan*, rev. ed. (London: 1963); Kazushi Ohkawa and Henry Rosovsky, *Japanese Economic Growth: Trend Acceleration in the Twentieth Century* (Stanford: Stanford University Press, 1973); John W. Hall and Richard K. Beardsley, *Twelve Doors to Japan* (New York: McGraw-Hill Book Company, 1965); Chapters 9 and 12; Mikio Sumiya, *Social Impact of Industrialization in Japan* (Tokyo: Japanese National Committee for Unesco, 1963); John W. Hall and Marius B. Jansen, eds., *Studies in the Institutional History of Early Modern Japan* (Princeton: Princeton University Press, 1968), especially Chapter 17; Ronald P. Dore, *Education in Tokugawa Japan* (Berkeley, California; University of California Press, 1965); Herbert Passin, *Education and Society in Japan* (New York: Teachers College, Columbia University, 1965); Ronald S. Anderson, *Japan: Three Epochs of Modern Education* (Washington, D.C.: U.S. Department of Health, Education and Welfare, 1959); Japanese National Commission for Unesco, *The Role of Education in the Social and Economic Development of Japan* (Tokyo: Japan Ministry of Education, 1966); Organization for Economic Co-operation and Development, *Educational Policy and Planning: Japan* (Paris: OECD, 1973); and Donald H. Shively, ed., *Tradition and Modernization in Japanese Culture* (Princeton: Princeton University Press, 1971), especially Chapter II.

either the process of Japan's economic development or the evolution of the Japanese formal education system, enough is known about the principal trends of each to point up that (1) formal educational institutions were already well-established prior to modern economic growth, and (2) once the economic growth process began and unfolded, formal education went through a series of structural elaboration as well as expansion. This background provides historical context for the quantitative analysis, presented in Chapter III, of the national "output" of educated human resources since 1868.

Phases of Japan's Economic Growth

Japan's "success" in reaching an advanced stage of economic development is the object not only of wide admiration but also of keen scholarly interest. One hundred years ago, the Japanese economy probably stood at a level, in terms of income per capita, not much different from many of the present-day developing nations. By some measurements Japan is now the second most advanced national economy of the world. Among the twenty or so major countries that today are predominantly industrial societies, the emergence of Japan from "backward" agrarianism to modern industrialization was based on one of the most rapid, sustained, and accelerating rates of long-term economic growth. As a result, by 1960 per capita income in real terms was of an order almost ten times higher than in 1880. Since 1960 it has increased at least three times. In the process, the nonagricultural sector of the population grew from 25 to close to 90 percent of the total in this period.

In recent years a scholarly focus upon the processes of economic development has begun to clarify why Japan succeeded in this accomplishment. No longer is it tenable to conclude that the Meiji Restoration signaled a reversal of trends and characteristics that had blocked Japan's modernization. Rather, there is considerable evidence that political, social, and economic conditions

that had been unfolding long before 1868 were highly congenial
for modern growth. Japan's "preconditioning" may be traced
back to at least the mid-eighteenth century, and includes, as we
shall discuss, the spread and upgrading of education itself. To be
sure, the economic advance was hardly dramatic until after the
Tokugawa regime had been replaced, and even then only by the
1880s at the earliest did it appear possible that modern growth
and industrialization would continue without faltering.

Taking a long-run view of the process, Ohkawa and Rosovsky
have depicted Japan's economic modernization by dividing the
past 140 years after 1830 into three major periods.[2] In their
analysis, a "preparatory" era of a half-century obtained from approximately the mid-1830s to 1885, during which the political
apparatus was transformed, modern manufacturing and international trade were initiated, literacy widely increased, and innovations based on Western science and technology markedly spread.
There followed a twenty-year period (1885-1905) during which
Japan initiated a "forced march" into industrialization by deliberately manipulating agricultural surpluses to support industrial
investments, stabilizing (and "sanctifying") new political and
economic institutions, and entering the world scene as a major
military power. From 1905 almost to the present, Ohkawa and
Rosovsky conclude, Japanese economic modernization has been
in a third period, one of self-sustained accelerating growth, although accompanied by only a gradual and agonizingly slow
eradication of a dual economic structure left in the wake of the
rapid change-over from a technologically backward agrarianism.
Some analysts see a fourth period, which Lockwood has labeled
Japan's "New Capitalism," commencing about 1952, when the
Japanese economy, having recovered from the disruption and
destruction of World War II, entered its most rapid and continuing growth experience. After 1960 especially, structural change

[2] See Ohkawa and Rosovsky, "A Century of Japanese Growth," in Lockwood,
State and Economic Enterprise, pp. 47-92.

in the economy has been notable, as seen for example in a sharp decline in the absolute size of the agricultural labor force and the growing preponderance of heavy and chemical industries.

For the purpose of tracing the development of education as related to human resource strategy, it is useful to refine the Ohkawa-Rosovsky and Lockwood periodizations to take account of sets of political decisions that have significantly affected Japan's educational structure. Six such periods are discernible. As in the Ohkawa-Rosovsky scheme, the first was a "preparatory" period, extending from about 1800 to 1870. In this era the Tokugawa educational institutions grew, differentiated, and adopted a wide variety of curriculum innovations. The second, from 1870 to 1890, overlapped the beginning of Japan's "forced march" into industrialization as the Meiji government experimented with establishing a "modern" school system and consolidated an educational structure that was to remain essentially intact for the next six decades. The third period, 1890 to 1920, during which Japan's industrial sector became self-sustaining, was one of structural elaboration, beginning first with the elementary and university levels and then the secondary, so as to produce a highly status-graded multitrack system. The decade of the 1920s constitutes the fourth period in which a major extension of the multitracking in formal education took place through the spread of vocational programs and training-within-industry, which had begun early in the century. After 1930 until the surrender of Japan in 1945, there is a fifth period, during which the educational structure was increasingly converted to serve the purpose of militarism, including direct manpower controls, overriding ideological indoctrination, and specific vocational training for heavy industry. With the end of World War II, the sixth period began and has continued to the present. This has been foremost an era of reconstruction, reform, and growth in education, attempting to provide equal opportunity for all, abandoning the formal multitrack system and then, especially after 1950, rapidly expanding secondary school and university enrollments. Only in the late 1950s did the government again begin to emphasize directly formal vocational training per se.

In the sections that follow, we first describe more fully the three phases of economic growth and then outline the major developments in the six periods utilized for identifying changes in the educational system. Our attention focuses primarily upon the years up to about 1905 when Japan achieved self-sustained industrialization and had already established a viable educational structure as the basis for generating industrial work skills and capacities.

Transition to Modern Economic Growth (1835-1885)

Despite the political decline of the Tokugawa Shogunate in its last three or four decades (as evidenced by political ineptness, financial and moral bankruptcy of some of the feudal leadership, rural discontent, and low population growth), the two and a half centuries of the Tokugawa regime established several conditions congenial for Japan's modern economic growth. Most important was that national unity replaced political fragmentation. With this came widespread acceptance of the value of industriousness not unlike the Protestant Ethic. Important sectors of the economy, although still almost completely agricultural, became commercialized and specialized, including spread of an effective monetary and financial system. Agricultural output and productivity increased, even though at a slow rate. Improved farming techniques became widely diffused. Traditional rural industries multiplied, with many farm families engaged in nonfarm by-employment. Cottage industry grew, often dependent on merchants for materials, finances, and markets in a so-called "putting-out" system. The central shogunal and local *han* (or clan) governments initiated the beginnings of a modern factory system. Many types of new manual skills merged in both the rural and urban areas: carpenters, blacksmiths, boatbuilders, coopers, dyers, stonemasons, tilemakers, cabinetmakers, plasterers, mast-makers, and so forth—usually organized in craft guilds. Restrictions on geographical mobility were relaxed, wage labor markets were spreading, and population was transferring from rural to complex urban areas. There was a wide-scale fostering and embracing of education, available to most segments of the populace and offered at various levels of learning. Thus, by the time of the Meiji Restoration, Japan was already infected with a spirit of change and had developed educational and other institutions conducive, or at least adaptable, to economic modernization.

The year 1858 perhaps represents the turning point in Japan's embarking upon modern economic growth. With the signing of the first commercial treaties with the Western nations in that year, Japan fully confronted the Euro-American world, with which it had had few contacts for many decades under the shogunal policy of seclusion. The end of national isolation was now at hand, for soon afterward foreign trade began to flourish, foreign goods invaded Japanese markets, and Japan quickened its interest in utilizing and catching up with Western technology. If nothing else, the Japanese faced the challenge of rapidly developing an understanding of the requirements and workings of advanced economies. The alternative that the Japanese perceived was foreign domination and, if the example of much of Asia could be taken seriously (which it was), colonial subjugation. The Shogun's government also feared revolt and uprisings by hans, mainly in Western Japan, which had never fully accepted the Tokugawa system.

Although the decade following 1858 was turbulent and one of great ambivalence and struggle, it was clear that the drive to catch up with the West would soon lead to abandoning institutions that had been geared to the delicately balanced feudal agrarian system. Despite the popularity of the slogan "Restore the Emperor; expel the barbarians," it was its first half, not the second, that became important in emphasizing the forces of change. Once the Meiji regime was installed, after only a year or two of hesitation and floundering, by 1870 its leadership was heavily committed to Japan's modernization, although as yet uncertain what form it should take.

Throughout the 1870s, the Meiji government concentrated on consolidating its political power, quelling revolt and dissension, and abolishing feudal institutions that might detract from national unity or impede economic development. The government decreed the end of the Tokugawa class and fief system, lifted all restraints on geographical mobility, reformed the system of land tenure, eliminated regional customs barriers, and structured agricultural tax levies to stimulate agricultural output. Further, new institutions and practices were initiated to underpin modern economic growth: establishment of a Ministry of Industry; crop reporting; agricultural experiment stations; rural extension services; importation of foreign teachers, advisers, and managers; dispatch of Japanese for study in the United States and Europe; construction and operation of the modern nation-wide communications and transportation network; finance and control of foreign trade; a modern military establishment with compulsory conscription; and a universal primary education system.

Once internal rebellion had been suppressed and economic stability achieved in the early 1880s, the preparatory period reached its culmination. It became clear to the Meiji leadership that the burst of private and public entrepreneurial activity that had already emerged was too haphazard and may have contributed to the economic collapse of the late 1870s. Following intensive studies of potential industrial development, the government thoroughly reformed its fiscal and monetary arrangements (as a direct result of severe inflation and depression), began to transfer its own industrial operations to more efficient private organizations, restructured and rationalized its own bureaucracy, and further revamped and expanded the educational system. By 1885, Japan was essentially ready to devote the full energies of its people to catching up with the West and achieving the long-held goal of a "rich nation, strong army." When this forced march into industrialization began, Japan was still fully a century behind Britain, a half-century behind France and America, and at least a decade or two behind Germany. Little economic improvement had actually been achieved from 1868 to 1885, but the foundations for growth surely had been consolidated.

Entering Self-Sustained Growth (1885-1905)

The two decades from 1885 to 1905 witnessed some of the most profound changes Japanese society has experienced. In this period, the new state was formally inaugurated; large-scale economic and political organizations—the government bureaucracy, the military, and the zaibatsu—were firmly established; and a close interrelationship among the economic, political, and military elites had been woven. Two successful wars, with China in 1894-1895 and with Russia in 1904-1905, convincingly demonstrated the organizational, military, and industrial prowess Japan seemed suddenly to have achieved. Industrialization fed upon military requirements and government support and protection, and was facilitated by agricultural growth, favorable world trade conditions, and population expansion. In the early 1890s, Japan became an exporter rather than an importer of cotton textiles. By 1903, Japan was the world's largest supplier of raw silk. At the end of the period, Japan's international stature sharply contrasted with the nation's seclusion half a century earlier.

Of particular interest was the development beginning in the 1880s of the nation's increasing reliance upon a mixture of private and public enterprises to manage the emerging modern industrial apparatus. Although the Meiji government had initially taken leadership in establishing plants and other industrial operations, many of these ventures proved financial failures; under political and financial pressures, government policy shifted toward encouragement of the growth of private enterprise. As a result, the government divested itself of a large portion of its manufacturing activities and resorted to a system of subsidies, tariff protections, and close consultation with private business leadership. The two wars, a sizable settlement indemnity from China, overseas territorial gains, and an end to the "unequal" treaties of 1858 were major political underpinnings for an industrial expansion that was becoming more and more independent of the agricultural sector for capital supplies. It was in these two decades that many of today's large modern enterprises first emerged—most private, some semipublic—for the manufacture of iron and steel, cotton yarn, silk filatures, paper, refined sugar, beer, cement, rubber, glass, chemicals, and numerous new products previously unknown to the Japanese economy. From 1885 to 1905, Japan developed the two conditions which Kuznets points out are necessary for a nation to enter upon modern economic growth. First, the Japanese had begun to accelerate the nation's growth rate *internally*, through improvements in production techniques, large-scale organization, and efficient management. Second, Japan completely transformed itself *externally*. By altering its political and economic relations with other nations, Japan gained an inflow of scientific ideas and technology, secured its position in world trade, and obtained a seat at the conferences of the major world powers.[3]

At the same time, the meeting of Kuznet's two conditions carried forward elements already present before the initial growth period began. Internal unity increasingly strengthened, resting upon a widespread popular acceptance, if not consensus, in support of the new state. This culminated in the proclamation of the Meiji Constitution in 1890, sanctification of the Imperial system,

[3] Simon Kuznets, *Postwar Economic Growth* (Cambridge: Harvard University Press, 1964).

and full development of universal education and compulsory military conscription as established facets of national life. The new communications and administrative networks rapidly disseminated an enormous influx of ideas and technology imported from the West. Within a single generation, Japanese officials, teachers, traders, merchants, and manufacturers became highly sensitized to all quarters of the globe—its products, markets, capital sources, technologies, and institutions. Although Japan's rapid rate of growth may be explained in part by the initially low level from which growth began, the chief explanations more likely reside in the human capacities the Japanese had already developed to utilize and modify available and growing stocks of knowledge and technology from abroad. As we will show, much of this capability rested upon human skills and talents previously accumulated through the Tokugawa education system.

Self-Sustained Growth and Economic Dualism (1905-1952)

The Russo-Japanese war signaled the conversion of the Japanese economy to self-sustained industrialism. By the end of World War I, more than half of the Japanese labor force would become non-agricultural, although the core of industrial activity long remained in light industry, particularly cotton textiles, and a majority of workers was female. As the principal earner of foreign exchange and no longer dependent on farm surpluses, the industrial sector increasingly used its own profits to turn to heavy manufacturing. The most marked accelerations in that direction came during the First World War, when Japan became a major supplier for the Allied Powers, and following the Manchurian Incident in 1931, when Japan first embarked upon its plan to create a Greater East Asian Co-Prosperity Sphere. Completion of a nationwide rail transport system, full operation of the giant Yahata steel mills, exploitation of hydroelectric sources, construction of extensive electric power networks, and a major expansion of shipbuilding and a merchant marine—all in the first decade of the present century—paved the way toward a larger and larger component of heavy industry in Japan's modern economy. By the early 1930s, for the first time, male industrial workers outnumbered female.

Although this continued restructuring of Japanese industry toward increasingly complex technology and heavy plant and equipment represented a substantial catch-up with the West, nonetheless it was confined selectively within the overall economy. Internal economic growth was highly uneven, and by 1905 it was clear that a dualistic structure had emerged. Side by side ranged some of the most highly advanced factories, equipped with the most modern technology and staffed by well-trained scientific and technical personnel, *and* countless small shops, utilizing rudimentary techniques and traditional labor skills. In addition, as part of the premodern sector, there remained six million farm households, which, while continuing to improve farm yields up to 1920, basically relied upon traditional family organization, primitive methods, and intensive labor.

As the Japanese economy expanded, both the modern and premodern sectors also grew apace—a characteristic that has continued until very recently. The dualism reflected pressing shortages of capital and natural resources, a persistence of "traditional" social relations and value systems, and to some extent the uneven acquisition of new technical skills and knowledge throughout a steadily growing population. Despite increasing industrialization, Japan's modern economy was as much a system of small and medium-size enterprises as it was of giant cartels and monopolies. As later chapters will demonstrate, the dualistic structure notably affected Japan's human resource strategy. Here it suffices to note that it probably contributed to a set of rigidly fixed channels for allocating skills and talents among selective economic activities which persisted into the post-World War II era.

On the other hand, improved techniques and managerial ingenuity often trickled down to the plethora of petty enterprises and agriculture, which in the aggregate contributed substantially to the overall growth rate. In part, this may be accounted for by the development of close-knit subcontracting systems between the large and small firms, whereby the latter often received assistance in financing, equipment, skill training, and management.

The events of the thirty-five years following World War I were hardly favorable to a rapid dissipation of the dual economic structure. The rise of farm productivity on the home islands appeared to have reached its limits; agricultural shortages loomed as population and urbanization continued to grow, requiring substantial imports of food staples particularly from newly acquired colonial possessions and encouraging militaristic elements bent on further overseas expansion. Until close to the end of the 1950s, the size of the farm population remained essentially the same (except for a decline during World War II due to the drain of military service), while the cities and towns absorbed the entire increase in population.

In the 1920s, moreover, the industrial sectors themselves stagnated, and many of the large organizations turned to rationalization and retrenchment. This was due in part to the sharp let-down following the World War I boom, but it also reflected the general contraction of world trade and limitations upon armaments at that time. Saddled with industrial overcapacity, the Japanese economy now witnessed its first large-scale industrial unemployment, which could be little relieved given the lack of a developed social security system. One consequence was a surge of labor and farm protest, inspired at times by left-wing ideologies that took their cue from the Russian revolution and often led by disaffected university graduates and other intellectuals. Even though the 1920s was an era of "liberalism" in Japanese politics (political parties for the first time came into control of the government, and universal male suffrage was established), the government felt compelled to contain or repress the protest, especially after the devastation of the Great Kanto Earthquake in 1923. Finally, in addition to the reduced level of economic activity after World War I, the Great Depression came early to Japan; by 1927, when financial panic gripped Japan, the world silk market was about to collapse; by 1931, Japan abandoned the gold standard. However, Japan began to emerge from the Great Depression earlier than most other nations, spurred on by a rising militarism following the Manchurian Incident of 1931.

The eradication of dualism was not an immediate objective as Japan reacted to the economic gloom of the 1920s by turning to political reaction and militarism. Improvement of Japanese economic conditions, the militarists reasoned, lay in colonial expansion and in establishing, under Japanese leadership and control, the Greater East Asia Co-Prosperity Sphere. From 1931 to 1945, the increasingly totalitarian government undertook to mobilize the existing economic structure in support of armament production and heavy industries upon which armaments depend. First priority in allocating labor, capital, and material went to steel, coal mining, electric power, shipbuilding, metals, machinery, and heavy chemicals. Subcontracting tightened, and small enterprise became even more firmly bound to their parental large-scale firms. Toward the end of the 1930s, the independent labor movement went out of existence and was replaced by a government-controlled labor front. With the attack on Pearl Harbor and Southeast Asia, total mobilization took effect. Strict controls were applied to labor mobility, capital investment, prices, wages, and the like. Education more and more stressed vocational subjects as well as ideological indoctrination. Only by 1944, especially after the effects of Allied bombings began to be fully felt, did total mobilization exhaust itself. Disruption of production and living patterns undermined the government's controls, and careful planning gave way to stop-gap measures. The final denouement, of course, followed upon the atomic explosions at Hiroshima and Nagasaki.

At the surrender in 1945, the Japanese economy was prostrate, its industrial plant in shambles. More than a third of Japan's productive capacity had been destroyed. Almost half the territory under Japan's control had been lost. With the beginning of the Allied occupation, enormous uncertainty beset Japan's economic future. There was a small prospect at the outset for substantial reconstruction of the modern industrial apparatus. While this was to change by 1947, when U.S. Cold War policy shifted to redeveloping Japan as a powerful industrial ally, the immediate postwar years saw a reinforcement of the dual economy. Population growth had resumed and, with the repatriation of six million Japanese from overseas, in alarming proportions. Millions sought to eke out a living in petty enterprise or returned to the family farms, many of which had been seriously run down due to the lack of adequate labor during the war years.

Yet it soon became evident that, with American financial and technical aid and then the boom prompted by the Korean war, the Japanese could quickly rebuild their economy to the highest prewar levels. This was achieved by 1952, the year the occupation ended. There is little doubt that the reconstruction period from 1945 to 1952 depended substantially upon a large backlog of suitable human skills and talents already present in the labor force. Although economic dualism had reemerged with full force, nonetheless the economy was now on the verge of undergoing changes perhaps even more startling than those that had occurred a half-century earlier.

Japan's "New Capitalism" (1953-1975)

Forbidden to rebuild a major military establishment, aided by American finance and technology, taking advantage of world trade expansion, and possessing a highly educated labor force, the Japanese nation bent its full energies to growth and expansion by the mid-1950s. While it could benefit by policies and habits that resulted in high rates of savings and investments, within a few years the economy—for the first time—also became a mass consumption society. A remarkable growth rate of GNP, averaging 10 percent per annum, was able to support not only a vast increase in modern plant and equipment but also rapid expansion of domestic consumer markets. Occupation reforms in agriculture, trade unionism, zaibatsu control, and education, among others, contributed to the outburst of both new entrepreneurship and new consumption patterns in Japan. Not only did the long-established large enterprises benefit from the expansion, but some medium-size firms became large ones, and some small firms, medium-sized. While public corporations and agencies still constituted a substantial sector of the economy, private enterprise, relatively free of government controls and restrictions, but encouraged by government "guidance" and favorable fiscal and monetary policies, flourished in the economic surge. A national policy of production "first and foremost" took complete hold.[4] By 1960, the demand for labor had risen so sharply that labor shortages became evident throughout the economy, especially among the younger workers or new entrants from school into the labor market. In that year, for the first time since the war, a notable absolute decline in the agricultural labor force set in, as farms rationalized, increasingly applied scientific techniques, and at the same time diversified and raised their acreage yields. Population growth also slowed down markedly with the end of the postwar baby boom.

In industry, one of the most significant developments of the postwar period, in addition to an increasing trend toward heavier industrialization, was product diffusion and technological diversification. Hundreds of new businesses fed the demands of the growing domestic markets and took advantage of favorable foreign trade opportunities. By 1960, a majority of industrial workers had for the first time become wage and salary earners—signaling the decline of unpaid family work and self-employment as the largest components of the total labor force. As in the West,

---

[4] See Kozo Yamamura, *Economic Policy in Postwar Japan: Growth vs. Economic Democracy* (Berkeley: University of California Press, 1967).

white-collar jobs were growing at the highest rates of all employed groups, reflecting both diversification of the economy through the spread of personal services and adoption of automation. With the population growth slowed by the mid-1950s (below European and American rates), the average individual's welfare leaped. Real per capita income roughly doubled from 1952 to 1962, nearing $500 per year, and has since more than tripled again, surpassing $1,500 by 1975. All of these trends also meant the gradual dissipation of economic dualism.

These developments do not imply that the Japanese economy has escaped severe problems arising from rapid industrialization—some are sure to worsen in the course of continuing structural transformation. While absolute poverty has virtually disappeared, disparities in income distribution and perceived relative deprivation have loomed—exacerbated by the rise in petroleum prices and general inflation—and have given rise to increased social tension and expression of social protest.[5] Yet to be developed are adequate investments in housing, transportation, social security, and other elements of a modern economic infrastructure. Urban areas have burgeoned but, despite the admirable aesthetic sense of the Japanese and recent efforts at improvement, remain unsightly, overcrowded, polluted, and impersonal. Certain rural areas have been depopulated and pauperized. The demands of modernization, moreover, have imposed heavy strains upon long-established social relations, as for example, the close-knit extended family patterns.

However, since 1945 the Japanese have exhibited the same strong characteristics for undertaking economic expansion as they did in the preparatory and initial periods of modernization. A great capacity to learn, adapt, experiment, save, and invest,

[5] See John W. Bennett and Solomon B. Levine, "Industrialization and Social Deprivation: Welfare, Environment, and the Postindustrial Society in Japan," in Hugh Patrick, ed., with the assistance of Larry Meissner, *Japanese Industrialization and Its Social Consequences* (Berkeley: University of California Press, 1976), pp. 439-492.

coupled with strong nationalism and pride in historical heritage, underpins determination to grow even though, as in the past, the process faces long-standing obstacles. Inadequate raw material and, until recently, capital supplies have always been obvious, holding down the expansion and diversification of domestic consumption, prolonging economic dualism, substituting labor for capital, and generating income inequalities. To this has been added labor shortages, pollution, and congestion in the past few years. A ready tendency to depend upon centralized controls and direction, while seeming to order the process of growth, also prolongs the tenure of a conservative elite leadership in both public and private spheres of life. This leadership is often more inclined to restrain structural shifts than to strengthen egalitarianism and support social change. One result is that, while "production first" remained until recently the dominant national policy, at the same time traditional organizational practices and freezing of hierarchical relationships persist, which delay desirable social overhead investment and the dissipation of status differentiations. Thus, despite the remarkable growth and change of recent years, Japanese society and economy remain a blend of modern and premodern elements. This blend is to be seen also in the historical strategy Japan followed in educating its human resources for modern economic growth.

The Tokugawa Heritage of Education

As in the case of economic growth, the roots of Japan's educational development had been planted well in advance of the Meiji Restoration. Indeed the Meiji government's decree in 1872 requiring universal primary education essentially attempted to consolidate and regulate the schools already in existence. The two and a half centuries of the Tokugawa era, especially its last 100 years, had witnessed an accelerating spread of formal education, a number of major curriculum innovations, and adjustments of the school system to changing social, political, and economic circumstances. In his recent study of the Tokugawa era, Dore points out that as early as the 1860s the educational, although not the economic, attainments of the Japanese population as a whole, despite low per capita income, probably had reached levels far beyond present-day developing nations and were even then abreast of Britain and France.

The reasons for this early development of education are not difficult to discern. Although by the mid-eighteenth century the Tokugawa system had begun to feel the strain of internal decay, the system had generated important economic and social innovations. Resulting political and social tensions gave rise to the seeking of knowledge and opportunities for learning new techniques and skills. Despite official prohibitions on social and geographical mobility, increasing economic activity occurred nevertheless, notably in the growth of monetization and domestic trade. Stagnation of the Tokugawa system had depressed the economic status even of the samurai class, especially those lower-ranked samurai as well as some segments of the peasantry, while witnessing the growing influence of merchants and craftsmen in the cities and towns even though they held the lowest status in the Tokugawa social structure. Under these circumstances, along with the perceived threat of colonial domination by the West, there grew widespread dissatisfaction with the existing political and social system. The dissatisfaction, in turn, contributed to a strong, nationalist-oriented drive for education throughout the population.

Dore aptly summarizes the great change in education that Tokugawa Japan underwent:[6]

It was not a literary society and hardly even a literate society which emerged when Tokugawa Ieyasu had finished his campaigns and completed the process whereby a nation of warring baronies was pacified and forced to accept the overarching authority of the Tokugawa house. . . .

[6] Dore (1965), pp. 1, 2, and 3.

The Japan of 1868, when the first major battles for two and a half centuries culminated in the Meiji Restoration, was a very different society. The warriors' arrogant scorn for the effeminate world of books was hardly anywhere in evidence. Practically every samurai was literate, most had at least a smattering of basic Chinese classics, some were learned in Chinese literature, philosophy or history, in Dutch medicine, astronomy or metallurgy. They were educated in great secular schools. . . .

By this time the majority of town dwellers with a settled occupation, and a good proportion of the farmers of middling status, were literate.

By 1800, "the richer merchants and village headmen were often as learned as the average samurai."

Especially advanced in these educational efforts was the strategic leadership group, the daimyo lords and their samurai retainers, who in the latter part of the Tokugawa Era constituted five to seven percent of the total population of about 30 million. Ironically, it was the dissatisfied members of these elite groups, especially the samurai, who were to launch the restoration movement and take the helm of the new Meiji government.

Formal institutions of higher education for daimyo and samurai heirs may be traced back as early as 1630 with the establishment of the Confucianist *shōheikō* in Edo, which became the model for similar colleges and academies, known as *hankō*, sponsored by the han governments. The first known domain school was established in 1755 in Kumamoto. By the end of the Tokugawa period, about 300 hankō were in existence, at least one in each feudal domain. In Edo alone the Shogunate operated 26 schools of higher learning primarily for the education of daimyo and samurai children, forced to remain in the capital city under the alternate attendance hostage system (*sankin kōtai*) of feudal Japan. Official concern was almost exclusively with preparing samurai for assuming administrative duties either in the entourage of the Shogun or in the fiefs.

The spread of formal education outside the home to include commoners accelerated markedly after 1800. By 1868 the number enrolled in schools had grown at least fourfold; probably as many as 40 percent of all boys and 10 percent of the girls were in attendance. In Edo alone, 86 percent of commoner children were enrolled. By the closing years of the Tokugawa period, school enrollments reached 1.3 million—approximately the same number enrolled when the Meiji government issued its compulsory education edict four years later.

The upswing of education was also reflected in a relatively high degree of literacy among the Japanese *before* the modern era began. On the average, close to 40 percent of the adult male population was already somewhat literate. As mentioned, it is estimated that literacy among samurai and the nobility was virtually 100 percent; but literacy rates also ran as high as 70 to 80 percent for the large city merchants, 50 to 60 percent for the artisans and small town trades, and at least 20 percent even for the peasantry.[7]

A formal school structure resembling a modern system had emerged during the Tokugawa era. Development of a level of higher education, officially sponsored by the Shogunate and the hans, has been mentioned. In addition, there were primary and secondary tiers of schools. At the elementary level, the chief development was the spread of *terakoya*, or "temple" schools, essentially equivalent to common or parish schools, which catered principally to the vast commoner population. Secular and locally operated, they stressed the teaching of the three R's with an additional smattering of morals and manners. Although they received no official sponsorship, the terakoya soon received government encouragement and multiplied rapidly toward the end

---

[7] Some take exception to the meaning of these figures on the grounds that "literacy" meant not much more than the ability to write one's name in Chinese characters. See Koji Taira, "Education and Literacy in Meiji Japan: An Interpretation," *Explorations in Economic History*, Vol. 8, No. 4, July 1971, pp. 371-394.

of the eighteenth century. In 1803, there were little more than 550 terakoya in operation. Sixty-five years later their number had grown to more than 11,000, employing some 17,000 teachers and enrolling at least 920,000 pupils. Edo alone in 1868 had 1,200 terakoya; but it is important to note that terakoya were found even in the smallest hamlets. They varied greatly in size, utilized rote methods of learning in a system of personalized teacher-pupil tutelage, and usually offered four to five years of instruction. The terakoya, thus, provided a ready-made base for the modern elementary school system organized by the Meiji government. In fact, the idea of universal primary education was hardly a novel idea to most Japanese in 1872; for more than half a century, proposals to convert the terakoya into a unified system, either on a national or han basis, had been frequently advanced.

The secondary education tier that had come into existence was somewhat less recognizable as such. The hankō provided some second-level education (as well as some elementary) for samurai children before they went on to their higher learning. Of greater importance at this level were the *gōgaku*, official local schools that admitted both samurai and commoner pupils to study in curricula well beyond what the terakoya offered. In some cases, gōgaku were downward extensions of hankō, but usually they were locally financed rather than directly supported by the han government, as the hankō were. The primary concern of the gōgaku was to prepare the growing cadre of lesser officials for carrying out local administration in behalf of the feudal clans. In the 1750s, there were probably fewer than 60 gōgaku, but by the end of the Tokugawa era their number had grown to 568 with close to 30,000 students enrolled.

In addition to the official hankō colleges, at the higher level of education a wide array of centers for advanced learning, known as *shijuku*, proliferated under private auspices—a feature that to the present day remains important in Japan's total education system.[8] Relatively little is known about many of the shijuku, since they appeared in a wide variety of forms and differed greatly in size, style, and subject matter. Typically they were composed of a single master surrounded by student disciples. The largest establishments, however, were major seats of education and rivaled the official colleges (one, founded by Fukuzawa Yukichi, was the forerunner of present-day Keio University). By the 1860s, probably 1,500 shijuku were active, with as many as 120,000 students in attendance. Open in most cases to samurai and commoners without distinction, leading shijuku were devoted to the study of new rather than classical subject matter and experimented with unconventional ideas. Students could gain entry from hankō and gōgaku and, in some cases, directly from terakoya; and shijuku became the principal source of teachers for the hankō and terakoya. Moreover, it is notable that many of the young samurai who later took the leadership in the Meiji regime had received a large share of their advanced education at the feet of famous shijuku teachers. Some shijuku became so well established that they were officially transformed to hankō and shogunal colleges.

One is struck by the sizable practical and vocational orientation of the Tokugawa schools, which were originally geared to the traditional status hierarchy upon which Japanese feudalism rested. Pure vocational training itself, of course, existed in the form of apprenticeships in the merchant houses and artisan shops. More will be said about these in Chapter IV, but typically an apprentice first received terakoya schooling until the age of 12 or 13 and then spent 9 or 10 years learning a trade as a member of his master's family and, upon completing the apprenticeship, often

[8] Still other types of private schools were in existence during the Tokugawa Era, such as the theological academies, or *shinjuku*, which offered instruction from elementary through higher levels. At the time of the Meiji Restoration, 200 shinjuku were in operation.

opened a branch establishment for his master. But, in addition, practical and vocational education appeared at all levels of the Tokugawa school system. The need for new subject matter was especially apparent in the closing decades of the Tokugawa era, when not only did the feudal system begin to totter but also numerous new industrial enterprises were founded, most sponsored either by the Shogunate or han lords—smelteries, foundries, glass and ceramic making, iron-sand refining, wax manufacturing, textile spinning, ship repairing, and other stirrings of modern economic activity. Terakoya were mainly concerned with imparting basic intellectual skills so that the general population could cope with commercialization of the economy, increasing work specialization and mobility, and the growing network of administrative arrangements emanating from the castle-town trade and governmental centers. Gōgaku, hankō, and shogunal schools stressed preparation of leaders for administration of the changes.

Samurai education, moreover, did not remain static. Despite its classical Confucianist base, especially after the mid-eighteenth century samurai schools increasingly pursued new subject matter, much of a practical and applied nature. In part, this resulted from what happened to Confucianist doctrine itself, which, while it continued training in both the traditional military arts (bu) and "learning" (bun), gradually came to concentrate upon the latter as the Pax Tokugawa continued and leisure time for samurai increased. Soon there emerged several competing "schools" of Confucianist philosophy, the newer approaches tending to stress the samurai's practical preparation for his changing administrative responsibilities. This development created a climate for individualistic thought rather than strict conformity, and in part explains the rise of the independent shijuku. Also, as Confucianist learning changed its character, advancement up the educational ladder came more and more to depend upon demonstrating one's ability, ambition, and merit; and, while open competition was confined mainly within the samurai class at first, heredity lost its importance to such a degree that by the end of Tokugawa the once-exclusive samurai schools were admitting promising commoners in considerable numbers.

At the same time, two other subject-matter streams were joining the educational changes occurring in Confucianist studies. These, too, despite resistance of tradition, increased the flexibility, practicality, and adaptability in Tokugawa education. The first was a growing emphasis upon "Japanese," rather than "Chinese," studies—stimulated by the increased awareness of national unity generated by the Tokugawa system. In 1790 the Shogunate founded the National Learning Institute (*wagaku kōdansho*) as its chief center for developing studies of Japanese language, literature, art, and history. The second was growing acceptance (although at times officially condemned) of "Western" studies, as the Japanese learned of the rapid technical and economic changes occurring abroad. Both developments, along with the shifts in the study of Confucianism, prompted new approaches in education at all levels toward scientific rationalism, receptivity to innovation, and vocational preparation.

As is well known, Tokugawa Japan never fully closed its doors to the West, permitting the Dutch after 1641 to retain a trading station at Deshima Island in Nagasaki harbor, through which streamed a steady flow of Western knowledge (and what the Japanese could not learn from the Dutch they could often learn through Chinese contacts). Official recognition of the need for Western learning appeared as early as 1684 when the Shogunate established the *temmon kata*, or astronomy office, for research in Dutch studies. By the 1740s, the Dutch language was being taught in the shogunal schools, and in 1756 the Shogunate established its first college of Western medicine, for which in 1771 a Dutch anatomy text was translated into Japanese. In 1811 the Shogunate established the *bansho wakai goyō*, or the Office for the Translation of Barbarian Writings (a descendent of the temmon kata and later in 1856 to become the *bansho shirabesho*, or the Institute for the Investigation of Barbarian Writings, the government's chief center for Western learning). This was a forerunner of Tokyo Imperial University.[9]

As Dore notes, the results were that, by the end of the eighteenth century, "anatomy and astronomy had been revolutionized, the first Japanese-Dutch dictionary had been published, and already there were students of Newtonian physics, of Western botany, geology, art, mathematics, and surveying methods."[10] A half-century later, a samurai could no longer count upon classical Confucianist training alone to gain entry into the governmental hierarchy. Rather, he was expected also to demonstrate knowledge of both Western science and "Japanese" learning. The study of foreign languages, too, had become a necessary prerequisite for the officialdom. Unfolding the secrets of Western science now became a major occupation, as well as a chief pastime, among the samurai in Japan, and led to increasing expertise in fields such as astronomy, chemistry, geography, mathematics, medicine, metallurgy, military science, navigation, and physics, and even in Western sociology, economics, and political science. It was soon apparent to many Japanese that, as Dore puts it, "the social institutions of their own country were not a fixed part of the order of nature and that they could, by conscious planning, be changed."[11]

Commodore Perry's appearance in 1853 spurred more experimentation with new knowledge and ideas. Many Western studies schools sprang up alongside the established educational centers, and even the latter increasingly ingested Western subject matter. The Shogunate founded a Western military academy in 1854 and a Western naval academy in 1857. At about the same

[9] See Michio Nagai, *Higher Education in Japan: Its Take-Off and Crash* (Tokyo: University of Tokyo Press, 1971), p. 22.

[10] Dore (1965), p. 30.

[11] *Ibid.*, p. 208.

time, the popular adult education centers, the *Meirindō*, began teaching foreign languages. By the end of the Tokugawa era, 28 hans had established official schools of Western studies, while their hankō and gōgaku were offering instruction in Western medicine, Dutch, and English. Most adaptable of all the schools were some of the shijuku that embraced a wide variety of Western subject matter. The influence of the West had also begun to affect even the terakoya curricula.

In view of this transformation, it came as no great surprise to most Japanese that a major tenet of the Meiji Charter Oath of 1868 proclaimed, "the seeking of knowledge throughout the world in order to strengthen the foundations of the Throne." Spread and change of education in the Tokugawa period, on both a public and private basis, had paved the way for a fully organized effort to provide a modernized educational apparatus for Japan. It was now virtually inevitable that education no longer would be utilized to maintain the old feudal order. It had run far beyond this. Having strengthened national unity, developed common value systems, enhanced the people's sense of a national history, implanted vocational orientations, adopted innovations, and facilitated communication and mobility, the education system now awaited consolidation to support Japan's consciously directed modernization efforts.

Experimentation in Early Meiji Education (1870-1890)

From the outset of the Meiji Restoration, education was a prime concern of the new leadership. In 1869 the government established an education study commission and merged a number of the existing colleges, essentially of Western learning, to establish Japan's first university, the *daigaku nankō*. A Department of Education, later to be made a ministry, was organized in 1871 to develop a national plan of education, which was set forth a year later. In 1872, the *kaisei gakkō* took the place of the daigaku nankō and added curricula in law, engineering, and mining.[12] During the same time numerous groups—the most famous of which was the 1871 Iwakura Mission—were sent abroad to study educational systems in Europe and the United States. Numerous foreigners, especially Americans, were brought in as consultants, advisers, and teachers.

The Educational Order of 1872 for a new school system called for the establishment of an ambitious nation-wide, unitary three-tier network of public schools. Most of the terakoya were to be converted to elementary schools, in which terakoya teachers continued to carry on the instruction while a next generation of teachers was being prepared in newly established normal schools. Hankō and gōgaku were transformed to middle and higher schools. Others were to be created.

The 1872 edict envisioned eight years of compulsory education as soon as possible for all children from six through thirteen years of age. This paralleled the official abolition of the feudal class system and the proclamation of universal military conscription, both adopted at about the same time as the decree. The model first chosen for administrative purposes was the hierarchical French prefectural and local district network under central government inspection. With one elementary school for every 600 persons, there were to be 53,760 primary schools. The elementary schools were to be grouped into local districts, each with 210 elementary schools. Every local district, of which there were 256, was to have a middle school, while 32 local districts were to constitute a single university district, for a national total of eight.

Actually the initial development of a nationwide public school system required little governmental financial investment. The Meiji government provided only nominal revenue support and continued to rely, as in the Tokugawa era, upon local finance, private enterprise, and individual tuition charges. Since the major changes were administrative, the new system was prem-

[12] Nagai (1971), p. 23.

ised upon continued growth of the population's longstanding eagerness for education, especially in support of advancing the nation's economic and military strength. It was the central government's function mainly to bring new ideas and knowledge into Japan (principally by importing foreign experts and sending missions abroad), while the local communities were to finance and administer the schools. Those who took the educational leadership, such as Mori Arinori, Tanaka Fujimarō, and Fukuzawa Yukichi, were engaged in a process of carefully examining foreign educational systems to determine what elements would be most suitable for Japan.

Under these arrangements, the 1870s proved to be a decade of educational experimentation in Japan. In part, this was due to the leaders' preoccupation with organizing the new state apparatus and stabilizing political conditions, but it also resulted from liberal attitudes in the government that stressed local determination. On two points alone did there seem to be unanimous agreement from the beginning—the eradication of illiteracy at the low end and the development of higher education at the most advanced level.

Although the French administrative system was adopted, there was no attempt at first to impose a uniform curriculum. This was more like the American approach. Study content was left to local determination, although the government leaders, relying upon educational specialists from Rutgers University, urged the schools to adopt American pedagogical methods and curricula. To achieve this, the new Department of Education spent 10 percent of its budget, and the Ministry of Industry more than 40 percent, throughout the 1870s for bringing in foreign advisers and teachers. Five thousand such foreigners came to Japan in this period.[13]

Popular response fell far below the government's hopes, how-

[13] Noboru Umetani, *The Role of Foreign Employees in the Meiji Era in Japan* (Tokyo: Institute of Developing Economies, 1971), p. 74.

ever. Despite the large-scale attempt to introduce foreign methods and subject matters, the school programs continued to vary widely, and traditional terakoya and gōgaku patterns changed little. By the end of the 1870s, only half of the projected elementary schools had actually been built; less than half the middle schools and only one center of higher education, renamed Tokyo University in 1877, were in operation. As a concession to intense objections, and even riots at the village and town levels, compulsory education was soon reduced to 16 months, spread equally over four years. Part-time attendance was permitted from 1879 to 1889. A new set of ordinances issued in 1879, which attempted to strengthen local determination of and responsibility for education (even calling for locally elected boards of education), backfired and was widely interpreted as a sign of the central government's disinterest in education. The lag in implementation eventually meant a 10- to 20-year delay in developing a literate labor force for industry.

As a result, voluntarism was abandoned and a higher degree of administrative centralization was instituted in the 1880s. Once the internal rebellions were quelled and economic stability attained, the government turned to consolidating the educational system as it did the state apparatus in general. In 1885, the movement toward central control culminated in establishing the Ministry of Education under the leadership of Mori Arinori. The Ministry of Education thereafter issued a stream of educational decrees that were to shape the school system for the following six decades. Three full years of full-time compulsory elementary education were decreed and in 1886 raised to four, going into effect in 1890. The ministry, moreover, now required the universal teaching of Confucianist principles, particularly by introducing the famous courses in ethics as an integral part of all curricula, and stressed Germanic educational philosophy and methods of instruction. Textbooks were standardized, military drill made obligatory, and nationalism and statism emphasized. Each prefecture now had to have at least one middle school and one normal school. Tokyo University became *the* "Imperial" university in 1886, including faculties of law, medicine, literature, science, engineering, and graduate studies. Normal-school students were subsidized, given military training, and now, as civil servants, required to teach in the national schools upon graduation (10 years in the case of men and five for women, later reduced to four and a half years). All school children had to wear standardized uniforms. Most significant for our purposes was the sharp distinction to be made between vocational and academic track middle-level schools.

With the promulgation of the Meiji Constitution in 1890 and the issuance of the Imperial Rescript on Education a year later, Japan's modern educational system had already taken decisive form, both in structure and curricula. Until 1945, the changes after 1890 were largely an elaboration of the existing system rather than any fundamental shifts in philosophy and subject matter. What emerged had been a blend of new and old elements, encapsulated in the slogan, "Western Science, Japanese Culture" (*wakon yōsai*).

Elaboration of the Modern Educational System (1890-1930)

Full development of Japan's formal educational system took place in the thirty years after 1890, the period in which modern economic growth became self-sustaining. By 1900 four years of compulsory elementary education had become virtually universal, and Japan was assured of attaining close to 100 percent literacy within a generation. Seven years later, mainly as the result of the wide spread of enrollment, compulsory schooling was extended to six years and successfully enforced by 1918, and could be made longer when attendance in a grade of a given school exceeded 70 percent of the relevant age group. By the turn of the century, although local financing of the common schools remained, and the national government still provided only 10 to 15 percent of the cost of the system, tuition charges were abandoned. While it proved unnecessary to expand the number of elementary schools, the upper tiers were on the increase. By 1902, there were 222 middle schools, and another Imperial University, in Kyoto, began to operate. Private secondary and higher education institutions were also rapidly increasing, as will be noted more fully below.

After 1890 the most significant expansion in the structure of the education system was the development of multitrack schools beyond the elementary level. A series of decrees culminating in the vocational school ordinance of 1899 fully delineated the multitrack system beyond elementary education. From this time on, there was a careful apportioning of school children among the several tracks made available, and rarely could a student switch from one track to another. Once students completed three years of elementary schooling, the sexes were separated, and at least five different tracks were open to boys, and three to girls.

In the case of boys, about 10 percent went from elementary school into a pattern of academic study comprising five years of middle school, three years of higher school, and, in the case of about half these graduates, three or four years of a university (where a very small fraction could later pursue an additional four or five years of graduate work). The remainder of those who went on from compulsory education entered vocational tracks. About 10 percent of the boys proceeded to a terminal seven-year sequence of middle and higher schools, which offered a variety of vocationally oriented courses. An equal percentage went to more specific vocational preparation, first by entering five-year middle schools, and then either three-to-five-year polytechnical institutes (the well-known *semmon gakkō*) or two-to-four-year normal schools. Only in rare cases could graduates of this latter track enter universities. It was especially in the polytechnical insti-

tutes that subprofessional and technician courses were offered—
in fields as diverse as medicine, dentistry, engineering, architecture, pharmacy, agriculture, music, art, foreign languages, the-
ology, physical education, commerce, and fisheries. For a still
smaller group, a somewhat lower level vocational track provided
two-year higher elementary schools, from which graduates entered terminal five-year normal schools or three-to-five-year
youth normal schools. From the last, some could proceed to
two-year normal schools or three-year vocational teacher training
institutes.

The girls had a much narrower selection. A small percentage
who completed elementary school entered an academic track
consisting of four- or five-year girls' high schools and then, for a
small fraction of them, three-year women's ordinary normal
schools or four-year women's higher normal schools. A much
larger number went directly from elementary school to three- to
five-year vocational schools, from which some could go to two- or
three-year youth normal schools or vocational teacher training
schools. The largest groups of girls who went beyond primary
education entered higher elementary schools from which they
could be admitted to five-year girls' normal colleges.

In addition to the publicly supported school system, this period also saw the flourishing of many private educational institutions. Geared as it still was to local financing and highly selective
among its various trackings, the public school system was unable
to cater to all the growing demands for secondary and higher
education. As in the Tokugawa era, private education sprang up
in numerous forms above the elementary school level. Until
World War II, in fact, 15 percent of secondary school enrollment
was in private schools. Especially important was the growth of
private colleges, which mushroomed after 1905. Although they
received no official recognition until the close of World War I,
private colleges rapidly became an important source of advanced
education as the need for training at this level became more and

more apparent for Japan's modernizing economy and social status system. Until 1945 they furnished more than half the university graduates. The creation of Imperial and other national universities lagged in the process; by 1910 there were merely four and by 1920 only six.

At a lower level there also began to spring up numerous private programs of "quasi-secondary" and "miscellaneous" education, principally for graduates of elementary school, which though not financed or sponsored by the government could gain official certification. These schools included technical training programs that the government had provided in plants it had established or in government operations such as arsenals and naval shipyards. They tended to combine both general education and vocational training, most on a part-time basis in connection with doing work. Prefectural governments, cities, towns, and even villages also established quasi-secondary schools as did numerous private industrial enterprises and other private organizations, as will be seen in Chapter IV. Perhaps the most neglected aspect of the study of Japan's modern educational development has been systematic treatment of the vocational training programs that spread throughout modern industry during the 1920s. While we reserve fuller discussion of this trend for later chapters, it is important to emphasize that in this decade enterprises made increasing use of within-industry secondary education and training programs for its new employees.

Despite the economic stagnation following World War I and modern industry's retreat into retrenchment and rationalization, Japan's educational expansion continued at a rapid rate. Middle school and higher education continued to grow throughout the 1920s. As a result, it became increasingly apparent that Japan had an "oversupply" of educated labor. Moreover, as we will discuss in Chapter IV, for the new organizational, technical, and skill needs of modern industries, the public school system remained poorly articulated. The rapid growth of modern industry after 1905, its great expansion in World War I, and its emphasis upon technological change and reorganization in the 1920s had made it difficult for the vocational tracks in the public school system to keep in line with industrial requirements. In addition to their inability to absorb the rapidly growing supply of university graduates during the 1920s, modern enterprises also could not utilize vocational school graduates with a high degree of effectiveness.

Militarism and Education (1931-1945)

The overabundance of educated labor was temporary. With the ascendancy of the military to political control after the Manchurian Incident, the Japanese educational system was swiftly subjugated to support ultranationalism. This included manpower controls for the expansion of heavy industry and also, under the direction of the military, "thought" control to suppress anything that might be considered subversive. These complicated events have been recounted elsewhere and will not be reviewed here.

With regard to education itself, the policy of the militarists was to push vigorous expansion at all school levels, with increasing stress upon direct technical and vocational training in addition to ultranationalistic indoctrination. By 1930 the government increased the number of national universities to 17 and then added two more by the time World War II began. Recognized private universities also grew in number, from 10 in 1920 to 28 in 1940. Universities, notably, shifted to more and more emphasis on science and engineering. Particular attention was given also to the training of teachers, with larger portions of school curricula devoted to morals and nationalism. Normal schools increased in number, were raised to college-level status, and placed under direct control of the Ministry of Education.

A further expansion in secondary education took place in the 1930s, particularly in the vocational tracks. Most notable was the growth of the quasi-secondary schools and programs of part-time education beyond required elementary schooling. Among the latter was the extension in 1935 of a system of youth schools, which, while first established in the 1920s as an anti-unemployment measure, now required attendance of all boys between 12 and 19 who did not go beyond elementary education. Most of these schools were devoted to vocational training and military drill, as a part of the overall manpower controls and mobilization. Similarly, many of the existing quasi-secondary programs within industry were expanded and readily converted to the new youth schools. In 1939 all males who entered industry from elementary schools were required to attend the youth schools on a part-time basis until they were nineteen. A step-up in compulsory military conscription also served this national educational purpose.

By the time Japan entered World War II, it was clear that the educational system had become the government's primary instrument for indoctrinating, mobilizing, and allocating the labor force. Military officers now took charge of the schools. As labor requirements increased, especially to meet the needs of military conscription for war industries, school curricula increasingly combined industrial work with school studies. In some instances as labor resources became exhausted, school-age children spent full-time at factory or other war work. The regimentation latent in the edicts of the 1880s thus took full effect.

Educational Reform, Reconstruction, and Rapid Growth (1945-1975)

Education was one of the first targets for major reform in the Allied Occupation following Japan's surrender in 1945. The Imperial Rescript was almost immediately voided. By the early 1950s there had been accomplished a wholesale restructuring of the educational system, a complete curriculum revision, decentralization of controls, and a major replacement of the teaching personnel (one-fourth of the prewar teachers were purged). One of the immediate goals was educational democratization; thus, multitracking and sex differentiation came to an abrupt end. Advancement to the tiers beyond compulsory education was open as a right to all who could qualify. The years of compulsory schooling were increased to nine, and a uniform 6-3-3-4 system (elementary, lower secondary, upper secondary, college) generally established, although part-time secondary schools were also made available.

Another immediate step was the eradication of ultranationalism from the curricula, including the end of the ethics course; American-style social studies now took a prominent place among the subjects taught. To upgrade and democratize teacher training, normal schools were made integral parts of universities and graduate training was expanded. The teachers themselves were encouraged to form one of the largest nationwide unions in a new labor movement that the Occupation eagerly fostered as part of the postwar reforms. Two hundred and forty-nine institutions of higher learning, many former technical institutes and normal schools, were recombined into a system of 68 national universities (at least one to a prefecture), all theoretically with equal status.

As will be shown in the next chapter, a major consequence of the Occupation reforms was a rapid growth in enrollments at the secondary and higher education levels. Despite the misgivings of many that the expansion would merely serve to lower educational standards, institutions of higher education in particular proliferated, numbering 245 public and private four-year universities and 320 two-year junior colleges by 1955. As Japan's economic boom proceeded, in 1972 the number of universities had grown to 379, and junior colleges to 491, with a total enrollment of more than 1.8 million.[14] Almost 40 percent of all senior high

[14] *Japan Report* (New York: Japan Information Service), Vol. XXI, No. 6, March 16, 1975, p. 3.

graduates went to higher education in 1975.[15] Seventy-six universities were supported by the national government and 32 by other public agencies. A large minority of all universities were offering graduate work and night courses. Junior vocational colleges, somewhat like the old technical institutes but upgraded to cover three years of high school and two years of college, were beginning to make their reappearance; in 1963 the government placed 24 such schools into operation and added 12 more in 1964, and increasing them to 63 by 1973. Also by 1973, there were more than 8,000 "miscellaneous" schools (*kakushū gakkō*) with nearly 1.3 million students, most in vocational or specialized fields, beyond the senior high or junior high level but outside the standard institutions of higher education certified by the Ministry of Education.[16] In 1976 an amendment to the School Education Law elevated a number of qualified miscellaneous schools to the status of higher education and redesignated them as special training schools (*senshū gakkō*). Almost 2,000 such schools qualified with a combined enrollment of more than 350,000.[17]

High schools also showed tremendous leaps in attendance, especially after 1955 when the economic boom was well underway. By the early 1960s nearly 60 percent of all junior high school graduates were going on to senior high school (in Tokyo alone the figure reached close to 80 percent). In 1976, the figure had risen to 92 percent.[18] The great difference compared to the presurrender period was that most of the high schools were "comprehensive," including both vocational and academic courses of study, although some vocational high schools had been retained. At the same time, for middle-school graduates who did not go on, quasi-secondary programs continued to flourish, especially in training-within-enterprise arrangements—although these now

[15] *Ibid.*, Vol. XXIII, No. 2, January 16, 1977, pp. 2-3.
[16] *Ibid.*, Vol. XXI, No. 6, March 16, 1975, p. 3.
[17] *Ibid.*, Vol. XXIV, No. 10, May 16, 1978, p. 3.
[18] *Ibid.*, Vol. XXIV, No. 10, May 16, 1978, p. 5.

occupied a smaller place than formerly at the secondary education level.

As in the prewar era, private schools continued to occupy an important place in Japanese education. Again the public school system was unable to adjust rapidly to the enormous change and growth that the postwar reconstruction, reform, and economic advance generated. In 1960, more than one-fourth of secondary education enrollment and almost two-thirds of the university students were in private institutions. Thus, the present period appears to exhibit the long-time tendency of the Japanese to combine in their educational system both private and public approaches to providing formal education.

In summary, a huge new apparatus for educational opportunities had been made available for growing segments of the young population to enter an era of increasingly diversified and advancing industrialization. Although the school system was no longer geared primarily to Japan's military strength and to nationalistic ideology, it drew upon an extensive structure that had its roots deeply planted in earlier history. While old attitudes persisted in the schools, authoritarian values have been giving way to democratic egalitarianism and individuation. The final outcome of the new system is still being shaped, but the quantitative effects in terms of supplying educated human resources for economic growth and industrial change have been quite discernible. It is to this point that Chapter III next turns.

III.

Educational Indicators of Japan's Human Resource Development

GENERALLY, Japan's human resource strategy since the beginning of the modern period may be seen in the quantitative "output" of its educational system. The relationship between the "output" and economic growth helps to delineate strategic choices that the Japanese made with somewhat greater precision than would a description of the development of Japan's educational system. In addition, quantification helps in making comparisons with the experiences of other nations.[1] Ideally, quantitative analysis of human resource development might also include data for items other than education, such as health and cultural values; but, since the focus of this study is on the direct generation of skills and capacities for industrial work, it is limited to educational attainment.

The sections that follow present three principal indexes at the national level of educated human resources as they have grown in Japan since early Meiji. Following the Harbison-Myers approach, which we accept as reasonably valid, these include: (1) enrollment ratios based on age groups as appropriate for cross-national comparisons at various levels of the educational and

[1] In this study, however, we do not attempt specific country-by-country comparisons with Japan. For such analyses, see, for example, Frederick H. Harbison and Charles A. Myers, *Manpower and Education: Country Studies in Economic Development* (New York: McGraw-Hill, 1965); C. Arnold Anderson and Mary Jean Bowman, eds., *Education and Economic Development* (Chicago: Aldine Publishing Co., 1965); and Frederick Meyers, *Training in European Enterprises* (Los Angeles: Institute of Industrial Relations, University of California, 1969).

training structure; (2) ratios of the number of persons per 10,000 population engaged in certain key professional and technical occupations usually required for advancing industrialization; and (3) proportions of enrollment at the secondary and higher levels of formal schooling in the major fields of study concentration.[2]

First we examine these three types of indicators in relation to the stages of Japanese economic development outlined in Chapter II and also demarcate sequential phases in Japan's human resource development. The latter utilizes the index of national educational attainment constructed by Harbison and Myers to categorize 75 countries, for which they gathered comparable data pertaining to the late 1950s. Although cross-sectional rather than historical, this index, according to the Harbison and Myers analysis, shows four successive stages of human resource development by country category. These stages are labeled Level I: Underdeveloped; Level II: Partially developed; Level III: Semi-advanced; and Level IV: Advanced. In their method of calculation, this index is a "composite" of the school enrollment ratios *above* elementary education. It purposely excludes elementary education because the primary grades presumably do not contribute directly to vocational preparation, even though undoubtedly they are extremely important as the basis for secondary and higher education which are assumed to make more direct contributions (see p. 80 below).

For the 75 nations taken together in the Harbison-Myers study, the composite index displays high correlation coefficients with major indicators of economic growth: positively, with per capita gross national product or national income, and, negatively, with the percent of active population in agriculture.[3] By compar-

[2] See Frederick H. Harbison and Charles A. Myers, *Education, Manpower, and Growth: Strategies of Human Resource Development* (New York: McGraw-Hill, 1964), especially Chapter 3, p. 36.

[3] *Ibid*. For the 75 countries taken together, these correlations respectively are .888 and − .814. A later study led by Harbison reexamined these correlations for 73 countries for 1960 and 1965 and found that the original and recalculated figures

ing the relationship between the indicators of economic growth and of the composite index for educational attainment in the case of Japan since the modern period began, we then identify the ways the Japanese experience follows or diverges from the Harbison-Myers correlations at each stage of human resource development. Finally, we examine the implications of divergencies in terms of Japan's particular strategy of human resource development.

Although later chapters return to this question more fully, the quantitative analysis by itself indicates that Japanese strategy historically has departed significantly from the "logical" strategy suggested by the Harbison-Myers correlations for nations to progress from lower to higher categories of human resource development.[4]

It is necessary to caution at the outset that numerous technical and conceptual problems plague the quantitative measurement of human resources and economic development for a nation at any given point in time or over time. Japan is no exception in this regard. The indexes for human resource development and economic growth probably contain errors of unknown magnitude. Available data are incomplete and have to be indirectly and often roughly approximated. The errors are probably compounded also by inconsistencies from one period to another, especially because of variations in definitions and concepts. For example, it is unlikely that a year in high school in the 1970s provides the same learning content as a year in high school in the 1900s. When international comparisons are made, in all likelihood the uncertainty increases even more, especially if demographic structures differ. Despite these pitfalls in measurement, recent studies of human resource development and economic growth for many na-

---

correlated 98 percent. See Frederick H. Harbison, Joan Maruhnic, and Jane R. Resnick, *Quantitative Analysis of Modernization and Development* (Princeton: Industrial Relations Section, Princeton University, 1970).

[4] Harbison and Myers (1964), Chapters 4 through 8, although one should note the authors' reservations on p. 178.

tions, including Japan,[5] have brought forth fresh compilations of data, which probably lessen the inaccuracies and, for our purposes, provide sufficiently reliable estimates at least to gauge long-run trends in Japan, to compare Japan with other countries at a national aggregate level, and to detect similarities and differences in Japan's overall human resource strategy compared to the Harbison-Myers "logical" model.

Enrollment by Levels of Education

Table I presents basic data for Japan's educational expansion in roughly five-year intervals from 1885 to 1975 in terms of estimated enrollment ratios in three schooling levels (1st, 2nd, and 3rd) utilized by Harbison and Myers. The series for each level is constructed in the same way as, or close to, those employed by Harbison and Myers in their original cross-sectional study of 75 countries.[6] The 1st level corresponds essentially to elementary schooling, the 2nd level to secondary schooling, and the 3rd level to higher education. For purposes of cross-national comparability, enrollment ratios for each level are the percentages of the population, respectively, in the age groups, 5-14, 15-19, and 20-24, inclusive, regardless of the actual ages of the students attending.[7] Although these are rates of enrollment rather than of

[5] For Japan, see *Japan's Growth and Education* (Tokyo: Japan Ministry of Education, 1963). This study relies on the "residual" method for measuring the contribution of education to economic growth. Unless otherwise noted, statistics cited in the present chapter are drawn from this source. In recent years, there has grown a large literature on the relationship between education and economic growth. See, for example, W. Lee Hansen, *Education, Income, and Human Capital*, Studies in Income and Wealth No. 35 (New York: National Bureau of Economic Research, 1970); and John Simmons, ed., *Investment in Education for Developing Countries: National Strategy Options*. Proceedings and Papers from a Conference on the Economics of Education, October 1973.

[6] Harbison and Myers, *Education, Manpower and Growth*, pp. 29-30, especially footnotes 15 and 16.

[7] Presumably, such common age groups permit uniform comparisons on an international basis. For any one country, they are not necessarily the "normal" age groups for attendance at each respective educational level; nor does the 1st

TABLE I.   Estimated Enrollment Ratios by Levels of Education in
Japan for Selected Years, 1885-1975

Year	1st Level[a]	2nd Level[b]		3rd Level[c]
		Excluding Quasi-Secondary Education	Including Quasi-Secondary Education	
1885	39.2	0.1	0.2	0.4
1890	35.2	0.1	0.3	0.5
1895	41.6	1.2	2.8	0.4
1898	45.6	2.1	3.6	0.5
1903	53.1	4.0	8.1	0.8
1908	50.5	19.8	27.7	1.2
1913	56.5	19.2	36.4	1.3
1920	60.2	25.7	48.9	1.8
1925	59.3	36.7	57.9	2.7
1930	61.1	37.2	73.0	3.3
1935	60.9	42.7	74.5	3.1
1940	60.2	49.6	90.0	4.0
1945	61.6	58.6	93.1	7.1
1947	58.7	63.9	87.9	6.4
1950	61.5	84.7	90.3	5.2
1955	61.2	98.7	109.9	7.3
1960	62.3	98.2	111.5	8.5
1965	57.4	101.8	114.6	12.0
1970	59.5	99.2	114.1	15.5
1975	60.2	115.6	130.3	23.0

[a] Percentage of age group 5-14 inclusive.
[b] Percentage of age group 15-19 inclusive.
[c] Percentage of age group 20-24 inclusive.

SOURCES: Office of the Prime Minister, Bureau of Statistics, *Japan Statistical Yearbook* (1964, 1971, 1975); Rōdō Undō Shiryō Iinkai, *Nihon Rōdō Undō Shiryō*, Vol. X (1959); Ministry of Education, *Japan's Growth and Education* (1963), *Gakkō Kihon Chōsa* (1960, 1965, 1970, 1975), and *Wagakuni No Kyōiku No Ayumi to Kongo no Kadai* (1969).

level necessarily coincide with the years for compulsory education. The ratios do not represent the percentage of a particular age group actually enrolled at a given level, but merely the enrollment regardless of age at the level as a percentage of the given age group. For example, in present-day Japan, typically children age 5 do not attend elementary school, while those age 12 to 14 attend middle or lower secondary school. As a result, with the exclusion of these age groups, Japan's sat-

actual school attendance or school completion (which, as Harbison and Myers point out, would be a more desirable index), this is probably not a serious difference for measuring educational achievement in Japan's case, since especially in the latter decades enrollment has been tantamount, except for natural attrition, to attendance and graduation.

In addition, Table I shows *two* enrollment ratios for 2nd-level schooling. One ratio excludes and the other includes "quasi-secondary" education (both as a percentage of the 15-19 age group), which as explained in Chapter II are programs beyond the elementary level that though certified are usually not part of the officially established formal school system. In Japan "quasi-secondary" education is usually labeled "miscellaneous" schools. The Harbison-Myers study does not present such an all-inclusive ratio for the 2nd level; but at least in Japan's case it is useful, if not critical, to take account of this type of education in analyzing Japanese human resource development and strategy because of the large role such schools have played in direct vocational training. The fundamental reason for estimating "quasi-secondary" education in Japan rests on the importance of the multitrack school structure prior to the end of World War II, to which was adjoined widespread utilization of training-within-enterprise programs.

Although the duration as well as the content of schooling at each of the levels in Japan has changed over time and is not strictly comparable with other nations, the variations fall within the year limits utilized by Harbison and Myers in their computations, and therefore no adjustments in the enrollment ratios have been made for this factor in Table I. After 1891 much of elementary schooling in Japan in fact lasted six years even though six years did not become compulsory until 1907. From the beginning, entry into higher education required at least 10 or 11 years

uration point for 1st-level schooling is about 60 percent of the population, age 5 to 14, while that for 2nd-level is above 100 percent of the age group 15 to 19.

of preparation, and the 3rd level lasted four or more years. The duration for secondary and quasi-secondary education, however, at all times ranged from two to seven years beyond the elementary years, depending upon the period and type of school or program. In all likelihood, this variation at the 2nd level makes for some upward bias in the secondary education enrollment ratios particularly in the earlier decades, but probably is of minor importance for making cross-national comparisons.

The data on school enrollment ratios amply support the oft-repeated observation that Japan gave highest priority to spreading elementary education in the structuring of the Japanese school system throughout the Meiji era (1868-1911). By 1885, when Japan's preparatory period for economic development had about run its course, a number equal to two-fifths of the estimated population, age 5-14 inclusive, was already enrolled in 1st-level schools. This enrollment ratio had about doubled since 1873, the year following the official establishment of Japan's modern school system. The ratio represented more than three million students, most of whom in fact were in the 6-9 age group attending the three years of elementary school compulsory at that time.

By 1895, the ratio of the 5-14 age group enrolled in the 1st level rose to slightly above 40 percent, and, following the Russo-Japanese War in 1905, the year that marked the end of the initial growth period for Japan's economic modernization, the ratio climbed to about one-half. By that time the population in the 5-14 age group had increased to around 10 million. This enrollment ratio was already approaching the demographic saturation point (that is, almost 100 percent of the 6-11 age group), so that when six years of elementary education actually were made compulsory two years later, it was little affected. During World War I the ratio for the 1st level did reach saturation, and since 1920 it has remained virtually unchanged at about three-fifths of the 5-14 age group. In fact, for the 6-11 age group, the years normally expected for elementary school attendance, by the 1920s enrollment was more than 95 percent and by 1940 close to 100 percent.

At the 2nd level, such a rapid expansion in the enrollment ratio to the point of saturation did not occur until much later. Throughout most of Japan's initial period of modern economic growth, secondary school enrollment as a percentage of the age group 15-19 inclusive remained minuscule. In 1898, when the population of this group was about 4.3 million, it was still as small as 3.6 percent, even including enrollment in quasi-secondary education. While 1st-level enrollment reached saturation in Japan by the 1920s, it was not until the mid-1950s that this became the case for the 2nd-level excluding quasi-secondary education; by then the 7th through 9th years of schooling, considered part of the 2nd-level in the Harbison-Myers analysis, had been made compulsory under the reforms of the Allied Occupation (although earlier planned but deferred by the Japanese government).

Only after the multitrack educational system had become widely instituted during the first and second decades of the present century did the enrollment ratio for the 2nd level as a percent of the 15-19 age group begin to rise notably, increasing in the single decade from 1898 to 1908 almost nine times for formal secondary education alone and close to eight times when quasi-secondary education is included. Following this initial outburst, however, formal secondary school enrollment rose more gradually. The 2nd-level enrollment ratio tripled from about one-fifth to three-fifths during the period from the beginning of World War I to the end of World War II, although it should be noted that the great bulk of these students (probably two-thirds or more) did not go beyond the equivalent of the ninth grade, normally age 13 or 14.

With the educational reforms of the Allied Occupation, the ratio for formal secondary education again increased rapidly, reaching more than 98 percent of the 8.6 million population in the 15-19 age group in 1955 (for the 12-17 age group normally expected to be attending secondary schools, the proportion rose from three-fifths to close to four-fifths between 1940 and 1947). This increase, of course, reflected the raising of compulsory education to nine years and the establishment of the comprehensive high school system under the reforms. By 1960, the ratio of 12th grade graduates to 9th grade graduates was more than 83 percent despite declining numbers due to lessened birth rates. By 1975, with few dropouts, more than 90 percent of the 9th graders went on to high school.[8]

When quasi-secondary education enrollment is included in the computations for the 2nd level, the increase in the 2nd-level enrollment ratio since 1908 has been considerably faster and steadier than indicated by the index for formal secondary education alone. Until the end of World War II, quasi-secondary education usually added between 50 and 100 percent to the annual enrollment ratio for the conventional 2nd level. (At the risk of overstating the case, in all likelihood this inclusive ratio would be even higher if data were available and included numerous local and private programs that were not officially registered or certified.) Inclusion of quasi-secondary enrollment indicates that a number at least one-fourth of the 4.4 million in the 15-19 age group were attending 2nd-level schools of all types in 1908 and more than one-half of the 5.8 million in the group by 1925. At the time of World War II, the proportion had risen close to the saturation point. It reached 95 percent (of about 8 million), but then dropped slightly as the single-track educational system replaced the multiple schools and absorbed many quasi-secondary education programs in the process. Although since 1950 quasi-secondary schooling has played far less of a role than in the prewar years, it was still significant enough to raise the 2nd-level ratio to

[8] See *Japan Report* (New York: Japan Information Service), Vol. XXII, No. 1, January 1, 1976, p. 8; and *Japan Labor Bulletin* (Tokyo: Japan Institute of Labour), Vol. 14, No. 1, January, 1975, p. 2.

about 110 percent of the 8.6 million in this group by 1955 and, even with attendance at senior high schools spreading rapidly, to more than 114 percent in 1965 and 130 percent in 1975.

Expansion of the enrollment ratio for higher education was, until recently, far less dramatic than for the 1st and 2nd levels of schooling. Until the end of World War I, the ratio, based on the age group 20-24 inclusive, failed to rise as high as 2 percent, although from 1885 to 1920 it had grown at least four and a half times (during which time the population of the 20-24 age group rose from 2.9 million to 4.5 million). The ratio notably increased throughout the 1920s and 1930s following the official recognition of many private colleges in 1918 and the establishment of several new state universities during these years; yet it was still only 4 percent of the 6.1 million of the 20-24 age group at the time of the outbreak of the Pacific War. (The percentages are no greater when the ages 18-21 or 18-22—those normally expected for college and university attendance—are used as the basis for computation.) Most of the increase in the ratio by 1960 to the level of 8.6 percent of 8.3 million in the 20-24 age group actually occurred during the Second World War, following which the percentage dropped and did not recover until the mid-1950s.

The major impact of the postwar educational reforms upon higher educational enrollments, therefore, has occurred since 1955. About one-tenth of the normal college age group (18-21 inclusive) was enrolled in 1960; but by 1967 this proportion reportedly had increased to almost 25 percent and by 1975 close to 40 percent. The 3rd-level enrollment ratio thus leaped from 7.3 to 23.0 between 1955 and 1975. In 1975, higher education institutions of all kinds admitted more than 38 percent of all 12th grade graduates, with about one-fourth entering four-year universities. Since 1960, in fact, Japan's percentage has been above that for France, England, and West Germany and has almost reached the American level.[9]

[9] *Japan Report*, Vol. XXIII, No. 2, January 16, 1977, pp. 2-3.

As the Japanese are well aware, the rapid spurt has created numerous problems of inadequate facilities and questionable academic standards, especially among the newer institutions of higher education. On the other hand, the recent change has converted Japanese higher education from an elitist to a mass system. Dramatic evidence of this are larger proportions of the young who are "doubly" enrolled at the elementary and secondary education levels in the private non-formal *gakushū juku* and *rōnin* (rejects) schools in their attempt to gain admission to universities and colleges.

Growth of High-Level Professional and Technical Occupations

In the process of economic modernization, under conditions of growing population, changing demographic structure, increasing urbanization, expanding industrialization, and rising per capita income, it is to be expected that the occupational constellation will change radically and shift more and more to modern professional and technical or "high-level" specializations. While it is not possible to examine here all the facets of occupational change that have taken place in Japan since 1868, Table II traces the increases that have occurred for certain high-level occupational groups usually considered among the most representative of these growth phenomena because of the specialized education, certification and/or prolonged training required for entry. The occupations include teachers in elementary and secondary schools, scientists and engineers, physicians and dentists, and supporting medical personnel (nurses, pharmacists, and midwives). Expansion of these occupations is shown by the ratio of persons engaged in each per 10,000 population for selected years, in some cases going back as early as 1880. No attempt has been made to adjust the ratios for changes in quality or level of training and preparation, so that in all likelihood the figures for the earlier years are upwardly biased in relation to the entry re-

TABLE II. Number of Persons per 10,000 Population Engaged in "High-Level" Occupations in Japan for Selected Years, 1880-1975

Year	Teachers, 1st and 2nd Levels[a]	Scientists and Engineers	Physicians and Dentists	Nurses	Licensed Pharmacists	Midwives	Total Population (in millions)
1880	5.5	0.0	9.6			4.9	36.6
1885	8.3	0.1	10.6			7.1	38.3
1890	7.1	0.3	10.1		0.7	8.2	39.9
1895	14.4	0.8	9.5		0.7	8.3	41.6
1900	17.5	1.5	11.2		0.8	5.7	43.8
1905	21.2	1.7	7.8		0.7	5.6	46.6
1910	25.8	2.0	8.0	2.0	1.0	5.6	49.2
1915	28.8	2.6	8.9	3.6	1.1	6.0	52.8
1920	31.2	4.1	9.3	6.3	1.3	6.5	55.4
1925	35.4	5.9	9.6	2.6	3.3	7.3	59.2
1930	38.5	8.4	10.8	11.9	3.0	7.9	63.8
1935	38.6	10.7	11.3	15.7	3.6	8.7	68.7
1940	39.6	14.2	12.4	19.2	4.4	8.6	71.9
1945	40.8	27.6[b]	2.5	4.4	1.0	2.5	78.1[b]
1950	71.8	30.9	12.4	15.6	5.5	8.9	83.2
1955	72.6	34.9	14.1	14.4	5.9	9.9	89.3
1960	74.5	42.3	14.6	19.9	6.5	5.6	93.4
1965	79.0	56.6	14.8	25.0	7.0	4.4	98.3
1970	76.9	80.1	15.2	26.5	7.7	2.7	103.4
1975	87.6	113.3	17.6	35.5	9.4	2.7	111.9

[a] Excluding quasi-secondary education, 1880-1945.

[b] 1947.

SOURCES: Office of the Prime Minister, Bureau of Statistics, *Japan Statistical Yearbook* (1964, 1971, 1975); Ministry of Education, *Japan's Growth and Education* (1963), and *Kyoiku Shibō No Kokusai Hikaku* (1971); Publishing Committee for Japan Education Yearbook, *Nihon Kyōiku Nenkan* (1963); Ministry of Welfare, *Isei 80 Nenshi* (1955), and *Ishi, Shikaishi, Yakuzaishi Chōsa* (1970, 1975); and Sano Yōko, *Nihon Ni Okeru Kagakusha Oyobi Gijutsusha No Suikei*, mimeographed (1978).

quirements for these occupations in more recent times. The ratios are computed from the number of school graduates in the appropriate fields of study, survival rates of the graduates, and occupational census data.

Comparison of the Japanese ratios with similar ratios in the Harbison-Myers study[10] indicates that, in the case of primary and secondary school teachers and of scientists and engineers, Japan until very recently lagged in the development of these professions. On the other hand, Japan appears to have made relatively fast progress in developing medical and dental professional manpower since the very outset of the modern period. These contrasts, while based on few occupations, reflect both the historical structuring of Japan's modern educational system and the occupational heritage from the premodern period.

Until 1900, the ratio for teachers was notably low, partly because of difficulties in transforming the instructional system of the Tokugawa period and partly because of the long process required to prepare instructors for the new school system. Even though the ratio more than tripled from 1880 to 1900, it still remained by the latter year at about the level that Harbison and Myers find associated with nations in the lowest category (Level I) of human resource development. The figures for Japan in these and later years up to 1945 no doubt are underestimated, however, because of large numbers of uncertified teachers who continued to carry on traditional private instruction or were engaged in quasi-secondary education. On the other hand, the almost exclusive concern of the Meiji leaders with first developing a universal elementary education system, using high pupil to teacher ratios, probably held down growth of the teacher ratio per 10,000 population. Even then, despite the rapid expansion of formal secondary education in the first two decades of the present century, the ratio less than doubled and, by the outbreak of World

[10] See Harbison and Myers, *Education, Manpower, and Economic Growth*; pp. 45-48, for this and other comparisons of high-level occupations cited above.

War II, expanded only about one-third more. Compared to the Harbison-Myers average, these increases merely advanced Japan into the partially developed category (Level II). By contemporary standards, therefore, the formal educational system of Japan was probably "understaffed" in the prewar period.

Immediately following World War II, a sharp rise in the teacher ratio took place under the impact of the educational reforms—to a level in 1950 only slightly below the mean average Harbison and Myers find for the nations in the most advanced category (Level IV) of manpower development. This was swiftly accomplished despite the purge by the Occupation authorities of about one-fourth of the teaching personnel, but it also reflected the absorption of previously uncertified teachers and the rapid expansion of teacher training at the university level. Although class sizes markedly increased, especially as the result of high birth rates in the immediate postwar years, the rise in the ratio indicated the actual capacity of Japan to expand its teaching profession.

Japan's "output" of professional scientists and engineers compared to other nations also lagged until recently. Although there had been a strong tradition of scientific and vocational education inherited from the Tokugawa era, Japan entered the initial period of modern economic growth with a mere handful of persons educationally qualified in these professions even by then-modern standards. Not until the mid-1880s, when graduates began to flow from the new industry training programs and the University of Tokyo or returned from study abroad, did there begin to emerge a group of professionally trained engineers and scientists in the modern sense. Nevertheless, the rise of these occupations was relatively slow throughout the initial period of Japan's modern economic growth (1885-1905). The ratio per 10,000 population was only 1.7 at the end of the Russo-Japanese War; although it more than doubled by the end of World War I and rose to 8.4 by 1930, the ratio was not very impressive compared to the average ratios found by Harbison and Myers for nations in comparable stages of overall human resource development. While in the 1930s and throughout World War II the ratio grew to approximately 25 per 10,000 population—as the result of the expansion of universities and increased emphasis on technical and scientific curricula—still it was only about half the average ratios found by Harbison and Myers for the nations most advanced in human resource development. Japan finally attained this level only in 1960. Since that time, the ratio for scientists and engineers has soared, almost tripling from 1960 to 1975.

The seeming lag in generating scientists and engineers in the course of Japan's modern economic development until the past decade may be explained in part by a relatively large emphasis upon training "middle-level," or semi-professional, technical personnel to work with the comparatively small group of professional engineers and scientists. As mentioned in Chapter II, the multitrack system at the secondary and quasi-secondary education level served in considerable measure to supply large numbers of semi-professionals and technicians, especially those educated in polytechnical institutes (semmon gakkō). The large increase in scientists and engineers since 1945 resulted in part from the replacement of the semmon gakkō with university-level curricula as part of the postwar educational reforms.

In the fields of medicine and dentistry, however, Japan has been endowed with relatively large stocks of high-level manpower from the outset of the modern period. Already in 1875 the ratio of physicians and dentists per 10,000 population was 6.75—a proportion, according to Harbison and Myers, that most developing nations do not achieve until a much later stage of human resource development. This relatively high initial ratio resulted from the traditionally established professions of medicine and dentistry inherited from the Tokugawa era utilizing Oriental medical arts. However, few of the early Meiji practitioners were trained in modern medical and dental schools; and maintenance of these professions depended on long-standing apprenticeship systems through close teacher-pupil relationships (often within families). Although the quality of those engaged in these professions at that time may be seriously questioned by modern standards, nonetheless, the ratio indicates the considerable attention the Japanese have long given to health maintenance and care.

By 1885, when Japan entered its period of initial economic growth, the ratio of physicians and dentists had risen to more than 10 per 10,000 population, reflecting the output of the newly established medical and dental schools. It remained at about this level for the next 15 years, probably in part the result of the need for health maintenance of military recruits under the compulsory service system. The ratio then declined to 7.5 by 1905 after legal licensing requirements had been tightened considerably and the traditionally trained practitioners were dying off, but it slowly climbed back to more than 10 by 1930. Since the early 1930s, the ratio has risen only gradually, except for a sharp drop during World War II, attaining 14.6 by 1960 and 17.6 by 1975. Unlike science, engineering, and teaching, following World War II and the postwar educational reforms there was no sudden spurt beyond recouping the postwar drop in the ratio. The ratio achieved by 1960 stood at about the average Harbison and Myers find for the nations in the most advanced categories of human resource development. That Japan has not gone much beyond this level for physicians and dentists probably reflects the increased requirements for training and licensing, no doubt due in part to controls over entry and qualifications exerted by organizations and members of these professional groups. By the 1970s, however, as Japan entered an era of greater emphasis on social welfare, it was apparent that there were serious shortages of medical personnel, especially in remote rural areas. This has led to governmental plans for expanding medical education facilities.

Some scattered evidence of Japan's emphasis upon middle-

level and semi-professional education in support of high-level occupations is seen in the figures given in Table II for nurses,
pharmacists, and midwives—although sufficient data for other
nations are not available to make meaningful comparisons at the
various stages of human resource development. Until as late as
1910, there were few professional nurses and druggists in Japan,
and in fact formal nursing training began only in 1915. The
number of midwives, as might be expected in the absence of professional nurses, was considerably higher, although after 1899
midwifery was tightly regulated by law. From World War I on,
all three occupations steadily expanded, except for setbacks during and immediately following World War II, and a drop in midwives after 1955. The ratio of nurses per 10,000 population has
shown the largest gain. It increased approximately five times between 1910 and 1930, nearly doubled between 1930 and 1940,
and almost doubled again from 1940 to 1975. The increase in the
ratio of licensed pharmacists has been less spectacular although
steady except for the interruption of the Second World War;
overall, the ratio grew at least nine times from 1910 to 1975.
Midwives have exhibited the lowest proportional expansion, less
than doubling their ratio from 1910 (when it was actually lower
than in the 1890s) to 1955, and then dropping rapidly as the
number of nurses and physicians expanded.

The magnitude of the increases of persons engaged in these
supporting occupations may also be seen in relation to the
number of physicians and dentists over the years. In 1880, midwives numbered half the physicians and dentists and, with some
variations, fluctuated between 50 and 80 percent up to 1960,
after which there was a steady drop to about 15 percent in 1975.
Until 1900, the number of pharmacists was merely 5 percent of
the physicians and dentists, but 20 years later it had grown to
about 15 percent; immediately following World War II there was
one pharmacist for about two physicians and dentists, and since
1950 the proportion has remained at that level. The failure of this

ratio to increase in recent years may be explained in part by the practice of physicians and dentists in Japan of handling medicines directly to patients and clients. The ratio of nurses to physicians and dentists has shown the greatest growth among these groups. In 1910, there was one nurse for four physicians and dentists, but from 1940 to 1970, nurses outnumbered the latter three to two, and by 1975 were double.

Trends in Study Fields

Still another indication of Japan's investment in middle-level support personnel for the high-level groups is seen by comparing the growth in the proportions of students enrolled in the formal secondary schools, whose major courses of study were technical or vocational, with the enrollment changes in major fields of higher education. Table III presents these data for selected years from 1875 to 1975. In general, until the 1960s, the trend at the secondary level of education was opposite that for higher education. Up to 1895, as Japan initiated her modern growth, most secondary education was general and nontechnical (this does not take account, of course, of the quasi-secondary education and private vocational programs then in existence); while higher education was devoted primarily, except for the period around 1890, to science and technology. In the mid-1890s only about 15 percent of the secondary school students were primarily studying vocational subject matter (agriculture, fishery, technical, commercial, etc.); but in higher education more than half the enrollment was in science, engineering, agriculture, medicine, dentistry, and pharmacy. During the succeeding 25 years, the percentage of secondary school students in technical and vocational curricula steadily increased, reaching about one-third of the total enrollment in 1920, and although it dropped in the 1920s, recovered in the 1930s, leveling off at about 30 percent by 1940. For the past 30 years the proportion has been fluctuating around

TABLE III. Percentage of Total Enrollments by Major Field of Study in Secondary and Higher Education in Japan, for Selected Years, 1875-1975

	Secondary Education[a]						Higher Education	
Year	General	Agri-culture	Fishery	Technical	Commercial	Domestic Arts and Others	Science and Technology[b]	Law, Literature, Economics
1875	100.0						58.3	41.7
1880	100.0						78.1	21.9
1885	100.0						71.5	28.5
1890	100.0						36.1	62.8
1895	84.7	3.6		4.0	7.7		50.2	46.6
1900	84.3	5.0		2.1	8.4	0.2	39.3	56.2
1905	79.3	8.0	0.4	2.5	9.0	0.8	26.7	68.9
1910	76.2	10.4	0.5	2.2	9.8	0.9	32.5	63.2
1915	68.7	11.5	0.3	2.2	10.3	7.0	36.4	58.5
1920	67.7	10.3	0.2	2.7	12.7	6.4	33.9	61.7
1925	70.6	6.8	0.2	3.3	12.7	6.4	32.7	62.0
1930	68.5	6.5	0.2	3.6	14.1	7.1	31.6	60.7
1935	63.0	6.7	0.2	4.2	17.0	8.9	35.4	58.2
1940	59.0	6.2	0.2	6.6	18.0	10.0	42.7	51.5
1945	64.2	7.9	0.3	12.1	10.0	5.5	44.2	33.4
1950	65.2	9.4	0.4	9.3	9.5	6.2	29.4	59.7
1955	59.8	7.8	0.5	9.2	14.3	8.4	24.2	55.5
1960	58.3	6.7	0.5	10.0	16.5	8.0	26.6	54.1
1965	59.5	5.2	0.4	12.3	16.9	5.7	29.1	53.2
1970	58.4	5.3	0.4	13.4	16.4	6.1	30.0	50.3
1975	62.3	4.5	0.4	12.7	17.3	5.8	29.0	49.1

[a] Excluding quasi-secondary education.

[b] Includes science, engineering, agriculture, medicine, dentistry, and pharmacy.

Source: Ministry of Education, Japan's Growth and Education (1963), and Gakkō Kihon Chōsa (1960, 1965, 1970, 1975).

this figure. Most of the increase since 1900 has been due to the growth of enrollments in commercial and technical curricula, although agriculture played a prominent role in the expansion from 1900 to 1920.

In contrast, after 1895 but with a slight upturn in the 1960s, the percentage of higher education enrollments in the science, engineering, and professional fields has tended to decline. By 1905, it had fallen from more than 50 percent to about 25 percent, although by 1910 it rose again to about one-third and stabilized at this level until 1935. In the wartime years, the ratio spurted upward to close to two-fifths, but after 1945 it dropped markedly to its earlier level of between one-fourth to one-third. The opening of many new universities and colleges as the result of the postwar reforms undoubtedly led to the expansion of the less expensive higher education programs such as the arts, humanities, and law, with far smaller increases in science, technology, medicine, and the like. Within the technical and professional fields, however, engineering and, to a lesser extent, science have steadily replaced medicine, dentistry, and pharmacy in relative importance, although the latter three accounted for a majority of this enrollment until as late as 1935.

If we compare these trends for Japan with the data presented by Harbison and Myers for the orientation of higher education toward science and technology among the nations at various levels of human resource development, the Japanese experience was not unusual—except for the relatively large enrollments in these fields in the early years of the modern period. In the case of Japan, however, it needs to be stressed that the long-run relative decline in emphasis on science and technology in higher education (except during the war period) should be viewed in conjunction with the sustained emphasis on vocation and technical study in 2nd-level education. Were more precise data available for quasi-secondary training, the contrasting trends probably would be even sharper.

Since most of the secondary and all of the quasi-secondary

education was virtually terminal until after World War II, it is apparent that, once the initial period of modern economic growth was well underway, Japanese human resource strategy concentrated increasingly upon technical, vocation, and semiprofessional schooling in support of relatively small groups of high-level manpower. Since 1945, however, as the result of the educational reforms and rapid industrialization, higher education no longer remained a special preserve for small professional elites; while secondary education, now opened to all, has become more and more general and a channel for direct entry into universities and colleges. This change has produced a major shift in the mechanisms for allocating the middle-level labor force among technical and semiprofessional occupations. One result, to be discussed in succeeding chapters, is that training-within-industry and enterprise programs have come to play an even greater role in Japanese manpower strategy than they already had.

Japan's Human Resource Development Related to Economic Growth

Table IV shows our estimates of the development of Japanese human resources in relation to economic growth and industrialization from 1885 to 1975, compared to the means, medians, and ranges for the same items utilized by Harbison and Myers in categorizing the 75 nations they analyzed. The "composite index of educational attainment" is the same employed in Harbison and Myers. This "composite index" is "simply the arithmetic total of (1) enrollment at 2nd-level education as a percentage of the age group 15 to 19 adjusted for length of schooling, and (2) enrollment at the 3rd-level of education as a percentage of the age group 20 to 24, multipled by a weight of 5."[11] As previously men-

[11] See *Ibid.*, pp. 31-32, for the authors' explanation of this weighting in the "composite index." They note that "higher education should be weighted more heavily than second-level in such an index. A weight of 10 and a weight of 3 gave somewhat different results, but not significantly different."

tioned, Harbison and Myers found that this composite index had the highest positive correlation coefficient with national income per capita of the various correlations they computed. It should be noted again that the index does not include enrollment at the 1st level because it does not contribute to a higher correlation.

For Japan's estimated economic growth, Table IV lists estimates of real per capita national income at prevailing exchange rates in U.S. dollars at best can be estimated from official sources.[12] For the degree of Japanese industrialization, the percentage of active population engaged in agricultural occupations is utilized. The means, medians, and ranges found by Harbison and Myers at each level of human resources development are also shown for comparison.[13]

In addition, we have computed *two* "composite indexes" for Japan: one excluding and the other including quasi-secondary education enrollments. For the latter, however, we have arbitrarily weighted quasi-secondary education by one-half to take account of likely shorter duration of the school year, part-time schooling, and less intensiveness of study than conventional secondary education. Although Harbison and Myers do not include quasi-secondary education in their computation of composite indexes, we wished to gauge what effect it had upon the Japanese index both because of its historically prominent role in Japanese human resource strategy and because of our contention that quasi-secondary education even though nonformal or informal was still another facet of the prewar multitrack system. The use of

[12] There are numerous difficulties in estimating per capita national income and converting it into U.S. dollars at prevailing exchange rates. The estimates here are based first on deflating current yen prices to 1960 yen prices and then converting the 1960 yen prices to dollars on the basis of the official fixed exchange rate of ¥360 to $1.00 that was in effect from 1949 until December 1971. After that time, because of flexible exchange rates, the conversion is based on ¥296.8 per dollar.

[13] In replicating the Harbison-Myers study, Harbison, Maruhnic, and Resnick found that by 1965 the means and medians of the composite index for each category of human resource development had advanced considerably. So had those

TABLE IV.   Estimates of Japan's Human Resource Development and Economic Growth, for Selected Years, 1885-1975, Compared to Harbison-Myers Categories

	Composite Index of Educational Attainment		Per Capita Income, 1960 dollars	Percent Population in Agriculture	Public Expenditures on Education as Percent of National Income
Year	Excluding Quasi-Secondary Education	Including Quasi-Secondary Education			
1885	2.1	2.2	56.8	75.7	1.8
1890	2.6	2.7	70.3	72.7	1.3
1895	3.2	4.0	81.5	69.7	1.2
1898	4.6	4.9	85.7	67.9	1.3
1903	8.0	10.1	85.6	64.5	2.3
1908	25.8	29.8	93.0	61.0	2.5
1915	25.7	34.3	110.7	57.3	2.1
1920	34.7	46.3	149.1	52.4	2.5
1925	50.2	60.8	181.0	50.0	3.4
1930	53.7	71.6	211.7	47.7	4.0
1935	58.2	74.1	225.4	45.1	3.3
1940	69.6	89.3	226.2	42.6	2.1
1945	94.1	111.9	n.a.	55.8	n.a.
1950	110.7	113.5	274.7[a]	49.7	4.7
1955	135.2	140.8	319.4	41.2	5.2
1960	140.7	149.3	460.6	28.7	4.7
1965	161.8	168.2	705.6	22.1	5.3
1970	176.7	184.2	1,154.7	16.5	4.9
1975	195.8	207.4	1,686.3	11.8	6.3

Harbison-Myers
Categories of Human Resource Development for 75 Countries, late 1950s

I. (Underdeveloped)					
Mean	3.2		84	83	3.7
Median	3.0		71	85	3.2
Range	0.3-7.5		50-170	59-90	1.9- 5.9
II. (Partially developed)					
Mean	21		182	65	2.1
Median	23		173	67	2.0
Range	10.7-31.2		57-362	53-81	0.8- 3.6
III. (Semi-advanced)					
Mean	50		380	52	3.1
Median	48		357	49	3.1
Range	33.0-73.8		73-1,130	26-85	1.4- 5.5

TABLE IV. *(Cont.)*

IV. (Advanced)				
Mean	115	1,100	23	4.2
Median	105	1,000	20	4.0
Range 77.1-261.3		306-2,577	5-50	2.2-7.1

[a] 1952

SOURCES: Office of the Prime Minister, Bureau of Statistics, *Japan Statistical Yearbook* (1964, 1971, 1975) and *Kokusei Chōsa Hōkoku* (1975); Ministry of Education, *Japan's Growth and Education* (1963), *Gakkō Kihon Chōsa* (1960, 1965, 1970, 1975), and *Chihō Kyōikuhi no Chōsa Hōkoku* (1955); Economic Planning Agency, *Kokumin Shotoku Tōkei Nenpō* (1978); Ministry of Labor, *Rōdō Tōkei Nenpō* (1952); Bank of Japan, Office of Statistics, *Nihon Keizai Wo Chūshin To Suru Kokusai Hikaku Tōkei* (June, 1977); and Frederick H. Harbison and Charles A. Myers, *Education, Manpower and Economic Growth* (1964), pp. 45-48.

this all-inclusive index, of course, may overstate the human resource development of Japan compared to other nations. It would be desirable to have parallel data for other countries.

The years when Japan stood in a particular stage of human resource development according to the Harbison and Myers study may be seen by comparing the composite index for Japan with the means, medians, and ranges of the four country categories in their study. As previously pointed out, these categories are labeled Level I (underdeveloped), Level II (partially developed), Level III (semi-advanced), and Level IV (advanced)—shown in the lower half of Table IV.

In this comparison, Japan clearly remained in the Level I category for human resource development at least until the beginning of the present century. Only after 1890 did Japan reach either the Level I mean or medium, measured by the composite index either excluding or including quasi-secondary education. In these years, both national income per capita and the percent-

---

for per capita income except for Level I countries, which remained about the same as in 1960. These revised findings do not affect our analysis of the Japanese case, since, despite the increases, there was little change in rank of countries and rank order correlations. See Harbison, Maruhnic, and Resnick (1970).

age of population in agriculture also appear to be well within the ranges associated with Level I. Because of unreliable output and population data, there has been considerable disagreement over estimating the level of real per capita income during the Meiji era (up to 1908 in Table IV). Although real per capita income may have been somewhat higher than shown in Table IV for those years, it is very unlikely that Japan emerged from the category of Level I countries (underdeveloped) in terms of per capita income during that period, or, for that matter, until the 1920's.[14]

Between 1903 and 1908, however, Japanese human resource development rapidly accomplished the transition to the Level II category even though per capita income did not. From the outset of the modern period in 1868, therefore, it had taken Japan 35 to 40 years to rise from an underdeveloped to a partially developed status, according to the Harbison-Myers ranking of educational attainment. By 1908, utilizing either of the composite indexes for Japan, the Level II median and mean of Harbison and Myers had been exceeded, reflecting the rapid spread of secondary and quasi-secondary education around that time. For Japan, in contrast to Level I, the duration of Level II was extremely short, perhaps as little as 10 years and no more than 15 years. On the eve of World War II, although there had been almost no change in the composite index excluding quasi-secondary education, the index with quasi-secondary education included had clearly raised Japan into the Level III range. By 1940, both indexes show Japan fully within the semi-advanced category.

At the same time, however, there appears to be a notable lag in the rise of Japanese per capita income compared to the Harbison-Myers figures for Level II nations. On the other hand,

---

[14] While GNP per capita and national income per capita differ, we ignore the discrepancies as not significant for the long-run comparisons of trends. For discussion of the basic national income statistics, see Ohkawa and Rosovsky, *Japanese Economic Growth: Trend Accelerations in the Twentieth Century* (Stanford: Stanford University Press, 1973).

the population shift away from agriculture was about as expected in the Harbison-Myers analysis.

Japan's rise to the Level IV category, while somewhat problematic in timing, also advanced well ahead of the indicators of economic growth and industrialization. Measured by either composite index, Japan took 20 to 30 years after entering the Level III range to reach the Level IV category. According to the index including quasi-secondary education, this was accomplished between 1925 and 1935, and, excluding quasi-secondary education, not until during World War II. The all-inclusive index places Japan near the mean for advanced nations soon after 1940, although without quasi-secondary education this does not occur until the early 1950s.

A notable drop in the all-inclusive index occurred as would be expected in the immediate postwar period, and the index did not recover until after 1950; but, even omitting quasi-secondary education, the composite index showed a steady upward progression after World War II. The difference in trend is due to the termination of the multitrack system, absorption of some quasi-secondary education into formal secondary schooling, raising of compulsory education from six to nine years, and, later, expansion of higher education. The rise in either composite index after 1945 was so rapid, however, that by 1960, Japan ranked after the United States, Australia, The Netherlands, United Kingdom, and New Zealand, but ahead of 13 other nations in the Level IV category when only formal secondary education is counted in the index. (If quasi-secondary education is added for Japan, only the United States led Japan in that year.)

Despite this seemingly remarkable progress in human resource development, Japan's economic advance from Level II to IV was hardly commensurate with the averages and ranges presented in Harbison-Myers analysis. As shown in Table IV, per capita national income, while growing about fifty percent from 1920 to 1940, failed to rise in this period even to the mean for the

Level III category, although the composite index for human resource development already had reached the most advanced range. Despite the rapid spread of education and although the proportion of the active population in agriculture continued to decline from one-half to two-fifths during these years, the shift into nonagricultural activities had considerably slowed. This relative slackening, of course, increased dramatically in the chaotic period immediately following World War II. By 1945, per capita income probably had dropped more than half, almost to the level of 1910, and only in the early 1950s did it recover to the 1940 level. However, data for per capita income in the immediate post-World War II period are so unreliable that no estimates are given in Table IV for 1945 and 1950. Only by 1952 do such estimates become reliable.

The proportion of the population in farming occupations swelled immediately after the surrender, rising to more than one-half in 1945 and then dropping gradually to the two-fifths level again by 1955. Yet, it was precisely in this period that Japan began to emerge as one of the leading nations in human resources development as measured by the composite index. Since 1955 there has been rapid progress in economic well-being and the extent of industrialization. By 1960, national income per capita finally exceeded the mean for Level III nations, and by 1970 it had more than quadrupled to exceed the median and mean of Level IV nations.

The effects of the recent dramatic rise in income and educational levels are seen in the sharp drop of the percentage of the population engaged in agriculture. By 1960 the proportion had dropped to less than one-third and by 1975 was little more than one-tenth. It would appear, then, that Japan has been in the midst of accumulating educated human resources at a high rate of intensity, perhaps similar to the era between 1905 and 1920—in advance of further economic growth and industrialization presumably to come.

Japan's Human Resource Strategy: Public and Private

These quantitative aspects of Japan's educational and training system amply support the oft-stated contention that, once Japan had passed through her initial period of modern economic growth, by the early 1900s, accumulation of educated manpower began to run well ahead of the human resource needs "logically" commensurate with subsequent levels of economic development. This accumulation "in advance" is perhaps the most notable feature specific to Japan's strategy of human resource development. Although we do not have data to provide direct supporting evidence, it is likely that the process of advance accumulation began much earlier, perhaps well before the Meiji Restoration in 1868.

Japan's strategy of advance accumulation was not solely the product of central government policy, although after the Meiji Restoration central government decisions undoubtedly provided the basic institutional framework needed to encourage the comparatively large upsurge of educated and trained manpower. The quantitative outcome rested heavily upon local and private initiative in addition to the actions of the central government. It is not likely, for example, that the central government would have been successful in expanding 2nd- and 3rd-level education even in the ultranationalistic period preceding and during World War II without the earlier local and private response to the demand for education and training. Similarly, the transition to the rapid growth of high school and university enrollments following the education reforms of the Allied Occupation depended to a major extent upon the earlier development of the elaborate network of education institutions established by the combination of central and local government and private organizations. This coalition of efforts and desires, also traceable to the Tokugawa era, has been a constant theme in the strategy of Japan's human resources. The recent postwar expansion of school enrollments at secondary and higher levels of education may be interpreted as a continuation of a thirst for learning and training long exhibited by the Japanese beyond relatively immediate requirements for economic development *per se*.

Although in the period preparatory for modern economic growth the Meiji government clearly took leadership in generating skills needed in the new industries, for the initial forty years the central government was overwhelmingly occupied with spreading elementary education throughout the population. Until the beginning decades of the present century, except for its control over a small and elitist higher education system, the central government devoted relatively small resources to expanding 2nd- and 3rd-level schooling. Education beyond compulsory schooling in those years was largely left to private and local initiatives. As discussed more fully below, this is reflected in the low rate of central and local government expenditures in Meiji Japan on education as a percentage of national income compared to Level I countries, also shown in Table IV. When the government finally undertook to spread secondary education rapidly after the Russo-Japanese War, this was mainly in response to a fast-growing demand from private and local sectors of the society for increased educational opportunities beyond the elementary level. The growth was not highly systematic but was structured to mesh into diverse private and local efforts.

Until the Occupation reforms after 1945, the central government remained far more hesitant about extending secondary and higher education to the population as a whole than it had been in the case of elementary schooling. At the 2nd-level, government policy was directed toward a system of multitracking in order to serve selective vocational needs rather than to uplift general education attainment. While the multitrack school structure may have provided adequate preparation for specific occupations and careers (and this is dubious, as discussed later), it is likely that the great bulk of the students who went beyond the elementary grades did not do so to gain a basic education that would increase their flexibility in labor markets but rather to assure access to specific enterprises for their working careers. The selectivity implicit in the policy of multitracking, furthermore, was buttressed—or, better perhaps, complemented—by the rapid growth of nonformal quasi-secondary education programs largely initiated at the local and private level and aimed mainly at supplying trained recruits for individual enterprises and communities. Within the framework of the dualistic economic structure that had emerged, and in view of the preponderant preoccupation of Japan's leadership with rapid industrialization and strengthening national unity, this approach seemed entirely "logical" to many Japanese.

What is of particular interest is that, despite the long lag at the secondary education level, it appears that Japan's human resource strategy nonetheless "autonomously" generated comparatively large proportions of "middle-level" human resources once economic development was fully underway; and, if the relatively low numbers of scientists, engineers, and teachers may be taken as representative of the development of the "high-level" talents required for economic growth, the strategy furnished an unusually large group of educated personnel to support, supplement, and assist relatively small groups of high-level professionals.

The resulting output of "middle-level" manpower, moreover, was large enough to staff important parts of the traditional economic sectors as well as the modern. Also, it endowed both sectors with readily expandable human resource capacities. In all likelihood, the spread of education beyond the elementary level through the complex network of secondary and quasi-secondary schools and miscellaneous programs made feasible the ready substitution of educated labor for capital and materials, almost always in short supply, by segmenting labor markets and channeling trained workers along specific routes into and within specific enterprises.

The Harbison-Myers analysis suggests that, from the outset of economic development, a nation should give "absolute priority" to 2nd-level schools and the achievement of a "balanced" system of elementary, secondary, and university education in order to lay the basis for rapid and stable economic growth.[15] As seen in the quantitative measures, Japan's experience only in part followed this strategy of human resource development. A conscious formal program on a nationwide basis for the 2nd level was considerably delayed, established not much earlier than the military period of the 1930s and not becoming full-blown until after the postwar educational reforms. If there was a "balancing" in Japan, it depended to a major extent upon relatively uncoordinated local and private initiatives rather than central government planning.

Only since 1945 has there been a notable surge in the percentage of national income expended on education by government, reaching more than 5 percent at times since the 1950s and exceeding 6 percent in 1975. In fact, local government and private sources long provided the majority of the expenditures, although the proportion directly shouldered and indirectly subsidized by the central government gradually increased over the decades. As late as 1940, three-fifths of the expenditures still came from local revenue and even in the late 1960s about half was still local. Finally, it should be noted, private school expenditures have constantly increased—from 2 percent of total educational expenditures in 1902 to 14 percent in 1940 and 15.5 percent in 1960. In 1968 private expenditures on education were almost 30 percent of total public expenditures, and have probably remained at about that level since then.[16]

The postwar educational reforms required Japan's public policy to give increased priority to the development of secondary

---

[15] See Harbison and Myers, *Education, Manpower, and Economic Growth*, Chapters 4-8.

[16] See *Japan's Growth and Education*, pp. 191-194; and Ministry of Education, *Education in Japan: A Graphic Presentation* (Tokyo, 1971).

and higher education. In turn, this shift has severely strained the long-standing strategy of accumulating human resources through diversified channels of public and private educational and training institutions for selective allocation into the changing occupational structure of the economy. Elimination of the multitrack system has had the result of accelerating the rush into formal secondary education and into universities—if for no other reason than the lack of alternatives for seeking preparation and training for jobs. Although one effect of the change has been to strengthen the role of vocational and skill training within industries and enterprises, at the same time the system that had long been dependent upon an intricate interlocking of private and public, local and central educational and training institutions for allocating human resources in Japan's economic growth is threatened with dissolution. The next chapter elaborates the history of vocational education in Japan both in the public and private spheres and discusses how recent developments have brought into question the appropriateness of the combination that emerged over the years.

IV.

Industrial Training in Japan: An Overview

ALTHOUGH the new Meiji leaders in 1868 quickly recognized the need to develop industrial skills for Japan's modernization, they had no clear-cut plan for achieving this. It took at least thirty years after the Restoration for their strategy to take shape. Initially there was a build-up of a highly structured system of formal education including a variety of specific vocational tracks. However, after considerable experimentation in the schools and ministries, the problem of generating modern industrial skills was left largely at the operating enterprise level for solution.[1]

In this chapter, our purpose is to concentrate upon the efforts to spread general vocational training in Japan, both public and private, as a backdrop to the more detailed industrial-level cases that follow in Chapters V to VIII. This review helps explain why Japan eventually came to rely to a large degree on an enterprise-level strategy rather than a more general approach such as public vocational schools and training institutions. Also, we examine the implication of this strategy in terms of the degree of comprehensiveness and flexibility in skill training achieved, impact on the allocation of labor to industrial work, and the capacity of the enterprise training system to develop skills needed for an in-

[1] For a detailed history of industrial training up to the Second World War, see Sumiya Mikio, ed., *Nihon Shokugyō Kunren Hattenshi*, Vol. I and II (Tokyo: Japan Institute of Labour, 1971), and Ishihara Koichi, *Nihon Gijitsu Kyōiku Shiron* (Tokyo: Sanichi Shobō, 1962). See also Japan Ministry of Labor, *History of Industrial Education in Japan*, 1868-1900 (Tokyo: UNESCO, 1959), and *Wagakuni ni okeru Shokugyō Kunren No Shiteki Hatten Katei*, Vols. 1, 2, 3 (Tokyo: Japan Institute of Labour, 1969, 1970, and 1972).

creasingly sophisticated and diversified industrialization. The concluding chapter returns to this last point in assessing Japan's contemporary manpower problems as well as the model that Japanese experience provides for human resource strategy in present-day developing economies.

Initial Efforts of the Meiji Government

In establishing a modern school system the principal aim of the Meiji government was to prepare the young to enter a new, industrialized society. As already discussed, even before the modern period began, Japan had attempted to make formal education "practical." But formal education was not the only approach. Quasi-secondary schools, youth schools, and "miscellaneous" schools, concurrently with expansion of vocational curricula in the public secondary schools, became important supplements.

The first steps of the Meiji leaders for economic development included a systematic estimate of skill needs. These were based mainly on *Opinions on Industry*, a survey of potential industrial development by national and local leaders and administrators carried out in the 1870s, and published in the early 1880s.[2] *Opinions* also compared Japan with other countries, and the European experience became the basis for developing public vocational schools in the 1890s. The early policy makers soon concluded that Japan's needs for skill and vocational training could not be left to the haphazard workings of demand and supply in the labor market, but rather required coordinated, programmed efforts in both the public and private sector of the nation. As Taira has pointed out, however, Meiji leadership undoubtedly "deluded itself with ambitious designs about education."[3] In actuality, the approach was haphazard and progressed through trial and error.

[2] For data on *Kōgyō Iken* [Opinions on Industry], see Ōuchi Hyoe and Tsuchiya Takao, eds., *Meiji Zenki Zaisei Keizai Shiryō Shūsei* (Tokyo: Kaizosha, 1931-1933), Vols. 18-20.

[3] Koji Taira, "Education and Literacy in Meiji Japan: An Interpretation," *Explorations in Economic History*, Vol. 8, No. 4, July 1971, p. 393.

Initially, these government-sponsored programs concentrated upon training the poor and displaced such as the ex-samurai; only later was there a major effort focusing on young labor force entrants. Unlike the early policy for achieving universal primary education, vocational programs in the public schools did not become standardized and centrally directed for several decades. Instead there was a variety of approaches, formal and nonformal.

Throughout the first two decades following the Meiji Restoration, the new government and its agencies virtually took sole direction of the training of employees within the newly founded factories, arsenals, and offices—just as it did for the whole initial push to industrialize. In hopes of facilitating this, the Meiji government early decreed both the abolition of all previous barriers to labor mobility and the end of the long-established guild system among the traditional, shielded trades. As during the closing years of the Tokugawa period, training relied heavily on instruction by foreigners of recruits into the new work sites. Later, as the foreigners left, the more skilled Japanese workers directly instructed young recruits on the job. Most prominent of these vocational programs was the training of employees in the government-owned enterprises during the 1870s and 1880s. Except for the continuation of traditional craft apprenticeships in hopes that their skills would be useful in new industries, few other important instances of systematic training for new technologies and organizations appeared during these years in the private sector. Not until the government began to divest itself of ownership of industrial plants and enterprises in the 1880s were training functions for modern industry also transferred for private development. The importance of this early leadership by the government was that public enterprise had set a pattern for enterprise-level training programs; and, in a sense, through its own enterprises the government has remained a pattern-setter down to the present.

Despite the strong early resolve to foster widespread, publicly sponsored training systems, actual government support for the effort was minimal, and little was accomplished until close to the end of the nineteenth century. As already noted, resources for funding education in general proved meager; and these were allocated principally to developing universal elementary education, compulsory military service (which included an educational function), teacher preparation, and a single elitist university rather than vocational training. In fact, elementary education alone continued for decades to absorb three-fourths of all public expenditures on education; while secondary education, including its vocational training component, received barely 4 to 5 percent. Even as late as the 1920s, elementary education still accounted for two-thirds of the total and by 1940 more than half. In contrast, expenditures on secondary education, even after the elaboration of the vocationally oriented multitrack system, rose merely to between 15 and 20 percent a year of total outlays in the 1920s and then leveled off for the next two decades. Only when nine years of schooling became compulsory under the Allied Occupation reforms did secondary education require much larger proportions of expenditures, reaching more than 35 percent of public expenditures on education in 1968, by then finally equaling elementary school expenditures.[4] Thus, in the pre-World War II era formal vocational education programs remained relatively few, concentrated among the government ministries, for small select groups of skilled workers, administrators, technicians, and engineers. Nonetheless, vocational education directly aimed at meeting skill needs in the new emerging industries was first installed in the public schools in the 1890s. Central government ordinances in 1886 and 1894, relating, respectively, to middle and higher schools, began the earliest attempts to establish permanent in-

---

[4] Japan Ministry of Education, *Japan's Growth and Education: Educational Development in Relation to Socio-Economic Growth* (1962 White Paper on Education) (Tokyo: 1963), pp. 28-65 and pp. 94-95; and Japan Ministry of Education, *Education in Japan: A Graphic Presentation* (Tokyo, 1971), p. 51.

dustrial and vocational curricula within the public schools. Even then, agricultural and commercial courses, which had been planned as early as 1877, were not actually introduced into the public schools on a regular basis until the mid-1890s. With the adoption of a comprehensive ordinance in 1899 establishing a separate second-level vocational school track, the government attempted to foster formal vocation education on a far wider basis. In addition to middle-school tracks this ordinance also paved the way to establishing in 1903 the higher level semmon gakkō, to provide professional and subprofessional training in such fields as medicine, law, economics, commerce, and technical subjects. By 1905 the semmon gakkō numbered 63 and when they were abolished and/or absorbed in the new system of higher education in 1947, had grown to 368.[5] As discussed below, there was a continuing tendency for public school programs once established to shift upward toward higher levels of skill and professional education.

From the very beginning of the Meiji period, the central government did focus special attention upon the vocational training of school teachers, recognizing that all other advances in modern education depended on an adequate supply of appropriate instructors. While the first public normal schools were established in 1873, there followed a twenty-five-year period of experimenting with teacher training, utilizing a variety of approaches, but directed mainly toward basic education rather than vocational training. An ordinance in 1899 systematized the normal schools into higher, ordinary, and women's categories, which were respectively geared to the various levels of the general educational system and placed under direct administration of the prefectural and local governments. Normal schools themselves, of course, were strictly vocational. Graduates were required to teach and received the status of low-level civil servants, limited in their rights to academic freedom. Normal schools were not treated as a

[5] *Japan's Growth and Education*, pp. 150-151.

part of the more liberal university system (although some, notably the higher schools in Tokyo and Hiroshima, were later upgraded to this level).

Despite the early development of normal schools, however, little was done to include preparation of vocational education teachers. In fact, development of such programs on a notable scale waited until the mid-1930s. Probably one reason for the lag was that, from the outset, practical learning was considered sufficiently a part of the general education in the common schools that no particular need was perceived for specialized instruction. Only with the rapid expansion of heavy industry in the 1930s, coupled with growing militarism, did the government move to establish special normal schools for agriculture, physical education, and youth programs. By the end of World War II, there were 30 such normal schools, all of which under the postwar reforms were also absorbed into the new universities. Specialized vocational education teacher training was not revived until 1961, when in the face of growing labor shortages, especially among the young, the central government established nine new schools for preparing industrial arts teachers.

Ministry Vocational Schools

While vocational education in the public schools took several decades to emerge, new recruits into the early government-operated industries received a combination of vocational instruction, on-the-job experience, and general study. (Chapter V, which deals with the government-owned telecommunications and railway enterprises, provides examples of such early programs.) These pioneer efforts were the forerunner of the later wisespread utilization of quasi-secondary education programs by enterprises in the private sector.

Initially, from 1870 to 1885, modern industrial training in Japan was promoted under the direction of the central government, mainly by the Ministry of Industry and to a lesser extent by the Ministries of Internal Affairs, Finance, Navy, Army, and Education. As mentioned, in that 15-year period the Ministry of Industry allocated as much as 42 percent of its total budget to the salaries for foreign teachers, consultants, and experts who were brought to Japan to aid in vocational instruction in the imported technologies.[6] The Ministry of Industry almost immediately set up its own schools for telecommunications, steel and iron production, handicraft training (especially for females), lighthouse keeping, and mechanical engineering. These programs, too, tended to become increasingly sophisticated and were gradually upgraded. In 1878, for example, the ministry's school for mechanics became the *Kōbu Daigakkō*, a college for advanced training in civil, mechanical, and electrical engineering, architecture, applied chemistry, and metallurgy. When the new Tokyo Imperial University was established in 1887, the kōbu daigakkō became the University's Department of Engineering.[7]

Because ministry vocational schools tended to rise into higher levels of formal education, the ministries organized a new series of programs for the training of all-around factory workers, the so-called *seisakugaku kyōjō*. Bringing together several of those programs, the Ministry of Industry in 1882 established the Tokyo Craftsman School (*shokkō gakkō*), which regularly offered courses for comprehensive training of apprentice workers. But these, too, tended to become elevated. In 1890, after establishment of an attached apprenticeship program, the Tokyo Craftsmen School itself became the Tokyo School of Technology. Before the turn of the century, Niigata became the site of still another well-developed craftsman program run by the Ministry

---

[6] For an analysis of the transfer of Western technology at that time, see Saegusa Hakuo et al., *Kindai Nihon Sangyō Gijitsu no Seiōka* (Tokyo: Tōyō Keizai Shimpōsha, 1960). For materials on foreigners employed in Japan, see Umetani Noboru, *Oyatoi Gaikokujin* (Tokyo: Nihon Keizai Shimbunsha, 1965), and *The Role of Foreign Employees in Meiji Era in Japan* (Tokyo: Institute of Developing Economies, 1971).

[7] Japan Ministry of Education, *Gakusei 50 Nenshi* (Tokyo: 1922), pp. 174-176.

of Industry. At the same time, of special significance for training fully skilled workers were the arsenals and shipyards under the control of the army and navy ministries, which established systematic programs particularly in the fields of metallurgy, mechanics and construction. All of these, however, as in the case of the Tokyo Craftsmen School, tended to lose their original character of preparing all-around skilled workers as they moved on to training higher-level specialized engineers, technicians, administrators, and the like. Another example of upgrading was the forerunner of the present Hitotsubashi University, which began in 1874 as the Tokyo Higher School of Commerce and Economics.

Systematizing Public Vocational Education

Throughout the Meiji period, then, the initial concern of the central government for preparing workers for employment in the new industries shifted steadily toward the training of higher-level specialists. In turn, this shift entailed increasing the effort to install vocational education in the newly developing public school system. With the establishment of the education ministry led by Mori Arinori in the 1880s, government responsibility for basic vocational training began to shift from the Ministry of Industry to the common school system under the direction of the Ministry of Education. This change occurred just as the government began to divest itself of many of its own industrial enterprises and turn them over to private management and ownership. Mori nonetheless believed that public schools rather than industry should now provide the basic training for industry. In anticipation of the shift, as early as 1883 the government drafted regulations regarding the rights and responsibilities of employees and workers, including relations between masters and apprentices, designed mainly to hold apprentices within workshops in order to improve their skills.

Most important was the series of new government ordinances

issued by the Ministry of Education, notably in 1886 and 1894, dealing among other matters with vocational education curricula as part of the formal establishment of the multitracking system in the common schools. In these decrees, the Ministry of Education set forth specifications for acceptable programs for apprenticeship, vocational teacher training, and agricultural, technical, commercial, navigation, fishery, and industrial education in both elementary and quasi-secondary schools and in the professional and semi-professional semmon gakkō. In the 1894 order, the government for the first time provided subsidies for publicly operated quasi-secondary education, notably apprenticeship schools and supplementary vocational schools. Later in 1914, since private schools also had begun to flourish with the outburst of industrial activity of that time, the central government began to provide local governments with financial support for private programs provided they met prescribed standards set by the ministry for both general and vocational education. In the background was Japan's first major labor standards law, the Factory Law of 1911, which during the next 27 years implemented a series of steps protecting female and child labor.

As already seen in Chapter III, public quasi-secondary vocational education made notable gains in the years between the Russo-Japanese War and World War I. In response to Japan's industrial surge, there was a mushrooming of officially recognized programs, usually called technical supplementary schools, which numbered more than 14,000 by the end of the period. In addition 12 new semmon gakkō had been established as well as at least 80 lesser technical institutes.

Because of this hot-house growth, the government mounted a series of investigations of how best to rationalize the burgeoning school system. These culminated by 1920 in a set of major revisions in the laws and regulations covering vocational and technical education. The main thrust of the changes was a consolidation of many existing programs and the encouragement of new, local vocational schools to be established by prefectures, cities, towns, villages, chambers of commerce, trade unions, and other public and private organizations. Another major objective of the changes was to ensure that all approved programs would place heavy emphasis upon moral indoctrination as well as providing military drill. Standards were raised for common school curricula in agriculture, industry, commerce, fishery, and navigation; night vocational classes were expanded; and financial support of private industrial training and female vocational education was increased. In general, it was at this time that the minimum duration of the approved upgraded quasi-secondary schools was set at two to four years. Later in 1930, new regulations for the quasi-secondary education programs raised again both curriculum standards and the amount of practical instruction. By 1935, 95 upper level and 15 lower level industrial schools were operating with official recognition.[8]

The central government particularly utilized this growing network of programs during the prolonged depression of the 1920s, which was worsened during the disruption caused by the Great Kanto Earthquake in 1923, to enact the Youth Training School Law of 1926. This law required all boys who had not gone beyond the six years of compulsory elementary education or into supplementary extension courses to enroll in designated quasi-secondary schools for vocational training, military drill, and nationalistic indoctrination. Those who completed the required programs were excused from a half-year of compulsory military service.

Following the Great Depression and the Manchurian Incident of 1931, the militarists stepped up their campaign to gain complete control over the educational system in line with their de-

---

[8] Ōuchi Tsuneo, *Totei Seidō to Gijitsu Kyōiku* (Tokyo: Kyōchōkai, 1936), 283, 286; and Sumiya Mikio, ed. (1971), Vol. II, pp. 229-246. See also Okamoto Hideaki, ed., *Sangyō Kunren 100 Nenshi* (Tokyo: Japan Industrial and Vocational Training Association, 1971), pp. 96-103.

mands for strengthening heavy industry and emphasizing ultranationalism. The thrust of the militarists began with vocational
training and eventuated in establishment by the government in
1935 of the so-called Youth Schools, replacing the earlier Youth
Training Schools. The Youth Schools absorbed many of the
15,000 private and public quasi-secondary education programs in
operation at that time and injected into their curricula a heavy
emphasis on military training. Beginning with about 17,000
schools, by 1942 the Youth School system expanded to almost
24,000.[9] An amendment to the law in 1939 stimulated further
expansion of the Youth Schools by taking over private training-
within-enterprise programs. This amendment placed all firms
with 200 workers age 16 or more and certain special smaller firms
under the jurisdiction of the Ministry of Health and Welfare and
required three years of training for these workers.[10]

With the outbreak of the Pacific War, the Youth Schools became a key part of the government's overall effort both to regulate industrial manpower and to conduct basic military training.
As such, they became a chief means for assuring that all males
who did not go beyond elementary education would continue to
receive the stipulated combination of vocational training, military instruction, and moral indoctrination as "industrial soldiers."
However, the Youth Schools did not supplant the formal public
secondary vocational schools. The latter continued to grow in
number from about 1,000 in 1930 to almost 1,800 at the end of
World War II, and by 1943 more than 125,000 workers had received training in these schools.[11] On the other hand, in 1943 the
central government consolidated the entire vocational education

[9] Sano Yōko, *Nihon ni okeru Setsuritsu Kikanbetsu Chūtō oyobi Jun-Chūtō
Kōygō Kyōiku no Suii* (mimeo.) (Tokyo: Institute of Management and Labor
Studies, Keio University, 1964), p. 32.

[10] Japan Ministry of Labor, *Rōdō Gyōseishi* (Tokyo: Rōdō Hōrei Kyōkai, 1961),
pp. 943-944.

[11] *Ibid.*

system through a single regulation designed to centralize its administration (as had been done for the middle and higher schools also), to fortify ultranationalistic indoctrination programs, and to increase the stress upon the importance of industrial work as a patriotic duty. The government also took over direct control of all normal schools, semmon gakkō, and other semi-professional schools.[12]

Thus, throughout the prewar and war period, a large array of government-sponsored vocational schools, secondary and quasi-secondary, was in operation under increasingly centralized direction of the military. These included, in addition to those already mentioned, elementary and advanced technical schools, apprenticeship schools, vocational schools, technical supplementary schools, commercial schools, navigational schools, fishery schools, specialty schools (cooking, typing, etc.), technical educators schools, agricultural military drill halls, fishery military drill halls, and so forth.

Yet, despite this wide variety of public vocational schools, these institutions proved unable to provide the skills needed by Japan's rapidly expanding modern industries. As it turned out, they served principally to recruit and channel youth who became clerical and administrative personnel, particularly in small and medium-size enterprises, rather than skilled manual operatives for enterprises with new and complex technologies. A main reason for this outcome apparently was the low quality of training actually provided and the inability of the schools to keep abreast of changing technical requirements. Still another reason was the government's growing preoccupation, especially after the militaristic period began, with strengthening nationalistic and moral indoctrination of the young. As discussed later in this chapter, despite the far-flung government efforts, in actuality industrial

[12] Japan Ministry of Education, *Sangyō Kyōiku 50 Nenshi* (Tokyo: the Ministry, 1966), pp. 160-164.

skills training remained largely within the enterprises themselves.

Postwar Reforms in Public Vocational Education

A major undertaking of the educational reforms under the Allied Occupation was to incorporate and upgrade the highly diversified vocational and industrial training programs into the new "comprehensive" secondary schools now open to all elementary school graduates. The newly enacted Fundamental Law of Education and the School Education Law, the key laws of educational reform adopted early in 1947, instituted some vocational orientation at each school level. Aside from these changes, however, the only other provisions for industrial training were to be found in the new Labor Standards Act of 1947 and its requirements for apprenticeship and for working conditions. Under the education reforms, pre-vocational education such as handicrafts and home economics was placed in the elementary school curriculum. In the lower or junior high schools, vocational courses were to be offered covering home economics, commerce, technology, agriculture, and fishery; and in a few select senior high schools, specialized curricula were set up in these vocational fields.

However, since the overriding objective of the reforms was to make certain that general education would eliminate ultra-nationalism and establish a democratic outlook among the children, it is questionable how serious these efforts at vocational preparation actually were. The level of success in improving vocational and industrial education was inconspicuous. Demand for entrance into the few specialized vocational high schools, for example, was well below the planned capacity, especially as the new, popularly elected local school boards made little effort to equip them properly or to recruit qualified teachers. The failure of the public school system to absorb adequately the diverse vocational tracks established in the prewar period was probably one reason that private enterprises and government agencies continued to maintain and expand their own training programs. [13]

Lack of articulation between general and vocational education led to the enactment in 1951 of the Law for the Encouragement of Industrial Education, which permitted both the central government and local school boards to institute specific vocational courses by providing public subsidies for this purpose in either the public schools or private organizations. This act revived industrial training centers and vocational guidance institutes similar to those established in the late 1930s. It was followed in 1953 by the Law to Encourage Science Education, which met similar objectives by establishing a science service center in each prefecture to assist local elementary schools in developing their curricula in the basic sciences in high schools, colleges, and universities that instituted technical courses in formal vocational education departments. The plan was strengthened with the establishment of the Science and Technology Agency by the central government in 1956.

However, expansion of technical education in the formal school system was resisted by educators on the grounds that it would undermine the objective of developing well-rounded citizens for a Japan committed to nurturing democratic values. They feared that undue emphasis on vocational education would too easily revive the totalitarian tendencies of pre-World War II and recreate a status system based on multitracking. Manpower planning, they felt, should not rely primarily on refashioning the education system, but rather upon such factors as breaking down immobility in labor markets, generating greater standardization of skill training across enterprises, giving support to the modern-

[13] See, for example, Japan Productivity Center, *Industrial Skill Training in Japan* (Tokyo: Japan Productivity Center, 1959), pp. 2-5.

ization of small and medium-size industry, and reducing oligopolistic controls exercised by the large modern enterprises. Achievement of closer articulation between formal education and industrial training was seen to lie first in these areas, especially if more were done to implement various legislation for public vocational training already in existence.

A number of underlying factors, however, have increasingly supported public efforts by the schools to expand industrial and vocational education. The agricultural population has been declining swiftly as better economic opportunities beckoned farmers and their families to the cities. High school education rapidly approached the saturation point, so that distinctions between blue-collar and white-collar work based on level of education began to evaporate. Trade union pressure, in addition to continuing shortages of young workers, after 1960 helped to compress wage scales and to raise wage levels in general. Japan's economy became increasingly diversified, with greater emphasis upon the production of consumer goods and services. Factors such as these have threatened training programs that are tied largely to length of service and permanent employment only within a specific enterprise.

With labor shortages looming by the end of the 1950s, the government enacted more direct measures to improve vocational education. Most important was the Vocational Training Law of 1958. This act, discussed more fully below, consolidated the 1951 law, established public vocational training centers, offered subsidies for approved in-plant programs, and, for the first time, set testing standards for various skilled occupations. Then, in 1962, in a move reminiscent of the earlier semmon gakkō, the government authorized a new set of 17 technical colleges for junior high graduates, which combined three years of high school and two years of post-high school education; most were operated by the central government and a few by prefectures and private organizations. By 1972 the number of these schools had increased to 63, with a total enrollment of almost 50,000.[14] However, private enterprises at first tended not only to disregard these new government-sponsored programs but also to expand their own internal programs. Only by the end of the 1960s when reliance on these institutions ran into problems of limited skill flexibility in the face of increased labor mobility did interest grow in expanding vocational training outside the enterprises.[15] Before discussing these recent trends we turn to the historical review of training *within* enterprises in general.

Emergence of Enterprise-Level Training and Education

Despite the initial impetus provided by the Meiji government, throughout Japan's modern industrial history private efforts in the field of technical and vocational training have overshadowed the central government's role. Except for the very early decades of the Meiji era and the World War II period, public education played only a supplementary role in vocational training. The common schools seem to have served primarily as the means for orienting the labor force to entering employment in the plethora of small and medium-size firms that sprang up alongside the relatively few large enterprises. The small and medium-size firms tended to combine both traditional and modern techniques and methods of production, so that they did not require highly sophisticated and changing skills to the degree the large firms did. As mentioned, not until after World War II, following the Occupation reforms, did the central government even take on the bulk of the financing required for vocational and industrial training offered in the public schools. Rather, despite the many

[14] Japanese National Commission for Unesco, *The Role of Education in the Social and Economic Development of Japan* (Tokyo: Japan Ministry of Education, 1966), pp. 87-94; and *Japan Report* (New York: Japan Information Service), Vol. XXI, No. 6, March 16, 1975, p. 3.

[15] Hideaki Okamoto, "Vocational Training in Japan," *Japan Labor Bulletin*, (Tokyo: Japan Institute of Labour), Vol. 9, No. 1, June 1970, p. 48.).

government ordinances, regulations, laws, and subsidies, the financial onus for providing training was left largely to local authorities, private organizations, and individuals. Until the outbreak of the Pacific War, individual tuition charges and private contributions alone usually accounted for up to 90 percent of the total financing of these programs.[16] Nonetheless, it is notable that families and individuals readily responded to training opportunities even under these burdensome conditions.

The large private enterprises played an especially crucial role in training. Until the imposition of tight manpower controls in the early stages of World War II, it had been left to the individual firm to determine its exact requirements for training and education for specific skills and knowledge. There were a number of reasons for this:

First, despite the state's leadership in embarking upon modernization and economic growth, its basic viewpoint was that each family and individual had responsibility for and a stake in achieving a sense of participation in national development through their own efforts. The government provided only the initial motivation through a basic education that stressed loyalty and hard work. After that, it was up to the individual himself, his family, or local community. No doubt, this approach reflected the lack of available capital for investing heavily in public education at all levels at the same time; but basically there was the belief that the ordinary citizen would quickly respond to the appeal of Japan's new nationalism.

Second, "localism" had long had strong foundations in Japanese society and in government policy. Thus, the central government hesitated to tamper with local attachments lest paradoxically the very goal of national unification might be jeopardized in the process. When in the 1870s and early 1880s the new state almost failed, in part as the result of the disruption of long-

[16] Japanese National Commission for Unesco, *The Role of Education in the Social and Economic Development of Japan.*

standing regional and local political and social arrangements, the central authorities recognized a need for carrying over elements of decentralization from the Tokugawa era. Education was a prime candidate for this role.

Third, establishment of a uniform public education system itself initially proved much slower than had been hoped for. Particularly, as noted, technical and vocational education as well as the secondary level in general lagged far behind the spread of the formal elementary schools and the building of high quality universities (which were difficult tasks in themselves). This left a vacuum that could be filled only by local and private efforts as new skills for the spreading industrialism were demanded. Traditional methods of imparting skills, such as the master-apprentice and patron-client (*oyabun-kobun* or *oyakata-kokata*) systems of training, met some of the needs during this transition, although, as we shall see, inadequately.

Fourth, when the Japanese economy did begin to leap forward, technologically and organizationally, it was too late to wait upon the then-established public educational system to provide the needed vocational training, especially for the specific manual skills required. Technological and organization changes were appearing sporadically, suddenly, and selectively. It was an unpredictable and uncertain process. Under these conditions, occupational standardization could not occur, making uniform training difficult and expensive. Major firms borrowed or adapted distinctive foreign technologies that made it impossible either to utilize traditional craftsmen and their apprentices or to establish standardized training courses across enterprises above the simplest skill levels (as in cotton textiles). Yet, the need for particularized skills grew so rapidly and unpredictably that each modern enterprise strove to find and retain its own skilled labor supplies. In all likelihood, moreover, technological specialization by enterprise led to further technological specialization in face of the skill shortages and high labor mobility despite a general condition of an excess supply of unskilled labor throughout the period. A publicly supported vocational training system did not appear technically or economically feasible under such conditions of uncertainty.

Finally, even if the public schools could have developed sufficiently sophisticated technical and vocational training, in Japan's dualistic economy, highly diverse levels of technologies emerged together. This was reflected in the industrial structure with its various types of enterprises, ranging from the most modern to the most primitive, with all sorts of hybrid varieties in between. As explained in Chapter II, industrial "dualism" was a major reason for the development of the multitrack school system, since the labor requirements of so many levels had to be satisfied simultaneously. The multitrack system, however, served mainly to allocate graduates among the various levels of the economy rather than provide any specific training directly suitable for each level.

This situation was unlike that found in many present-day developing economies where there is usually an enormous gap between the modern and premodern sector of industry. Under the variegated technical conditions of industry in Japan, it was difficult to develop a coordinated education system that could provide standard training programs through the public schools alone. Specific enterprise training within the modern firms instead had to serve this function and thus, in a sense, came to constitute still another educational track beyond the compulsory years of universal public schooling. After all, as Taira points out, even as late as 1910 only two-fifths of the male labor force and slightly more than one-fifth of the female had completed the six years of compulsory education.[17] This development, of course, sharply contrasted with the emergence of higher education in Japan, which, soon after modern industrialization began, came to rely almost exclusively upon colleges and universities for recruit-

[17] Taira (1971), p. 375.

ing the would-be policy makers, administrators, engineers, and other high-level professional personnel in industry—in fact, probably to a greater degree than in the American or British experience.

Role of Patron-Client System

Premodern patron-client apprenticeships systems had long existed in the traditional craft guilds, old merchant houses, and native artisan (*shokunin*) shops for many decades prior to the Meiji Restoration, and they continued well into the modern era. Patron-client systems emerged from the traditional tight-knit family-like group structures that may be traced back over centuries. Only by the 1920s, however, did modern enterprise training take full hold in most major companies, although formal enterprise-level training programs for factory operatives (*shokkō*) trace their beginnings to the 1880s. In 1899, for example, shokunin were still the dominant type of worker in Tokyo: by one account, 113,958 in 296 trades and 66,148 establishments with only 43,556 factory workers (shokkō) in 424 factories, and as late as 1916 shokunin still outnumbered shokkō more than 12 to 1 in Kyoto.[18]

Although the new Meiji government abolished the artisan guilds in the early 1870s in order to erase a part of the feudal heritage and open the economy to increased labor mobility, it was exceedingly difficult to eradicate the traditional relationships of the patron-client system, which as will be seen in the succeeding chapters, persisted in numerous forms at work sites. Even though special training schools were established in the new modern industries, management continued to rely heavily upon patron-client ties for training workers within the factory or mill, since most plants at the outset employed the traditional artisans

[18] Rōdō Undō Shiryō Iinkai, *Nihon Rōdō Undō Shiryō* (Tokyo: Tokyo University Press, 1963), Vol. 2, p. 241.

in hopes of adapting their skills successfully to the new types of work. While labor was generally abundant for unskilled work, there was not only a severe shortage of skills everywhere but in some local areas industry was unable even to attract unskilled workers, especially males. As a result, enterprises continued to rely upon patrons as labor recruiters and agents to bring in workers from remote geographical areas to work with them or their henchmen.[19] The government itself had recognized the continuing need for these mechanisms by issuing new regulations in 1885 that encouraged reformation of the old artisan guilds under the new name of trade associations.[20]

The persistence of patron-client entities indicates the failure in Japan to systematically reorganize and restructure labor markets on occupational, interregional, industrial, and national lines. Apparently, it was assumed that "natural" economic processes would bring these about. Patron-client labor market arrangements in Japan were probably little different than those found in many other developing economies. They represented a highly decentralized labor market structure in which personal relationships were the key element in matching jobs and individuals. By virtue of experience and personal connections a patron typically was skilled in certain techniques required in modern enterprises; but he kept them as secret as possible and passed them on to loyal client members of his retinue in piecemeal fashion. Thus,

[19] Koji Taira, *Economic Development and the Labor Market in Japan* (New York and London: Columbia University Press, 1970), pp. 101-127. See also Solomon B. Levine, "Labor Markets and Collective Bargaining in Japan," in William W. Lockwood, ed., *The State and Economic Enterprise in Japan* (Princeton, N.J.: Princeton University Press, 1965), Chap. XIV, pp. 633-667; and "Labour Market Segmentation in the Economic Development of Japan" in Subbiah Kannapan, ed., *Studies of Urban Labour Market Behavior in Developing Areas* (Geneva: International Institute for Labour Studies, 1977), pp. 107-115.

[20] Notably trade associations formed in the building trades with some success. See Koji Taira, "Industrial Revolution and Factory Labor in Japan," *Cambridge Economic History of Europe*, Vol. 7, Part 2 (London: Cambridge University Press, 1978), pp. 166-214.

the patron was in a key position to gain access to work in various firms and to supply workers who had some knowledge of needed skills. However, a patron-client entity operated over a limited work area and, indeed, strongly resisted expansion into a broad market structure. One patron-client relationship did spawn others, but in general they remained closed. On the other hand, a patron would readily move his retinue from one work site to another in response to the highest bidder, opening the way to such widespread mobility as occurred before World War I.

The shift to shokkō from shokunin type workers required almost two generations. While the transition from the one to the other represented a distinct change, they had in common close identification of the employees with the immediate work organization and employing firm. Moreover, in most cases the change-over was not abrupt but occurred gradually, and usually both the traditional and new training systems were blended and carried on simultaneously within a major firm.[21]

When the enterprise-level programs finally became a major element in Japan's "modern" employment system, in contrast to the patron-client arrangement, they relied upon direct recruitment from schools, career-long work commitment, length-of-service and age-wage payment (nenkō), company-provided welfare, and early retirement. The types of enterprise-level training, like other components of Japan's employment system, continued to depend upon both traditional methods and modern innovations, relying heavily upon long-standing patron-client relationships within the firm. As the young workers completed training under patrons within the new modern enterprises, especially as semi-engineers and technicians, they usually continued to work in the factory which first recruited them and in turn themselves became patron-like types in imparting knowledge to the succeeding groups of new recruits. Thus, the traditional style of patron-client relationship persisted within the place of employment—an

[21] Ishihara (1962), pp. 124-137.

organizational feature notable in modern plants down to the present day.[22] Only later did the concept of permanent "key" employees of the enterprise emerge to replace the patron-client entity.

Yet, as the old patron-client system gradually gave way to direct management control, the modern enterprise frequently faced sudden gaps between existing available skills and the new technological requirements, especially when sharp changes in technology were introduced.[23] Establishment of organized training schools and programs within the major enterprises was one attempt to meet this problem. However, despite the persistence of patron-client patterns, little resembling the traditional apprenticeship system reemerged in industry. In their quest for "instant" skills, firms could not wait for the all-round training and tutelage provided by comprehensive apprenticeships. Instead, training was usually directed toward specific needs, dictated by the new technology brought in from abroad.

Gradually replacing the craftsmen who had risen through the traditional apprenticeship were the so-called "key" workers who now were to receive successive training and retraining over the duration of much of their working careers within a given enterprise. These workers were not trained to their fullest capacities for any one type of work but were available within a company for ready transfer to work a variety of tasks as required by changing technology. This system provided the enterprise with a high degree of flexibility in utilizing the workers permanently in its employ—another characteristic that has continued to the present day. The "key" worker approach made it difficult for common

[22] See Robert E. Cole, *Japanese Blue Collar: The Changing Tradition* (Berkeley: University of California Press, 1971); and Ronald P. Dore, *British Factory-Japanese Factory: The Origins of National Diversity in Industrial Relations* (Berkeley: University of California Press, 1973).

[23] Sumiya Mikio, *Nihon Chinrōdō Shiron* (Tokyo: Tokyo University Press, 1955), pp. 216-239; and *Nihon Shokugyō Kunren Hattenshi*, Vol. I, p. 102. See, also, Ishihara (1962), pp. 74-85.

craft and occupational groups to emerge across enterprises, as had been the case in Western countries or even among the traditional Japanese artisans. As long as training was partial even though continuous, and technological change came in distinctive, incremental, and sudden forms, a "key" worker increasingly became tied to a particular firm. His skills were not likely to be of use to any other large enterprise.[24]

Moreover, in boom times such as the Russo-Japanese War and World War I, the major firms were inevitably threatened with skill shortages, labor piracy, and worker unrest. Management's reaction, as might be expected, was to strengthen the devices to tie their skilled and potentially skilled workers to the firm. This was still another reason for the gradual decline of the traditional patron-client system and the abandonment of traditional apprenticeships; for the patron usually had the power to move his retinue from one place to another, depending on the state of the economy, and thus could raise costs and disrupt a firm's growth and stability. He also had the power to settle labor disputes, which were occurring with greater frequency.

For several decades beginning about 1910, management in the modern enterprises fought the grip of the patrons, gradually substituting the "key" worker system as a means of wresting away the control of the training of new workers. The price for this was: 1) lifetime employment commitments, 2) seniority wage payments, 3) welfare benefits, 4) training and retraining programs in response to immediate technological requirements, and 5) acceptance of a Factory Law in 1911 that provided Japan's first legislated labor standards on a comprehensive scale.

Transition to Work Force Segmentation

In order to compete with patrons, managements of large-scale enterprise usually felt compelled to reaffirm their own benevo-

24 Levine, "Labor Markets and Collective Bargaining in Japan."

lent paternalism, or "welfare corporatism."[25] This took the form
of emphasizing the traditional ideology of local and family-like
ties within the enterprise in the quest for worker loyalty and immobility. In addition, modern enterprise managements found it
to their advantage to abandon reliance upon "outside" agents for
carrying out recruitment and training and to undertake these
functions themselves.

Thus, modern firms tended to avoid the open labor market in
searching for skilled workers. Instead they turned to the formal
schools for directly recruiting new workers who were to be
"reared from the young." While direct recruitment from school
appeared to be similar to the old apprenticeship system, in actuality it was more an attempt by each modern enterprise to
"capture" a supply of potential skills for exclusive use over the
long-term. In this context, educational level itself did not become an important factor for determining the level of wages
among companies even in the same industry, although it was important within the firm's hierarchy. The larger and more modern
the firm, the more likely that workers of a given age and level of
education over time would do better financially than their counterparts in smaller firms. Usually, the elementary school
graduate in the large modern enterprise would soon earn more
than the middle-school graduate in the small traditional company
even though both had the same age, length-of-service, experience, and possibly skill. The differential in favor of the large-
company employee was a reward not only for skills specifically
useful to the large company but also for the potential of acquiring
additional specific skills within that enterprise.

Welfare corporatism embraced only those workers who could
gain permanent status as "key" workers in the company. The new
school graduate upon being hired first became a probationary
employee, who in the eyes of the supervisor or engineer to whom

[25] We are indebted to Ronald Dore for this term to describe the Japanese employment system. See Dore (1973).

he was assigned for training had to demonstrate his ability and loyalty in order to gain permanent status. Unlike apprentices elsewhere, he was paid a wage for learning his work, and wage progression was a sign of gaining status. Once he cleared the probationary period he could count on rising up the status ladder, receiving regular increments in pay, and constantly learning new skills and tasks. Temporary hires were left out of this system.

Management exercised considerable care in granting admittance to recruits destined to become "key" workers. Recruits had to have impeccable references and personal connections, were required to have completed upper-elementary schooling, and to show excellent health. New workers were usually subjected to severe physical, ability, and personality tests in order to decide who would become permanent. In part, high qualifications were demanded to overcome the opprobrium which industrial work had earned previously when marginal members of the labor force had been recruited. Especially for low-income farm families, the pay possibilities of the new employment system were attractive and, given the training and advancement opportunities, far more so than sending children on to higher levels of education that would likely be a continuing burden to themselves and relatives. For this system of welfare corporatism, management began to elaborate special professional personnel divisions within their organizations to take charge of the multifaceted aspects of permanent employment, including recruitment, training, and general education. A major aspect of their functions was the maintenance and strengthening of employee morale, loyalty, satisfaction, and harmony, since interfirm mobility could not be counted upon to remove dissatisfied employees.

"Key" workers thus came to constitute the permanent work force of large modern enterprises. Those who were rejected as "key" workers remained for their careers on the fringes of the organization in the category of "temporary" employees, not ever likely to be admitted to the training process, and often drifting back and forth between the family farm and a given factory. The temporary workers, of course, tended to insulate the "key" work force from adverse labor market conditions and to strengthen further the emerging training-within-enterprise system. As a result, external competition for labor among the large enterprises eventually was reduced to a single port-of-entry: new school graduates. Workers hired from other sources would be employed only on a temporary basis and, if by chance they became permanent, then usually at a discounted wage compared to what they would have received if they had been employed directly upon school graduation. Welfare corporatism thrived on this segmentation of the labor market.

Japan's system of segmented employment has persisted to the present, although the reasons for the persistence differ from the reasons for the origins of the system. Indeed, with the economic slowdown of the early 1920s there seemed to be little economic rationale for employers in large-scale modern industry to continue the single port of entry and the continual piecemeal, within-enterprise training approach. Potential labor skills by then had become abundant as the result of increased population, primogeniture on the farms, spread of education, urbanization, and depressed economic conditions. Moreover, as seen in Chapter III, public vocational education was receiving increased attention and government support. Under these conditions, one reasonably might have expected segmentation to break down and more open labor markets reemerge.

The chief explanation for the persistence does not seem to be solely economic. Politics and ideology were equally important. The "liberal twenties" of Japan was a period of great social ferment, which the economic depression of that time exacerbated. Ideological conflict was intense, especially following the Russian Revolution, the emergence of large-scale unemployment, and the growth of new radical groups, particularly in newly formed labor unions. As a result, large modern enterprises did not wish to tamper with the recently established employment arrangements. It was widely feared that this would merely fan the flames of labor discontent and threaten to undermine the economic structure that already was precarious because of intensified world competition.

Japan's ruling elite recognized that the most immediate threat after World War I to segmenting the employment system was the rise of trade unionism, even though at that time the labor movement was torn by ideological divisions between the communists, socialists, and anarchists, and by the conflict between the traditional labor patrons and the new intellectual managers. Direct labor-management confrontation loomed on a wide scale especially because, with the gradual decline of the patron-client system, oyabun could no longer be counted upon to settle conflicts in the shop. In the face of these developments, employers fell back upon the historical traditions of familyism, loyalty to superiors, and nationalism. They tended to give greater and greater emphasis to the virtues of the closed-employment system. While this was especially so for the white-collar "company member," it also reached down into the manual work force core of "key" skilled employees. Lifetime employment guarantees and steady progression in compensation and welfare benefits based on length-of-service—and corresponding to life-cycle needs—became ready-made practices to keep out "radical" elements, to dispense with collective bargaining, and to maintain harmony within the plant. As an integral part of these rewards and benefits, managements also strengthened training-within-enterprise programs—based on incremental learning of new skills plus an emphasis upon loyalty to the company and the immediate work group.

In this context, as further explained in the chapters on individual industries, many large firms embraced "scientific management" with its array of techniques such as time-and-motion studies, personnel aptitude testing, and even "employee participation."[26] By the mid-1920s Youth Training Schools, sponsored by the government to strengthen discipline among new young employees, easily gained acceptance. Backing up the system came revisions of the Factory Law, introduction of some social insurance schemes, adoption of a measure of male suffrage, efforts at conciliation and mediation in labor disputes, and a crackdown on left-wing radicals under the Public Police Maintenance Law of 1926. All of these developments served to strengthen rather than weaken work-force segmentation by enterprise. To managements of modern firms in those years, such practices were viewed as "rational" in spite of Japan's increasing and plentiful supplies of educated labor.

Wartime Labor Control and Its Postwar Impact

The segmented work-force system further tightened in the following two decades for still other reasons. As militarism gained ascendancy throughout the 1930s and with the onset of the Pacific War, government leadership recognized in Japan's employment practices an important instrument for achieving both labor control and popular indoctrination in ultranationalism. While Japan's shift to heavy and chemical industries from light industry after 1931 placed even greater strains upon skilled labor supplies (for the first time demand for male workers in industry outran the demand for females), the segmented hierarchical work forces were utilized to allocate workers efficiently. The whole arrangement seemed like sets of regiments, battalions, and other military units going into battle. Labor pirating, which had emerged once again, was severely condemned; and, although major firms had to draw so-called "half-way" or "mid-term" employees away from small and medium-scale enterprises to meet their skill needs, this was usually accomplished without dis-

[26] See Kenji Okuda, "Management Evolution in Japan," *Management Japan*, Vol. 5, No. 4, 1972, and Vol. 6, No. 1, 1972.

rupting the established hierarchy among the permanent workers by deliberately "discounting" the wages, benefits, and status of these experienced recruits.

These developments culminated in the labor freeze and the wage control orders of the late 1930s and 1940, and then in 1943 wholesale shifts, ordered by the government, of workers from less essential consumer goods production to more essential wartime industries and enterprises. In order to achieve tight enterprise identifications in view of possible disruptions from the movement, the government established the Industrial Patriotic Labor Association (*Sampō*) as a principal means for allocating labor among firms and organizations. In its wake, trade unions were driven out of existence. All of this meant a redoubling of skill training efforts *within* the enterprise itself.

The wartime experience under Sampō, with its heavy stress upon fixed attachments and identifications at the enterprise level, had much to do with the even firmer hold of the permanent employment system in the major enterprises during the post-World War II period. Now, however, the lifetime attachment concept was considerably extended. In the chaos immediately following Japan's surrender, economic and psychological security for the modern Japanese industrial worker lay in maintaining his close identification with his firm. The great outburst of labor unionism, now strongly encouraged by the Occupation authorities as a major democratizing reform and meeting little resistance from employers or the government, in large part reflected this drive for security. Characteristically, the unions organized on an enterprise or plant basis, encompassing all who could claim status as permanent employees and making no distinction between white- and blue-collar workers. Usually, a union's jurisdiction embraced the many "half-way" workers who had joined or been allocated to the given firm during the period of labor shortage. The success of unionism, whatever its weaknesses, otherwise rested on fastening most of the work force securely within the enterprise itself at a time of enormous uncertainty. This principle of enterprise-based unionism applied not only to the employees already regularly on the payroll but also to new recruits.[27]

Continued labor market segmentation, now supported by enterprise unionism, inevitably meant that training would be all the more concentrated among permanent workers of a large company. With lifetime attachment extended to so many more blue-collar workers than previously, management had little alternative but to concentrate training efforts within the firm itself. In a sense, therefore the new unions traded off the training function to management in order to assure employment security for their diversified membership. The result was to reinforce work-force segmentation by enterprise and to extend within-enterprise training programs even further.

As the Japanese economy emerged from its chaotic state by the late 1940s and soon afterward reembarked on rapid growth and technological change, once again the need for flexibility in skill training appeared. Management could afford to undertake the enormous amount of training and retraining involved as long as growth was taking place and most additions to their work forces continued to come from the unskilled new school graduates hired at relatively low wage rates under the length-of-service pay system. In addition, with the Japanese education system now undergoing a revolutionary structural transformation as the result of Occupation reforms in which major emphasis was given to general education rather than to vocational training, the major enterprises could look for little assistance in obtaining sufficient skills from the schools. Both short- and long-term training had been left to the enterprises themselves.

[27] See Solomon B. Levine, *Industrial Relations in Postwar Japan* (Urbana, Illinois: University of Illinois Press, 1958); and Kazuo Okochi, Bernard Karsh, and Solomon B. Levine, eds., *Workers and Employers in Japan: The Japanese Employment Relations System* (Princeton, N.J.: Princeton University Press, 1973).

On the other hand, in the sectors where small and medium-size enterprises abounded but which provided comparatively few permanent employment guarantees, training needs became especially critical if these firms were to survive in competition with the rapid technological advances of the major companies. The postwar upgrading of general education and broadening of university opportunities were especially beneficial for these firms. Following the establishment of the Japan Productivity Center in 1955, supported at first by American technical assistance funds, large-scale training facilities and programs, carried out by outside agencies both public and private, were launched primarily for the benefit of the smaller companies. So was the vocational training legislation. It is noteworthy, however, that the large firms continued to operate on their own.

Recent Pressures on Enterprise Training

Since the early 1960s, the piecemeal but continual training programs among the segmented work forces of the major enterprises have been subject to heavy pressures for modification that may result in much broader-gauged approaches. A number of factors appear to account for this trend. These include labor shortages, quickening labor mobility, increasing standardization of technologies, product diversification and automation, higher educational levels and stronger aspirations of workers, changing worker values, and management reorganization including changes in supervisory functions. However, the transformation is not as yet entirely clear cut. Enterprise "consciousness," supported by enterprise-type unionism, delicately structured worker status hierarchies, length-of-service and age payment systems, company welfare arrangements, and continuing (although weakening) economic dualism, remain severe obstacles to any rapid change-over from established training patterns.

Nonetheless, many large enterprises that have long prided

themselves on their own special schools and training programs have begun to feel the strain of maintaining their own institutions. The squeeze in the labor market derives from the sustained high rate of economic growth and the decline in new school graduates as the result of a decrease in birthrates and an increase in school duration. The resultant shifts in labor demand and supply led throughout the 1960s and early 1970s to above average increases in starting wages for the young worker and increased mobility among the new labor force entrants, many of whom now shop around for the highest paid starting jobs and often scorn lifetime employment with a single company. With their rising educational backgrounds, the young workers often find that they are adaptable to a wide range of tasks and that their experience in one job may indeed be transferred to another, even in a different company.

At the same time, particularly as the major firms incorporate more and more sophisticated technologies and organization, the permanent workers already in their employ, especially the older members, seem less able to adapt to the new skill requirements—or they are not encouraged to do so by some managements. Partly, this is because of changes in methods, machinery, materials, work flows, and the like that have taken place under conditions of rapid industrial change, for which older workers are believed less prepared because of their lower levels of formal education. Union resistance often makes it impossible for management to reallocate these workers through layoffs and discharge or even in transfers, so that some firms have resorted to ingenious means of creating new organizational hierarchies, utilizing subcontractors, employing temporary and outside workers, developing diversified product lines, establishing subsidiary companies, and introducing ability and merit pay elements into the wage system, without in most cases disturbing existing permanent attachments and relative social statuses of employees.

Another factor is that management organization itself has begun to change, although the change is probably still in its early stages. By the mid- or late 1950s, it had become clear that in many cases established managerial organization in large firms was incapable of taking advantage of opportunities for growth and development in the rapidly expanding Japanese economy. The high degree of management centralization with functional divisioning, characteristic of most large firms, fell short in carrying out the planning and coordination required for rapid technical innovation, diversification, expansion, mergers, and cost reduction. Existing methods of organization—symbolized by the so-called *ringi* decision-making system—had grown up in an era of selective monopolization and industrialization, premised on capital shortages (and, hence, concentrations in the zaibatsu), abundant labor supplies, and tight-knit patrimonial employment arrangements. With the aid of outside agencies, such as the Japan Productivity Center and the Japan Industrial Training Association, and considerable cooperation from American companies and American military, management groups, especially their younger members, began an attack on the established organizational system that continues to the present. Firms began to abandon managerial centralization and accompanying narrow specializations by function and to create new staff departments for overall planning and broad strategy. In turn, this meant a broadening or enlarging of functions down through the organization including first-line supervisors, and a recognition that authority as well as responsibility had to be decentralized. A result of the new trends was a call for much broader training for the management members as well as employees and for basing compensation more and more upon ability and responsibility rather than seniority.

At the level of first-line foreman, the changes in technology and organization required new training techniques. Some of the most popular were Training-Within-Industry (TWI) and Job-

Relations-Training (JRT), which were introduced from the United States soon after the end of World War II. By the mid-1950s, more than 825,000 supervisors were trained in the use of these methods.[28] It was no longer possible in some cases to treat the foreman, for example, as simply the all-knowing, fully experienced "key" worker or oyabun in his work group. Perhaps he still could be entrusted with paternalistic functions in dealing with subordinates, but over the years he had lost any role in hiring, firing, and training to the specialized personnel departments. Workers themselves were learning to do jobs with standardized techniques without the direct aid of foremen; at the same time the specialized staff and technical personnel were determining training needs and carrying out training functions. What this meant, of course, was a further disruption of established patron-client relationships within the work shops, and in the transition the work supervisor at times found himself increasingly in an ambiguous position vis-à-vis his subordinates.

The upshot of these trends is that training requirements for the major firms have been changing from those provided through the long-established within-enterprise training institutions. Although work-simplification, as the result of mass production and automation, and worker "participation" in workshop decision making, have meant the continuation of in-plant training, many managements are increasingly skeptical that all the training needs of their work forces can be met in this way, even if couched in a framework of enterprise attachment, status hierarchy, and welfare corporatism. The question now being gradually approached, particularly with the recent reestablishment of technical higher schools and the expansion of public vocational training centers, is to what degree training activities should be shifted to outside agencies.[29]

[28] Ryoichi Iwauchi, "Adaptation to Technological Change," *The Developing Economies*, Vol. VII, No. 4, December 1969, p. 430.

[29] Okamoto (1970), pp. 10-17.

On the other hand, many managements look upon the new developments with considerable trepidation. They have long had enormous faith in promoting company loyalty and career progression within the enterprise as chief motivations for assuring productivity increases and high work effort. Managements often fear that plants will be disrupted as the result of tensions between old and young workers if the segmented enterprise employment systems are abandoned and strong enterprise consciousness declines. Also, since the exact nature of technological change and training needs remains unpredictable, they feel that abandonment of "inside" in favor of "outside" training programs is risky. In most cases, however, management is seeking some type of reconciliation between established systems and new institutions. Increased worker participation in management is seen by many as a possible solution, while the government's chief response has been the promotion of an "active" manpower policy and program as described below.

In summary, Japan's historical manpower strategy for modern industry concentrated upon developing and accumulating skills within specific enterprises rather than throughout the economy as a whole. Thus, instead of fostering open labor markets for the ready transfer of skills from one sector to another, from one occupation to another, or from one enterprise to another, the general approach was to make available educable workers at all levels of industry. The multitrack school system, even with its vocational components, allocated students to a sector of the economy but not to specific work. It was then up to the individual enterprise to provide specific training. The modern large-scale enterprise responded to this approach by continuously building skills piecemeal as required *within* their own organizations and utilizing skills in a highly flexible manner almost solely within their own or subsidiary organizations. Open markets existed only for older unskilled workers as temporary workers in modern industry and among the small and medium-size firms. Connections between such external labor markets and the closed systems of the enterprises were limited, with ports of entry and exit confined mainly to new school graduates and, on a temporary basis, to experienced workers in times of boom or rapid technological or organizational change.

This strategy encountered few difficulties as long as the Japanese economy experienced steady population and labor force growth, compulsory secondary education was not yet universal, and technological advances were introduced on a relatively selective basis. To be sure, bottlenecks occurred when there were sudden increases in labor demand, as for example during the Russo-Japanese War, World War I, and World War II. After each of these periods, however, accumulation of skills within enterprises quickly resumed; and no doubt, the availability of skills in each enterprise work force was a major factor in pulling Japan through the dark days following the surrender in 1945 and in contributing to rapid recovery and expansion of the Japanese economy in the 1950s. This meant, in essence, the continuation, if not the strengthening, of the "key" worker system and the concomitant piecemeal but continuous training within the plant or enterprise. In turn, each modern enterprise maintained its distinctive separate employment system, and standardization of jobs and occupations across enterprises failed to emerge until quite recently. For the economy as a whole, or even at the industrial, regional, or occupational level, external labor markets played minor roles in the development of human resources.

Emergence of an "Active" Manpower Policy

Since the late 1950s, however, there has been growing concern that the closed employment and training systems may prove inadequate for the continuing growth and structural change anticipated for Japanese industry. While the final chapter goes into this problem more fully, it is useful to outline the recent development at this point before taking up the human resource strategies utilized at the industry level.

By the early 1960s, the single major port of entry into firms, namely school graduation, had become too narrow to channel the labor required by the rapidly expanding industrial enterprises. Reliance on school graduation presented a serious dilemma for skill training, let alone Japan's employment system as a whole. Since work force hierarchies in modern firms have been firmly based on gradual upward progression in skills, length of experience in a given company, and level of education which the worker begins with, it was possible for managements to maintain such hierarchies only so long as workers could be flexibly allocated within the enterprise, retired relatively early, and replaced by new school graduates. On the other hand managers hesitated to open the enterprises to mobility through external labor markets because it ran the risk of seriously disrupting the status systems that had emerged and, at the same time, of generating high turnover among the younger workers dissatisfied with the need to wait their turn to rise up the status, income, and promotion ladders. Under such conditions, internal training systems could be wrecked without viable substitutes.

Recognition of the problem led to a number of experiments in personnel administration such as introducing intensive within-enterprise training programs for older employees, simplifying work, enlarging jobs, and implementing quality control programs, and job classification and evaluation. These have also meant increased emphasis upon company loyalty, incorporation of ability and merit factors in individual wage payments, worker participation in shop problems, larger responsibilities for work supervisors, and the like. However, while expanding internal training activities to retain the advantage of within-enterprise flexibility, management also began to insist upon greater public efforts to upgrade potential recruits through outside education and vocational preparation.

The first thrust in this direction was the Vocational Training Act of 1958. Before adopting this landmark act, the Japanese government had long concentrated vocational preparation primarily in the school system. Yet, as we have already discussed, except at the highest levels of human resources there was a notable lack of coordination between vocational training in the formal schools and skill needs of modern industry. Government legislation to develop industrial skills outside the schools and enterprises had been relatively feeble—at best geared to meet immediate problems of unemployed or dislocated workers. The government gave little consideration to active promotion of industrial skill training through direct sponsorship of separate vocational institutions articulated with organized labor markets for such skills. Although as early as 1883 the government had enacted regulations for master-apprentice employment relationships, had set working standards for miners in the 1890s, and had legislated the protective Factory Act for woman and child labor in 1911, it did not go so far as to couple these with vocational training institutions and labor market organization. Initial recognition of the need for the latter appeared in 1921 with the passage of the Employment Exchange Act, but this was actually an attempt to discourage workers from leaving their farms and shifting to urban areas in a period of severe economic depression. It was followed by similar "emergency" measures for public works employment and the youth schools attached to enterprises in the depressed 1920s. While the employment exchanges played a significant role in the 1930s and war years in transferring and providing training for skilled workers from medium and small firms to the expanding heavy industries, they remained supplemental to the closed employment systems that were taking firm hold in the large modern enterprises.[30]

[30] Organization for Economic Cooperation and Development, *Manpower Policy in Japan. OECD Reviews of Manpower and Social Policy No. 11* (Paris: OECD, 1973).

First glimmerings of an "active" governmental policy for manpower development emerged with the postwar labor reforms. Beginning in 1947, the new Labor Standards Law identified 15 occupations for standardized skill training (two years later this was increased to 31 occupations), but these aimed at preventing worker exploitation under the guise of training. Also, in the same year, the government adopted the Employment Security Law to replace the 1921 Employment Exchange Law, setting up Japan's first broad-based unemployment insurance system and a much wider network of public employment offices. In 1949 the Emergency Unemployment Countermeasures Law was adopted to provide relief projects for 300,000 workers displaced under the disinflationary impact of the Dodge Plan. TWI, JRT, and related training techniques were introduced first in the government-owned National Railways, and through the Employment Security Law in 1950 were offered throughout industry in general under government auspices. Probably, one of the most notable developments was the sponsorship, with American assistance, of the Japan Productivity Center (JPC), beginning in 1955. The JPC's training activities have been especially useful for small and medium-size enterprises. Yet, in 1954 there were merely 28,000 enrollees in the public vocational training institutes established under these various measures, and in 1958 only 62,000 in programs within enterprises that had received official certification.[31]

Adoption of the Vocational Training Law in 1958 thus represented the government's first major effort at a wholesale long-term reorganization of skill training and labor market structure. The new act called for setting up public vocational training institutes, in-plant programs, and skill trades testing.[32] Notably, the

[31] Ikuo Arai, "Notes on Institutions and Policies for Manpower Development in Japan," *Industrialization and Manpower Policy in Asian Countries* (Tokyo: Japan Institute of Labour, 1973), p. 151.

[32] For an analysis of the experience under the 1958 Law, see Hideaki Okamoto (1970), pp. 4-7.

new approach provided both for directly operated training centers set up by prefectural governments and for company-level programs run by individual or groups of enterprises according to central government standards and with its financial support. The Japan Vocational Training Association was also established in 1958 to promote the new training activities. Special legislation to assist and retrain displaced garrison force workers and coal miners, handicapped persons, and unemployed dock workers followed in 1958, 1959, 1960, and 1963; while in 1961 the government adopted the Employment Promotion Projects Law with a far-flung network of vocational training for unemployed, older, and handicapped workers, and in 1963 strengthened the retraining functions of the public employment offices. By the early 1960s the 1958 act had led to establishment of a sizable number of short-course vocational training centers, almost 400 in all, and of more than 1,000 training programs run in cooperation with individual companies or groups of companies.[33] All these schools aimed mainly at adults rather than new school graduates in order to bring into balance the rapidly changing demand and supply conditions for labor skills. Despite these efforts, the Act of 1958

[33] The act established two types of public vocational training institutions eligible for financial support: (1) "general" and "advanced" centers set up by prefectural governments for basic training of new labor force entrants for six months to one year and for training of displaced workers for two months to one year; and (2) "comprehensive" or "advanced" centers, operated under the Employment Promotion Projects Corporation for "specialized" training for two years, for job instructor training, and for some displaced workers. In 1976, there were 201 "general" centers, enrolling close to 130,000; and 211 "advanced" centers with almost 85,000 enrollees. See Japan Ministry of Labor, *Labour Administration in Japan* (Tokyo, 1971), p. 18; and Japan Ministry of Labour, *Vocational Training Administration in Japan* (Tokyo: undated), p. 9.

In addition, the act authorized support for private in-plant training programs initiated by individual or groups of employers that met standards set by the Ministry of Labor and received approval from the prefectural government. By 1974, more than 1,100 plants and groups received such authorizations, and the number of trainees exceeded 73,000. See Okamoto (1970), and *Vocational Training Administration in Japan*, p. 66.

failed by far to reach its initially announced ten-year goals of training 1.55 million new skilled workers, upgrading 1.39 million experienced workers, and refreshing 420,000 foremen. By the late 1960s only about one-half of these targets had been achieved.[34] Moreover, those involved were primarily workers in small and medium firms. Very few new school graduates attended—perhaps not more than 10 percent of the enrollees.

As a result, the government turned to an even more active manpower policy. In 1966, it adopted the Employment Measures Law, which aimed at achieving full employment, matching labor supply and demand, and developing and utilizing every worker's potential abilities. The objective was to shift the role of the vocational training centers decisively from correcting ad hoc imbalances in the labor market to preparing workers for long-term careers. The "failure" of the 1958 act, it appears, lay in the reluctance of junior and senior higher graduates to enter the vocational training schools (only about 10 percent did so) because they still did not perceive these schools as important channels for upward mobility and employment security compared to enterprise programs.[35]

Implementation of the 1966 law began with the Basic Employment Measures Plan adopted by the Japanese Cabinet in March 1967. Its ultimate objective was to break down enterprise and other segmentation in the labor markets and to promote worker mobility, and as such was a portion of Japan's comprehensive 15-year national development plan at that time. It was followed in July 1969 by wholesale revisions in the 1958 Vocational

[34] At the time the 1958 Act was adopted, the Japanese government estimated that there were unfilled vacancies for 800,000 skilled workers, or about 15 percent of the skilled labor force. By 1965 this estimate was revised upward to a shortage of 1.8 million, or 22 percent of the skilled labor force, and it remained at that level until 1970. See Okamoto (1970).

[35] See Robert E. Cole and Shun'ichiro Umetani, "Manpower Training and Employment in Japan," *Monthly Labor Review*, Vol. 98, No. 11, November 1974, pp. 43-45.

Training Act, which were put into effect as the National Vocational Training Plan in 1971. Additional amendments were made in 1972 and 1974. The plan aimed at increasing by two to three times the volume of training programs by the mid-1970s that would emphasize "life-long training" rather than ad hoc labor market adjustments. It included skill training, adult as well as youth training, and expansion of the skill-testing programs. Under the plan, an Employment Council made up of 20 academic experts was established in the prime minister's office to advise the various government ministries on implementation.[36]

It remains to be seen what impact Japan's new "active" manpower policy has had or will have. By 1975 there had been only small expansions in the number of training centers and trainees, although the types of programs had been considerably diversified and program content improved. Following the oil embargo and other "shocks" to the Japanese economy in 1973, economic growth came to a virtual halt for the next two or three years. At the same time it became increasingly clear that basic shifts in the structure of the Japanese economy would likely emerge. This meant for the time being a shift back to concern with unemployment rather than long-term labor market restructuring. The temporary solution was exemplified by the new Employment Insurance Act of 1975, subsequently expanded, which provided wage subsidies to employers who retained workers who would otherwise be laid-off, discharged, or retired from their enterprises.[37] Aside from this setback, there has been little evidence of any further loosening of the segmented work forces, although the new policy may be affecting placement of new school graduates in their first jobs and extending the retirement age of older workers.

[36] For a description of the programs as of 1975, see *Vocational Training Administration in Japan*.

[37] See Masayuki Nomiyama, "Employment Stabilization Fund," *Japan Labor Bulletin*, Vol. 17, No. 1, January 1978, pp. 7-8.

In conclusion, Japan still faces the problem of devising a successful overall human resource development strategy that began with the attempt to industrialize 100 years ago. However, the decision whether to invest in training through public or private facilities, or in what proportion and coordination among them is probably more difficult today than it ever has been. While efforts in both spheres will be made as long as the Japanese economy experiences expansion and technological diversification, Japan may no longer rely on accumulation of skills mainly *within* major enterprises to meet its manpower needs. The loose combination of general education provided by the government and specific vocational training provided by enterprises appears to be becoming obsolete. We return to this problem in the final chapter.

In the next four chapters, we trace by groups of industries the particular strategies that the Japanese developed historically to meet their respective needs for human skills at the enterprise level. We begin (Chapter V) with the steel and shipbuilding industries, concentrating on skill training in the years up to World War II. The industries are treated together because of their close technological and economic relationship and the decided influence of prewar government policy in both industries. Railways and telecommunications are also taken together (Chapter VI) because of their early beginnings and direct government ownership and operation. We then turn to the private industrial sectors. Banking, textiles, and mining are examined as a group (Chapter VII) because of their premodern histories and their rapid development as private labor-intensive industries soon after the outset of the Meiji Restoration. Finally, we deal with a set of more recent, capital-intensive, major industries (Chapter VIII) in the private sector, heavy machinery, electrical equipment, and chemicals.

V.

Training in Basic Industries: Steel and Shipbuilding in the Prewar Period

THE mark of a nation's advance into modern industrialization is the development of domestic iron and steel manufacturing on a major scale and the use of the output for sophisticated heavy machinery, modern weapons, and complex products such as large ocean-going vessels. Although Japan's modern economic growth followed the familiar path of first emphasizing light industry, particularly textiles, conscious attempts to establish a heavy industry base began even prior to the Meiji Restoration.[1] It was clear to the Tokugawa leadership that with the arrival of Perry's Black Ships Japan's national independence was threatened. The threat almost immediately gave impetus to efforts at building a military establishment that could rely upon a modern domestic iron and steel industry to produce armaments required for effective defense against foreign invasion. By the late 1850s the shogunal and clan governments were vigorously pursuing this objective—a pursuit that would become even hotter for the new Meiji government with its sloganized resolve to build "a rich country, a strong military." However, high resolve alone was not enough to generate rapidly the needed human and material resources. Although nationalism and government centralization undoubtedly

[1] See Hisashi Kawada, "Industrialization and Educational Investment in the Meiji Era" in *Educational Investment in the Pacific Community* (Washington, D.C., The American Association of Colleges for Teacher Education, 1963), pp. 39-54; and Koji Taira, "Industrial Revolution and Factory Labor in Japan," *Cambridge Economic History of Europe*, Vol. 7, Part 2 (London: Cambridge University Press, 1978), pp. 166-214.

contributed significantly to Japan's eventual success in developing basic heavy industries, almost half a century was to elapse before this goal was actually achieved.

The efforts of the Japanese to produce their own iron and steel began with the objective of constructing modern naval vessels and military weapons capable of defending the nation against the world powers. From the beginning, then, the steel and shipbuilding industries were intimately intertwined. It is notable that during the first decades of their development, both industries shared the same management and, to a major extent, work forces.

Despite the limited objective, however, serious obstacles were encountered from the outset. It became quickly apparent that not only were there especially large capital requirements, which Japan did not possess, but that despite a long history of indigenous iron-making the Japanese had neither the complex organizations nor the skills required for rapid creation of these industries. The process of developing the two industries proved quite painstaking, and it was not until the 1890s that Japan possessed sufficient quantities and qualities of each critical production factor for steel and ship production. A culmination came in the construction of the government-run Yahata iron and steel mill in 1901, the largest integrated works in the Orient at that time, and the subsequent rise of the Japanese shipbuilding industry to a leading world position by the time of World War I.

Training in Shipbuilding in the Pre-Meiji Period

Acquiring a modern navy was foremost in the minds of Japanese political leaders from the mid-1850s on. One of the first actions of the Tokugawa government in 1853 following Perry's appearance offshore was to rescind its long-standing prohibition originally proclaimed in 1609 against construction of large ships and to order the building of Japan's first modern shipyards at

Nagasaki and Ishikawajima. However, there was also keen awareness that Japan possessed virtually no skills to organize and manage such large undertakings, let alone engage in actual construction of modern vessels. Japan had had little experience as a seafaring nation, mainly as the result of the two and a half centuries of Tokugawa seclusion; and, although boatbuilding guilds had long existed, the craft produced were merely for local fishing and coastal trade. The native artisans employed in traditional boatbuilding used simple technologies and primitive materials hardly suitable for constructing naval vessels considered modern in the mid-nineteenth century.[2] (Yet, almost by chance, in 1853 at Hata a shipwrecked Russian admiral directed the construction of the first modern ship built in Japan using native laborers.)

Yard construction was the first step for building modern ships. Most of the important yards in existence today trace their beginnings to the period just prior to the Meiji Restoration. In 1853, the Shogun founded the Uraga yard near Edo; the Mito daimyo, a loyal supporter of the Tokugawa regime, began the yard at Ishikawajima, also near Edo; and the Satsuma, or Shimazu, clan, which was hostile to the Shogunate, launched construction of a yard at Kagoshima. In 1856 the Tokugawa government initiated the yard at Nagasaki, which was completed in 1861. Throughout the 1860s yard construction continued to spread. In 1865 the Shogun began the Yokosuka yard; by the mid-1860s the Saga and Kanazawa clans also had completed theirs.

This almost feverish activity would have been impossible without the assistance of numerous foreign advisers, teachers, technicians, engineers, and craftsmen, who over the next several decades appeared in Japan in considerable numbers and with sizable financial inducements. Also foreign-made machinery was indispensable. Eager to obtain a foothold in newly opened Japan, Western powers readily responded to requests for assistance

---

[2] Arisawa Hiromi, *Gendai Nihon Sangyō Kōza* (Tokyo: Iwanami Shoten, 1960), Vol. V, pp. 104-108.

from both the Shogun and domainal governments. Initially, the Dutch provided most of the help, since they were already best known to the Japanese from their presence allowed during the Seclusion Era on the island of Deshima in Nagasaki harbor. As early as 1849 the Satsuma clan had translated a Dutch book on the building of steamships. In 1855, Dutch naval officers instructed some of the first Japanese workers, mostly indigenous craftsmen, employed at the new shipyards. A year later Dutch teachers took charge of instruction at the Shogun's new naval navigational school established at Nagasaki in 1855. It was the Dutch, in fact, who provided Japan with her first steamship—an outright gift to the Shogun of the 250-ton *Kanko Maru* for the purpose of demonstrating shipbuilding techniques. In addition to the *Kanko Maru*, Japan soon received or purchased several naval training vessels from England and the United States as well as Holland. Also, more Japanese students were beginning to go abroad to most of the Western seafaring nations, but especially Holland, to study shipbuilding and navigation.

The most important accomplishment under Dutch supervision was the completion of the yards at Nagasaki and Kobe, including the establishment of a training school at Nagasaki where 14 Dutch officers instructed 160 Japanese government officials and artisans in navigation, shipbuilding, maritime equipment, gunnery, steam engine operation, mathematics, and related subjects.[3] In 1863, the central government established a second navigation center, also under Dutch tutelage, especially for training samurai from the various clans loyal to the Shogun. That year some 15 Japanese were studying shipbuilding in Holland.

The almost complete reliance upon the Dutch for assistance in shipbuilding was short-lived. By the early 1860s, the Dutch had been displaced by the British and French, although the Americans and Russians were also active. The British worked especially with the so-called Southwestern clans, who in their long-standing

---

[3] Nihon Kōgakukai, *Meiji Kōgyōshi* (Tokyo: Kōgakukai, 1925), pp. 431-432.

hostility toward the Shogun, sought Western technology in order to increase their military strength and overthrow the Tokugawa regime. On the other hand, the French particularly earned the favor of the Shogunate in taking charge of the Yokosuka ironworks and shipyard, replacing the Dutch there in 1865. Under the direction of L. Verny, a French engineer, some 45 French engineers and mechanics instructed about 2,000 Japanese in most shipbuilding techniques from smelting to rigging. French-built machines were utilized for this. The Japanese trained by the French were drawn from a variety of sources: samurai, who served as the managing officials and clerks; traditional artisans, still in a feudal hierarchy of guild craftsmen, whose skills the French attempted to adapt directly to modern shipbuilding; inexperienced farm boys, who became on-the-job trainees and helpers under senior workers; and convict labor, for common and unskilled work.[4] Some of these graduates later became top personnel in both naval and private establishments.

This program, however, did not turn out modern engineers and technicians. While the Shogunate attempted at Yokosuka to train engineers and technicians only from the samurai class, following the Restoration, in an effort to indigenize the highest-level skills and to lessen dependence upon foreign personnel, the government opened these training programs to commoners. Presumably a sizable number of commoners were among the 37 engineering candidates and 50 or more technician trainees reported attending the Yokosuka school in 1876. In all likelihood, the admission of commoners alongside the samurai enhanced the attractiveness of this industrial work, then generally still held in low esteem and subject to frenetic turnover. The French teachers, although gradually dwindling in number, remained at Yokosuka for at least twenty years continuing to supervise virtually all aspects of iron ship construction.

The new yards became the major sources of skilled and semi-

[4] *Ibid.*, p. 433.

skilled workers for other yards being built and for workshops in related industries. As early as 1870, the first modern warship built in Japan—the 138-ton *Chiyodagata*—was completed at the Ishikawajima yard in Edo, with a 60-horsepower engine furnished from the Nagasaki yard, by workers originally trained by the Dutch at Nagasaki, and for the first time without foreign supervision or assistance. In the early years of shipbuilding, the labor market for shipyard workers was quite open and highly mobile. Trainers at Yokosuka often became chief workmen and shop heads at the new naval arsenals, shipyards, and factories at Nagasaki, Ishikawajima, Heta, and other locations.[5] Although the Meiji government attempted to retain the workers trained at Yokosuka, it appears that this effort was not successful. As a result, Yokosuka actually served as the training center for the entire industry.

Since there was virtually unlimited freedom of movement for the shipbuilding workers, managements soon began to offer special inducements to hold these employees within yards. One such incentive, possibly a forerunner of the lifetime employment system, was the granting of special status, such as *jōyatoi* (regular staff membership), which allowed exemption from military conscription and provided extra benefits in exchange for the promise to remain in the enterprise's employ. Jōyatoi contrasted with daily hired craftsmen and casual common labor. However, even these advantages fell short of preventing the high degree of worker mobility at that time. Much of the movement was due to the close personal relations between master workmen as patrons (*oyakata*) and their young apprentices (*kokata*), who usually moved together. To counter this, managers at yards like Yokosuka attempted to organize formally their own internal groupings of leaders and followers. This approach apparently

---

[5] Japan Ministry of Agriculture and Commerce, *Shokkō Jijō* (Tokyo: Seikatsusha, 1948), Vol. II, pp. 10-12 and Vol. III, pp. 167-170. See also Sumiya Mikio, ed., *Shokkō Oyobi Kōfu Chōsa* (Tokyo: Koseikan, 1970), pp. 81-83.

achieved little success in the 1870s and 1880s, since a wide social gulf separated the managers from the workers, and the informal patron-client groups remained. Basically, acute competition for an extremely short supply of skills, reinforced by a geographically spread network of patrons, caused the high turnover of client groups at the yards.

Nonetheless, training furnished at Yokosuka fitted the skill needs of the new shipbuilding industry rather well. While the French offered special instruction to help the young recruits master modern subjects such as drafting and mechanics, at the same time the latter were learning traditional techniques on the job from patron-master draftsmen and older artisans employed in the shops. Few of the recruits actually completed the programs planned and conducted by the French. As soon as they acquired some knowledge of both foreign and indigenous skills sufficient to cope with the varying technologies in the different shops and yards, they would be off to another site, especially under the willing guidance of their patron-masters.

In these early years also, those destined to become top-level personnel later were exposed to a variety of learning experiences at home and abroad. For example, Hida Hamagorō, who during much of the Meiji era became a Japanese leader in ship design and engineering, began his career at the training school in the Nagasaki yard, then studied in Holland and the United States, and returned to become chief supervisor of ship construction first in the Tokugawa and then the Meiji government. Another prominent case was Ueda Torakichi, who began his shipbuilding career helping the Russians build the vessel at Heta in 1854 (which was copied at a number of other yards). Later he moved on as one of the native craftsmen to work with the French at Yokosuka and then was sent by the shogunal government to Holland to assist with the construction of a warship which the government had ordered from the Dutch. Upon returning to Japan, Ueda took charge of the iron-making plant at the Yokosuka yard.

Given the absence of technical schools in Japan, this peripatetic learning process was probably necessary for developing enough comprehensive knowledge and skills required at that time for modern shipbuilding.[6]

The results in actual ship production were slow. Up to 1870, Japan had built only two modern steamships entirely on her own, and these together totaled a mere 57 tons. Even ten years later, while the number of modern ships produced in one year had increased to 40, total tonnage was barely 3,000 tons. As yet Japan could build nothing more than small iron ships. Also construction of traditional sailboats remained far in the lead and stayed there until 1900. The major boost to modern shipbuilding in Japan came only with the Sino-Japanese War, when in 1895, Japanese yards turned out 45 steamships totaling 5,500 tons. But the shift to modern vessels was not really assured until the Russo-Japanese War. In 1905, the total number of modern ships produced reached 103 for an aggregate 30,000 tons. The successful development of shipbuilding in Japan not only depended on generating skills for shipbuilding but waited also upon mastering modern iron and steel making.

Beginnings of Modern Iron and Steel Making

Indigenous ironmaking had been well developed in Japan for many centuries and had culminated in the invention of an ingenious seesaw bellows (*tatarabuki*) in 1691. However, traditional technology proved entirely inadequate to provide iron and steel for modern ship construction and armaments. Native methods were applied for making western firearms from as early as the sixteenth century,[7] but advanced Western technologies, while known to the Japanese, had not been successfully exploited even by 1853. In 1833, there had been an unsuccessful attempt at

[6] Nihon Kōgakukai (1925), pp. 431-432, 439, and 447-449.

[7] Nippon Steel Corporation, *History of Steel in Japan* (Tokyo: 1973), pp. 4-9.

Nagasaki to apply Western techniques to the manufacture of small arms and ammunition, and in 1843 there had been a similar failure in trying to build a Western-type iron furnace. When Perry arrived offshore Japan, Japanese cannons were still being made of copper and brass. Almost immediately, however, *A Study on the Seven Metals of the West* appeared, written in Japanese in 1854 by the government's leading translator, Baba Sadayoshi. This was the first time that systematic information on Western processing and manufacturing methods for iron and other substances became available.[8]

Recognizing Japan's military and technological backwardness, the shogunal government's initial step after Perry's appearance was to commission the Mito clan, a close blood-relative supporter, to construct a modern iron foundry and to commandeer necessary skilled workers from throughout the nation. Led by Ōshima Takato (1826-1901), a lower samurai of remarkably diverse engineering and scientific talents, the Mito group successfully completed Japan's first fire-brick factory in 1854 and then a year later began building Japan's first reverbatory furnace. Ōshima had learned the technology by translating a Dutch book on cannon casting. By 1857, Ōshima was directing the construction of a Western-type refinery for pig-iron production at Kamaishi, a mining town with excellent iron ore located on the Pacific coast in Iwate, soon to become Japan's first major center for iron and steel making (until the establishment of the Yahata mill in 1901).[9] No foreign equipment was imported for this development; the native *tatara* method continued to be used in the blast furnace. By 1868, ten of these furnaces operated at Kamaishi, producing 3,000 tons of pig iron per year.

Ōshima had studied Dutch medicine as a boy, but as an adult he became interested in Western science and technology, gen-

[8] *Idem.*

[9] Kamaishi Iron Works, *Kamaishi Seitetsusho 70 Nenshi* (Tokyo: Fuji Steel Corporation, 1956), pp. 7-15.

erally mining, metallurgy, and engineering. Before his assignment to Mito, Ōshima was already well known as the builder of Japan's largest cannon, having been sent by his native clan at the age of 21 to study Western gunnery at Nagasaki. In his native Morioka (near Kamaishi), where he served as court physician for the daimyo, he lectured his fellow samurai on modern ordnance. After serving as the chief engineer at Mito to construct the Kamaishi works, he was dispatched in 1860 to Edo to establish a school for the study of chemistry, physics, mechanics, mathematics, and Dutch. Two years later, he was employed by the Tokugawa government to take charge of all Dutch language instruction and to supervise a comprehensive survey of natural resources in Hokkaido, especially the coal deposits there. In addition, as mentioned, he drew up the plans and guided construction of the Kamaishi Iron Works. Following the Meiji Restoration, Ōshima was appointed both professor of engineering at the new Tokyo University and a top official of the new Bureau of Mines within the Home Ministry.[10] Crowning his career, he later became president of Japan's Mining and Metallurgical Institute.

In 1874, Kamaishi became the chief site under the Meiji regime for developing modern iron and steel production. The mines were state-owned. In line with the early Meiji policy for industrial development, the Kamaishi works were designated a "model" plant for private entrepreneurs to emulate. Almost immediately following Ōshima's initial efforts to start up the works in the late 1850s, the Tokugawa government had turned Kamaishi over to private operators; but the Meiji regime repossessed the works once it was realized, as the result of a survey conducted by British engineers, that Kamaishi had potential as a model manufacturing establishment. Like other operations inherited from the Tokugawa, Kamaishi by 1874 had become a hodgepodge of traditional and modern techniques, materials,

[10] *Ibid.*, pp. 11-15.

and products. In order to achieve full modernization, the Meiji government now employed some 200 British engineers, technicians, and craftsmen at Kamaishi and at the same time brought Ōshima back as chief assistant to the newly appointed British manager. New British blast furnaces and other equipment were installed. By 1880, Kamaishi was producing 15 tons of pig iron per day.

Despite these steps, Kamaishi was unable to overcome major obstacles to achieving modern iron and steel production. For example, the prohibitive cost of importing coking coal, which Japan possessed only in very poor quality, forced the British overseers to continue to rely upon low-quality local charcoal. Although there was some success in producing relatively small amounts of suitable iron for modern products in general, it was clear that the works were unprofitable. Kamaishi had neither sufficiently solved the technical problems nor obtained large enough markets to achieve economies of large-scale production. Indeed, mining was suspended after three years, when charcoal supplies ran out. An attempt to use coal from Kyushu as coke also failed. As a result, in 1883, the Ministry of Industry, which by that time had taken direct charge of Kamaishi, decided to abandon the works entirely in the face of severe financial crises besetting the Meiji government at that time.

The failure at Kamaishi was due to the problem that faced the Japanese from the beginning: the inability to adapt equipment, techniques, and materials from abroad to Japan's native conditions. Similarly, the government had experimented with an iron works at Kosaka that toward the end of the Tokugawa period had begun under private management. Here, too, foreign equipment and indigenous raw materials were found to be inappropriate for one another. Two more decades of trial and error were required before this problem was solved satisfactorily.[11]

On the other hand, the Meiji government's production of steel

[11] *Ibid.*, p. 17.

at its new arsenals and shipyards was meeting with far better results. Here, however, the product was highly specialized, and the military insisted upon meeting exact specifications. The foreigners whom they employed as advisers and managers also tended to be specialists in armaments and were selected for their particular rather than general knowledge. A conspicuous success in producing steel with Western equipment for the first time in Japan was the Tsukiji arsenal in Tokyo, which relied heavily upon engineers from the Krupp factories in Germany. In 1880, the most promising Japanese engineers and technicians at Tsukiji, in turn, were sent to Krupp for study. Contrasting with the experience at Kamaishi, by 1882 the Tsukiji plant, which utilized an imported Western mill, was producing high quality steel for tools appropriate for manufacturing armaments. During the following decade, several additional arsenals proved equally successful in using highly selective techniques in making special steels. The Yokosuka and Kure naval arsenals especially became adept in applying methods learned from French engineers. In 1892 Japan's first open-hearth furnace was operated satisfactorily at the Osaka army arsenal.[12]

Kamaishi did not die with the government abandonment in 1883. Rather, as part of the government's divestment scheme in 1887 the works were sold to Tanaka Chōbei (1834-1901) and his son. An imaginative private merchant with favorable political connections, but without any particular knowledge of iron and steel making, Tanaka was convinced that Japan would soon require its own basic steel capacity for general product development. He also acquired the Kosaka Iron Works, naming his new establishment the Kamaishi Kozan Tanaka Iron Works, and brought together craftsmen who had previously worked in the government iron and steel undertakings at Kamaishi. For the first few years, the Tanaka works fared little better than the government had, but it did succeed in producing steel for weapons,

[12] Arisawa (1960), Vol. II, pp. 23-24.

water pipes, and other modern products of high enough quality to find sufficient markets. During this time, Tanaka was fortunate to secure the services of Noro Kageyoshi (1855-1923), then an engineering professor at Tokyo University and formerly a student of Curt Netto of Freiberg, who taught at Tokyo, and of Ōshima Takato, in the methods of iron making. Bringing a number of his own students with him, Noro utilized Kamaishi for a variety of experiments and in 1894 succeeded in constructing Japan's first coke blast furnace. Following the earlier example of Ōshima, Noro scientifically attacked the problem of adapting foreign techniques and materials to the special Japanese conditions and even demonstrated that suitable steel could be produced in quantity using Japan's poor quality coke.[13] It was with this development after 40 years of experimentation that Japanese iron and steel making began to catch up with the West.

Yahata Steel: Japan's Leap Forward

The redevelopment of Kamaishi by the Tanakas and the success of the military arsenals—with their steady accumulation of management and operating skills—made it possible for Japan's political leadership to formulate plans for establishing a full-fledged basic steel industry in Japan that would integrate pig iron and steel making. The problem of making basic steel had also been eased as the result of the war with China, since Japan had now gained access to adequate supplies of suitable iron ore in Northern China and Manchuria. These plans culminated in 1901 with the opening of the Yahata mills on the coast of northern Kyushu as a government venture. Construction had begun four years earlier.[14]

Debates over whether the government should resume development of a basic steel industry had been underway ever

[13] Kamaishi Iron Works (1956), pp. 41-86.
[14] For the company's full history, see Ishikawa Hirokatsu et al., *Yahata Seitetsu* (Tokyo: Meiji-Shoin, 1962).

since Kamaishi was sold to Tanaka; but only in 1895 did the Japanese Diet, itself established but four years earlier, finally adopt legislation for construction of the Yahata plant. The immediate impetus for this act had been the Sino-Japanese War, which had dramatized Japan's great dependence upon importing foreign materials and equipment and consequent drain upon scarce foreign reserves. The new law also had the back-up of the work and study of Noro and his associates at Kamaishi.

Despite Tanaka's success at Kamaishi and the general policy of encouraging private enterprise, the government was unwilling to leave the development of Yahata in private hands. On the one hand, basic steel manufacturing was too crucial for national defense and economic growth; on the other, private entrepreneurs did not appear capable of bringing together sufficient capital and skills for the undertaking. As it turned out, Yahata tended to draw its managerial personnel, technical employees, and skilled workers from many sources: private industry, the government civil bureaucracy, the military, and foreign nations.

In 1898, when the Yahata enterprise was actually initiated, the government began to send engineers and administrators abroad to study foreign steel-making technologies and to determine the technical arrangements most suitable for Japan's needs and conditions. The Yahata site was selected after a careful study in Germany by Imaisumi Kaichiro (1867-1942), a student of Noro who was to become the first head of Yahata's steel-making department. As a result of these investigations, the Japanese government concluded that German methods, especially those at Krupp, were the most appropriate. This decision was taken despite the fact that Japanese iron and steel makers were more familiar with British techniques. However, German engineering and design were considered less sophisticated and thus more easily mastered by the inexperienced Japanese. In constructing and then operating Yahata, German engineers, technicians, and craftsmen, especially from the Gutehoffnungshutte A. G. Company, were brought to Japan to supervise the building and to instruct the Japanese in operations. At the same time, Japanese administrators and engineers continued to be assigned for study at German plants and then return to Yahata. By 1901 a blast furnace, open-hearth furnace, rolling furnace, and rolling mill began operation. Particularly influential in instructing the Japanese and recruiting German engineers to go to Japan was Adolf Ledebur, the famous metallurgist of Freiberg.

Although it was expected that the Germans would furnish the necessary techniques for efficiently utilizing the materials and equipment at the new Yahata mills, the German methods proved less than suitable, and numerous technical difficulties plagued the building and early operation of the Yahata Mill. Thus, the Japanese engineers were once again thrown back upon their own ingenuity.[15] What followed was similar to the previous experience at Kamaishi. Again Noro Kageyoshi, along with Ōshima Michitarō, another of Japan's leading metallurgists and engineers and the son of Ōshima Takato, took the helm at Yahata and, aided by a team of their own students, went to work on the technical difficulties peculiar to the Japanese situation. The results were a series of imaginative adaptations of the German methods culminating in the successful operation of the mill. Indeed, Noro's success in improving coke furnaces even surpassed the level of quality production in America. This experience heightened Japan's confidence in her own ability to proceed with iron and steel production without further foreign assistance. Thus, by the time of the Russo-Japanese War (1904-1905) most of the German technicians had left. In turn, the Japanese success at Yahata bolstered the reputation of the graduates of the old Ministry of Industry school, now the engineering department of Tokyo University, which had become the chief source of engineers and technicians for work in developing heavy industry in Japan.[16]

[15] Arisawa (1960), Vol. II, pp. 26-30.
[16] Yamazaki Toshio, *Gijitsushi* (Tokyo: Toyō Keizai Shinpōsha, 1961), pp. 81-84.

Throughout this development, as mentioned, Yahata drew upon human skills and talents from a variety of domestic and foreign sources, but rapid Japanization was undoubtedly achieved mainly because of the availability of engineers trained at Tokyo University and abroad, technicians and experienced craftsmen from the earlier efforts at Kamaishi and the military arsenals, and administrative and clerical personnel experienced in various government agencies. At first, as at Kamaishi earlier, the principal training technique utilized in the new mill was to rely upon small work teams composed of a key skilled worker and a number of unskilled subordinates. Once such teams were assembled and organized, not only were the Yahata mills in a position to operate successfully but could look forward to rapid expansion. As discussed later, Yahata now was able not only to generate for itself skilled workers through within-enterprise training programs of its own but also became a principal supplier of skills to other heavy industrial plants. The fact that Yahata became the principal supplier of basic steel needs of the expanding military establishment—and thus was assured of a protected and growing market—also facilitated these developments.

Rise of Modern Shipbuilding

Full development of Japan's modern shipbuilding industry waited upon the success of the Yahata operations. As mentioned earlier, the Japanese effort to establish modern shipbuilding also began in the 1850s, but progress was slow and piecemeal at best, and until the early 1900s the industry was still largely devoted to repairing and maintaining foreign-built vessels. Nonetheless, the accumulation of skills in the 30 or 40 years up to the Russo-Japanese War came to play a key role just as it had in the case of launching the Yahata mill.

One of the first moves of the new Meiji regime in 1868 had been to take over all private as well as government-owned ship-

yards. It also inherited all the shogunal and domainal military arsenals. To coordinate these operations in 1870 the government
organized the Shipbuilding Bureau within the War Ministry, and
two years later the bureau became a component of a separate
Naval Ministry. It was clear that shipbuilding was basic to the national government's aim of developing a major naval and commercial fleet in the attempt to provide military security and to lay
the basis for increasing international trade.

The Meiji government concentrated its resources for shipbuilding first at Nagasaki and Yokosuka-Yokohama. It immediately closed the yards that had already been built at Kagoshima
and Uraga and suspended operations at Ishikawajima in Tokyo for
three years because of the acute lack of resources. The newly established Ministry of Industry was given responsibility for the
Nagasaki facilities and engaged the help of British and French
engineers. Then, in 1871 the Ministry of War reopened the
Ishikawajima yards, placing Hida Hamagorō in charge. With the
assistance of foreign technicians, the War Ministry established in
1875 a major new installation in the form of the Tsukiji Military
Ordnance Bureau in Tokyo, which was merged with the Ishikawajima shipyards. Four years later, the government began
building the Osaka Iron Works with the advice and supervision of
British and German engineers at the site of the Fujinagata yard,
one of the small private operations the government had taken
over and at first had closed down. Thus, by first concentrating
resources in a few yards and then expanding step by step the
Meiji leaders attempted to avoid the scattering and fragmenting
of skills and capital that had occurred in the previous experience
with modern ship construction.[17]

Despite this rationalization, little actual headway in constructing modern vessels in Japan was made for several years. Capital
and labor skills still remained woefully inadequate. Japan continued to depend largely upon foreign sources for management,

[17] Arisawa (1960), Vol. V, pp. 112-13.

materials, and equipment. As already noted, the result was that, following the internal political disturbances of the late 1870s and the financial crisis of the early 1880s, the government decided to abandon direct attempts at developing modern shipbuilding as well as other industrial enterprises.

In time, under its general divestment policy, the government turned to private enterprise for development of the shipbuilding industry. The first decision in this regard was to grant lease rights for the then near-defunct Ishikawajima yard to Hirano Tomizo, who for ten years had been a works manager at the Nagasaki yard. When this operation proved successful, the Naval Ministry in 1880 leased the Yokohama iron works also to Hirano for the manufacture of marine engines. Hirano, it should be noted, relied heavily upon Archibald King, a British engineer, for managing these enterprises. With the financial assistance of Shibusawa Eiichi, the famous financier, and other leading Japanese investors, Hirano steadily expanded the Ishikawajima yards.[18]

The shift to private operation of modern ship construction was virtually complete by the mid-1880s and laid the basis for the emergence of several companies later to become major zaibatsu complexes, especially Mitsubishi and Kawasaki. Mitsubishi, then under Iwasaki Yatarō, who was deeply involved in developing a shipping company, took over the Nagasaki yard in 1881 at a low purchase price; ten years later it began construction of its own yard at Kobe. Also, Kawasaki Shōzō, the adventurous entrepreneur, was able to "borrow" the government-owned yard at Hyōgo in 1880 and eventually purchased it from the government in 1887.[19] The Osaka Iron Works was turned over to private operations in 1881 under the control of H. Hunter from England. Two years later, Hida Hamagorō from Ishikawajima started up

---

[18] For this company's history, see Ishikawajima Heavy Industries Co., Ltd., *Ishikawajima Jūkōgyō Kabushiki Kaisha 108 Nenshi* (Tokyo, 1961).

[19] For the histories of these companies see Mitsubishi Shipbuilding Co., Ltd., *Sōgyō 100 Nen no Nagasaki Zōsensho* (Tokyo, 1951); and Kawasaki Heavy Industries Co., Ltd., *Kawasaki Jūkōgyō Kabushiki Kaisha Shashi* (Kobe, 1959).

his own yard at Hakodate. In all these instances, the private entrepreneurs continued to rely upon foreign engineers, advisers,
and technicians, most of whom had had by then more experience
with shipbuilding in Japan than the Japanese themselves. At
Nagasaki, for example, the Mitsubishi firm depended primarily
upon a ship expert from Glasgow who earlier had managed the
government iron works at Osaka.

Even with the transfer of ship construction to private hands,
the government continued its policy of stimulating construction
of modern Western-style ships in Japan. In 1885, the government prohibited any further building of old-style Japanese vessels and increased its subsidies for modern ship construction.
Moreover, throughout this period, the government remained the
principal customer for the industry, laid down building specifications, and encouraged a flow of skilled workers into the shipyards. On some occasions, the government actually arranged for
the transfer of craftsmen from government-owned operations to
the private yards; the military arsenals, in particular, became a
chief source of supply for trained and skilled workers.[20]

Government-sponsored training continued as the primary device for developing modern skills at all levels, for shipbuilding
skills remained a crossbreed of old Japanese and new Western
type vessels. The naval academies, established soon after the
Restoration at Edajima, Kure, and Kobe, provided a steady flow
of marine engineers, who typically were sent abroad for study,
returned to assignments in the arsenals, and then transferred to
the shipyards. Similarly, the shipbuilding college of the Ministry
of Industry, which was begun in 1880 as one of the forerunners of
the engineering department of Tokyo University, continued as a
key source of high-level engineers and technicians.[21] The government's craftsmen's school, *shokkō gakkō* in Tokyo, established
in 1881, furnished skilled workers trained in modern shipbuild-

[20] Nihon Kōgakukai (1925), pp. 173-197.
[21] *Ibid.*, p. 433.

ing techniques. By the 1880s, the principal sites for training workmen for modern ship constructions were the Yokosuka Naval Arsenal, the Mitsubishi yard at Nagasaki, the Osaka Iron Works, and the Ishikawajima yard in Tokyo. At the same time, a supply of trained workmen from various government factories and arsenals flowed steadily into the shipyards. By the late 1890s, it should be noted, the Yokohama Naval Arsenal still employed more skilled workers than all the private shipyards combined. Throughout this period, training at the arsenal remained largely under the supervision of foreign engineers, technicians, and managers.[22]

By the time of the Sino-Japanese War, therefore, there had occurred sizable accumulations of workers skilled in modern shipbuilding techniques—enough so that Japan could finally contemplate the launching of a full-scale ship construction industry rather than merely engaging in the repair and maintenance of vessels imported from abroad. It was in this context that Kawasaki Shōzō began Japan's first overseas shipping line that was soon to extend to India, the United States, Europe, and Australia. Also, the ready availability of skilled manpower prompted the enactment of the Law to Encourage Shipbuilding and the Law to Encourage Shipping in 1896, which provided additional subsidies that increased with vessel size, granted tariff protection for the construction of steel vessels, and imposed Japan's first restrictions on foreign ship imports.

Most important of all was the decision to build the Yahata mills in order to assure a domestic supply of steel for ship construction and related industries. Between 1893 and 1905, there was again feverish activity in establishing new shipyards: the Yokohama yards were completed in 1893; the Yasuda zaibatsu reconstructed its yard at Toba in 1896; the Higo yard at Hiroshima started up and the Uraga yard was rebuilt in 1900; Kawasaki completed its Kobe yard in 1905. Another milestone was the construction of

[22] *Ibid.*, pp. 453-454.

the first Japanese-made turbine marine engine at the Mitsubishi yard in Nagasaki by the mid-1890s.

With the availability of domestic steel, the onset of the Russo-Japanese War brought full-blown development of the modern shipbuilding industry in Japan. Japanese-built tonnage for the first time exceeded foreign imports; and at the same time, as at the Yahata mill, the Japanese yards soon were dispensing with the services of foreign engineers, technicians, advisers, and managers. Foreign licensing agreements mushroomed in their stead. By 1910 the Japanese navy had placed its last foreign order, and with domestic-built vessels as its backbone joined the ranks of the most powerful navies in the world. With 26 companies in the industry soon after the war with the Russians, Japan had become the sixth largest shipbuilding nation, behind Great Britain, Germany, the United States, Norway, and France. Between 1906 and 1915 domestic-built tonnage increased ten times; and with the advent of the First World War, Japan suddenly rose to third place after the U.S. and U.K. in tonnage produced. Only a shortage of skilled labor held Japan back from a higher rank; employment in the yards rose fourfold. In fact, the 1896 law was repealed as it was no longer necessary for stimulating the industry.

While the steady accumulation of experienced manpower was a critical ingredient in the growth of Japanese shipbuilding after 1905, the piecemeal approach to training in the years up to the first decade of the twentieth century no longer appeared adequate to sustain further growth of the industry. The few yards, factories, and arsenals that had been the principal sources of skilled labor could not be depended upon for sufficient supplies of such workers. Furthermore, with the shift of the industry from repair and maintenance operations to full-fledged ship construction, the technology became increasingly complex and integrated, requiring skills that had not yet been widely developed in the Japanese yards.

At this turning point, the private companies were still not well prepared to provide the needed training, for the scale of the private firms had remained small. Throughout the early period they continued to rely heavily on the patron-client system for labor requirements. However, by the early 1900s many of the older master artisans, most of whom served as oyakata in the private yards, were dying off or retiring. The traditional apprenticeship, handed down by the old, now-abolished, guilds was also disappearing. Within the expanding shipyards and other metalworking factories, the training of directly recruited workers was not yet systematic, left largely to the dwindling number of skilled craftsmen whose retinues new recruits would join. Teaching of skills tended more and more to be on-the-job, spasmodic and specific, rather than comprehensive or craft-oriented.

The rapid expansion of the shipbuilding industry after 1900 required that management itself organize and direct training programs to provide much greater numbers of workers skilled in more and more diverse tasks. The initial management response to the problem was to subcontract work to the outside oyakata craftsmen, who could gather kokata workers together from many locations. Although they worked in the shipyard itself, oyakata recruited, trained, and managed their own groups of trainees without company interference or supervision. On its own, management had little of the knowledge necessary to carry on effective instruction.

The decentralized oyakata system was especially characteristic of the shipbuilding industry, and in fact was formalized at the Yokosuka yard. The oyakata in turn developed networks of connections among all the yards and factories, so that a young manual worker would acquire skills by moving around from one work place to another under the auspices of his patron or master. This mobility undoubtedly contributed more to the spread of skills and knowledge about modern technologies than could training in any single work place or in a school. This system of skill development, of course, also fitted the prevailing patterns of close-knit groupings based upon patron-client relations.

However, the continuing existence of the oyakata-kokata system actually meant a never-ending shortage of skills and inadequate training procedures. Especially troublesome was the need to master the rapidly changing technology in shipbuilding. As large-scale factories and shipyards emerged by the time of the Russo-Japanese War, informal labor market arrangements, with the worker's training and advancement in the hands of powerful oyakata, began to erupt into widespread labor unrest. Aspiring craftsmen saw their best opportunities either in becoming oyakata, themselves, or in joining labor unions, or in self-employment. Those who could not look to such a future either remained untrained, dissatisfied with their lot as factory workmen and perhaps protesting, or gave up and returned to their farm villages. By the early years of the present century, it was becoming clear to the managers of the new modern shipyards that a rapid revamping of the training system was essential if the industry was to continue to expand.

Management's principal solution lay in taking training out of the hands of oyakata and developing within-enterprise programs operated and controlled by the company itself. However, this appeared risky. The skills available were still held by the eagerly sought-after mobile workers who had acquired their skills and knowledge in many scattered places. It was not easy for a management to give them up by substituting a long process of training within the enterprise. Yahata was to lead the way in this experiment for both the steel and shipbuilding industries.

Enterprise Training: The Yahata Model

As discussed in the preceding chapter, even though Japan's educational level began to rise rapidly after 1890, vocational training in the public schools lagged behind. The vocational education ordinance of 1899 was an attempt to rectify this situation, but the results were not to become visible on a major scale for at least two decades. Nevertheless, the spread of general education at the elementary level and the advancement of literacy, especially among the younger members of the population, facilitated the establishment of training-within-industry programs in the absence of a widespread and effective public school system for vocational and technical education. The most notable of these programs were those in the steel industry, centering in the new Yahata mill.[23]

The demand for skilled and trained labor skyrocketed in the steel industry during the first decade of the twentieth century. Following the opening of the Yahata operations in 1901, smaller non-integrated steel mills mushroomed in the private sector, depending in numerous ways upon Yahata itself, especially for technical guidance: the Sumitomo Iron Works in 1901, the Kobe Steel Works in 1905, the Kawasaki Shipbuilding Hyogo Steel Mill in 1906, the Nippon Steel Works in 1907, the Hokkaido Coal Mining Wanishi Steel Manufacturing Plant in 1907, the Manchurian Honkeikō Steel Company in 1910, the Korean Kenjik Steel Manufacturing Plant in 1911, and the Japan Steel Tube Factory in 1912.[24] With Yahata as the basic steel producer, the role of these mills was mainly to supplement the requirements of the government for armaments, ordnance, and railway equipment. Japan Steel Tube alone concentrated wholly on civilian needs, especially pipe manufacturing, using pig iron from India and scrap from the United States in its open-hearth furnace.

This ambitious expansion in steel making constantly suffered from shortages of capital, raw materials, and skilled labor. A major reason for establishing the mills in Manchuria and Korea,

[23] Nippon Seitetsu Co., Ltd., *Nippon Seitetsu Kabushiki Kaisha Shashi* (Tokyo, 1959), pp. 716-26.

[24] For the histories of these companies, see Sumitomo Steel Corp., *Sumitomo Kinzoku Kōgyō Gonenshi* (Osaka, 1957); Kobe Steel Corp., *Shinkō 50 Nenshi* (Kobe, 1954); Kawasaki Heavy Industries (1956); Nippon Seitetsu (1959); Hokkaidō Tankō Kisen Co., Ltd., *Hokkaidō Tankō Kisen Kabushiki Kaisha 70 Nenshi* (Tokyo, 1958); Nihon Kōkan Co., Ltd., *Nihon Kōkan Kabushiki Kaisha 40 Nenshi* (Tokyo, 1952).

for example, was to gain access to suitable iron ore deposits and to lessen Japan's dependence upon imported pig and scrap iron. The supplies of skilled workers required were quickly exhausted—as indicated by the considerable movement of these workmen from plant to plant, arrangements among the mills for sharing the skilled workers, and frequent attempts at labor piracy. These conditions, as in shipbuilding, starkly dramatized the need to organize the labor market and to systematize direct management of work forces within the new expanding enterprises.

With Yahata as the keystone, accounting for 70 to 80 percent of Japan's total steel production in these years, an intermeshing arrangement was developed whereby first Yahata and the military arsenals provided technical advice and lent skilled manpower to the private firms, especially to assure the dovetailing of production schedules to meet the government orders for materials. More important for long-run labor needs was the establishment of a formal training school for young craftsmen (*shokkō yōseijo*) within Yahata to serve as a model for the remainder of the steel industry and other metalworking manufacturing. It was hoped that the new direct training approach would not only turn out more productive employees but also become the source for skilled workers and supervisors throughout the industry. Thus, Yahata's new manpower training program was in a sense a revival of the earlier efforts of the Meiji government to operate model factories. This time, however, as a public enterprise, the venture was assured of capital resources, protected markets, and rapid growth.

As each enterprise began to take up its own specialized steel production (a trend that heightened with the onset of the First World War and the elevation of Japan as a principal supplier of industrial products to the Allies), the need for additional enterprise-based programs was increasingly felt. The example of Yahata's company training system was all-important in this process.

The public nature of Yahata's training program made it one

strand of the then-developing multitrack system in Japanese secondary education. Actually, the formal beginning of the Yahata program did not occur until 1910; in fact the private Sumitomo steel-making operation six years earlier had established the first worker dormitories in which an educational program for young recruits was provided under the instruction of company engineers and their wives. In all likelihood what had delayed the beginning of the Yahata school was the need first to bring the system of supervision under management control. This involved developing first-line supervisors directly responsible to the upper management levels rather than relying upon traditional oyakata control.

Also looming on the horizon was the passage of the Factory Law, which, although it was not finally enacted until 1911 and didn't take effect until 1916, had been debated within the government since the 1880s. The prospect of this legislation made it increasingly clear that employers would become more and more directly responsible for training the young workers they employed. In the 1916 ordinance that implemented the act, not only were such rules set down applying to factories with 15 or more workers but also the ordinance prohibited child labor (under 12 for day shifts and under 15 at night), regulated aspects of recruiting, hiring, and discharges, and required employers to provide continuing education for workers of school age. In this context, then, Yahata as a major government operation was expected to be a model for the innovations implied for direct management organization, responsibility, and control.

Yahata's new school began with a two-year training program for newly recruited young labor who had graduated from higher elementary school. Most trainees were 14 to 17 years old. Training consisted of both classroom and on-the-job instruction. At the outset the instructors were drawn from experienced craftsmen and foreign engineers still in Yahata's employ. The first class in 1911 had 66 trainees; the second a year later, 100. After that, the numbers admitted gradually rose, so that by the early 1920s Yahata could claim that its permanent members were composed almost entirely of either its own trainees or military veterans recruited because of their demonstrated acceptance of discipline and work with mechanical equipment. About one-fifth of the workers considered permanent actually had attended the new company school since 1910.

Thus, within a decade or so after launching its own internal training program, Yahata's employment system had become "closed," no longer dependent on oyakata of the old style. For workers to become permanent, access to the company now existed only through direct company recruitment of young school-age youths. This represented a dramatic change from the informal, mobile labor market that existed for this industry in Japan barely 10 to 20 years earlier. With retirements and deaths, the number of the old oyakata types rapidly declined. By the 1920s, key worker and supervisory posts were almost entirely occupied by long-term permanent employees. In fact, in-plant training and experience became such an overriding condition for continual employment that the workers who had attended Yahata's school established in 1910 fared less well than workers who had risen up the promotion ladder for the permanent employees. For example, in 1920 still only about 3 percent of those who had training in the company school had become supervisors; while more than 20 percent recruited into the enterprise on a permanent basis without completing higher elementary school and without attending the company school were in supervisory positions. In other words, what was still most crucial for learning skills in this period was the early and continuous employment of young workers rather than enrollment in the formal enterprise-operated school. In fact, there is evidence to show that many of the trainees left the company without completing the in-company training during this era. School trainees were to become far more important only after the steel industry turned to rationalization and rapid technological change in the 1920s.

It is notable in this context, however, that the formal education level of skilled workers at Yahata was not especially high; as late as 1934, less than one-third of the male production workers had gone beyond sixth grade and fewer than 3 percent had completed middle school. Most workers by 1934 had worked up through training programs at Yahata with minimal public school education; only one-tenth of the production workers had attended even vocational or technical schools outside the company. In the Yahata employment system at that time, formal education actually still counted for little in a worker's progression; the rewards of lifetime employment and increased wage payments depended instead upon early recruitment into the enterprise, training-within-the-enterprise, and continuous years of service in the enterprise. The principal education of these workers beyond the elementary years was the training received within the plant; the formal schooling they had had was merely preparatory or supplemental.

The Yahata type of in-company training pattern, as an integral part of a large firm's employment system, rapidly spread to other companies in the steel industry. Kobe Steel, for example, established a similar school in 1912. With these programs emerging as an alternative to public school vocational training, the latter tended to lag behind—the lag undoubtedly increasing as each enterprise developed its own particularized technology and engaged in its own specialized production and training.

In the aftermath of the First World War, moreover, when Japan entered a serious and prolonged depression, the steel enterprises moved to strengthen their internal formal programs despite the availability of surplus labor and the rise in the general level of education. Faced with depressed markets, each firm turned to increased rationalization, in which specialized skills had to be carefully nurtured and retained, and to selecting carefully only the most desirable workers for training. Thus, along with rationalizing plant equipment and internal organization, training programs received close, direct attention of management. Under these conditions, modern industrial managements considered it unwise to resort to open labor markets or to the school system for needed skilled training. Experienced workers available in the labor market were not apt to have acquired the precise skills required by any individual enterprise; students who had gone through the vocational track of the public schools also were hardly of more use to a given company than youngsters just out of elementary grades.

Another reason for management's reinforcement of intra-enterprise training programs in the 1920s was the rise of a radical labor movement during the immediate postwar years. The steel industry, Yahata included, had experienced the formation of labor unions among its workers during the war, when labor was in short supply. Both government and modern industry were hostile to unionism and instead fostered worker-management consultative councils or company unions. As a result, there now emerged even more concentrated efforts to structure "Japanese-style" labor relations—with an emphasis upon loyalty to the employer and harmony within the enterprise. In effect, this meant increased stress upon recruiting unsophisticated recruits from the rural areas to be trained from entry into the firm only within the confines of the employing organization for their lifetime work. Also, it meant continued lessening of dependence for training upon the established oyakata, informal on-the-job training, and outside educational institutions. Within this context, in turn, arose the systematic schemes for wage payments and welfare benefits tied to length-of-service for those workers who would become permanent employees of a given firm through its established training procedures.[25]

Intra-enterprise training actually became an integral part of the overall movement to rationalize industry in Japan. Industrial rationalization proceeded throughout the 1920s preparatory for

[25] Fujita Wakao, *Nihon Rōdō Kyōyaku Ron* (Tokyo: Tokyo University Press, 1961), pp. 67-80.

the shift in emphasis to heavy industry when Japanese militarism gained ascendancy following the Manchurian incident in 1931. An important culmination of the movement was the merger of Yahata itself with plants of six private steel enterprises to become the mammoth government-owned Japan Iron and Steel Manufacturing Company in 1933. The merger and expansion that followed assured Japan of a fully integrated steel-making operation with increased productive efficiency and control for meeting military requirements. Yahata's intra-enterprise training program turning out workers skilled in Yahata's specific technology facilitated the transition. By 1935, for example, when Japan Iron and Steel employed a total work force of 18,000, the average length of service was 11 years. Merely 2,300 had graduated from middle school or higher, even counting the advanced formal training at Yahata. The great bulk thus had not gone beyond the sixth grade of elementary education, from which most had been directly recruited upon graduation and then trained and held within Yahata.

As mentioned, Yahata's training system in the years of rationalization became closely geared to a finely graduated promotion ladder and elongated status hierarchy established within the enterprise. Newly recruited production workers, if selected to continue training beyond an initial basic level, could look forward to rising to the lowest of five supervisory positions (*gochō*). This usually required at least either five years of service or three years of formal training within the company. After three years as gochō, employees could qualify for the next higher position of *kumichō*, provided they passed examinations that demonstrated both advanced technical skills and ability to handle subordinates. Eventually, with further training and experience, the kumichō could become a salaried worker upon selection by the company president. Kumichō then became eligible for promotion to *kochō*, Yahata's closest equivalent of a production foreman. Highly successful kochō might then rise to the rank of *shokurō*, or managerial assistant, in which capacity the employee might also serve as an instructor in the enterprise training program. While few employees actually rose to the rank of shokurō, the elongated and carefully structured promotion ladder, based on a number of rising status rankings, no doubt served as a strong incentive for new workers to enter the successive steps in the company's training program. The institution of this promotion system, and its accompanying formal training program, demonstrated how thoroughly a modern enterprise such as Yahata had moved away from dependence upon external labor markets and oyakata influence to direct management control over the training of the regular work force within the enterprise. The transition took about two decades.

Yahata's management continually refined and upgraded its training programs. Initially, in 1910, there was a basic two-year program only for young recruits who had completed the four years of compulsory elementary school. Mornings were devoted to classroom work and afternoons to on-the-job instruction. Soon afterwards, the company instituted special day and evening classes along with on-the-job training for up to six months for all regular emplyees, not only the new recruits. Also, lectures on technical subjects were regularly given to all production workers, while courses on ethics and practical living were provided in the company's dormitories.

In 1919 Yahata began its most ambitious program with the establishment of a separate technicians' school to provide continual training and retraining of permanent employees. At the end of the 1920s, most employees enrolled in this school were experienced workers between 23 and 35 years of age. The technicians program, three years in duration, was similar to the semiprofessional education offered at the government-operated semmon gakkō, but the equivalent years of formal education for the latter was not required for admission. Basic instruction covered pig iron and steel making, rolling mill, coking, and furnace operations, mechanical, electrical, chemical, and civil engineering, and other technical subjects. Trainees who completed the first year's study of one of these courses could then be selected for a second year of advanced work in metallurgy or engineering; for selected graduates of the second year, an additional nine months of study was offered in highly specialized subjects. Such a highly developed training curriculum was designed to educate only the permanent members of the work force. For a worker to be admitted, he had to be recommended by his department or section chief and then pass a special examination. To advance beyond the first year of instruction, the trainee not only had to perform well in his basic course but also had to have at least three years of service at Yahata with a middle school background or seven years of service if he had only completed elementary school. Usually no one over 40 was admitted to the courses beyond the first year.

Another major training innovation came in the mid-1930s when the company, like most other major firms, established its Youth School in line with the central government's policy for educating and indoctrinating the new young members of the labor force. While Yahata had had some government-sponsored youth training from the mid-1920s on, the Youth School became all-embracing and far more systematic. Now every young worker was required to take a five-year combination of military and industrial training from the time he was initially hired. By 1939 about 5,000 workers at Japan Iron and Steel had received this training. The Youth School served especially as the means not only for improving the general quality of the new workers but also for meeting on-the-spot skill shortages—again, in line with the government's new "emergency" policies for mobilizing manpower and controlling labor market mobility. In connection with the Youth School, the company also upgraded the technicians' training program by requiring all workers between 14 and 19 years old to take a special two-year sequence in steel making and electrical work. Eventually more than 2,500 young workers com-

pleted this program. Also, experienced employees up to the age
of 35 were required to enter newly established two-year middle
level and six-month advanced level technical courses. Some
1,600 workers went through these programs.

As a result, by 1935 more than 10,000 employees of Japan Iron
and Steel had received some formal training within the company.
3,500 had graduated from the technicians' school or had been enrolled in special advanced technical courses. To carry out the
programs, the company maintained its own full-time instructional staff of about 15 persons and utilized an equal number on a
part-time basis. Soon after the formation of Japan Iron and Steel,
the training function loomed so large that it was reorganized and
centralized, eventually being designated a separate department
of the company in 1941.

Following the onset of World War II, Japan Iron and Steel further upgraded its technical training program by establishing a
special new school at a higher level for engineering and technician training (the so-called *kyōshūsho*). Employees who had
graduated at least from middle school or who had completed the
company's previously established advanced training courses
were admitted to this curriculum. Upon graduation they were
certified as technical assistants for the professional engineers in
the company. The instructors themselves were usually section
chiefs or university engineering graduates. By 1945, 600 workers
had completed the program. In effect, these tiers of training at
Japan Iron and Steel paralleled secondary and tertiary levels of
schooling in the public education system.

Training Within Shipbuilding Enterprises

While Yahata was Japan's leading example for institutionalizing
comprehensive training-within-enterprise in modern industry, a
parallel development soon began to go forward in shipbuilding.
The programs in shipbuilding, however, did not become as for-

mal or systematic as those in steel because shipbuilding was not as highly centralized and shipbuilding technology remained more varied. Although there was no attempt to consolidate the industry under government ownership as in the case of steel, shipbuilding still received a sizable portion of government guidance and subsidy. As already emphasized, the industry also was very closely related to steel and enjoyed a protected market— both factors that contributed to the systematizing of within-enterprise training programs. Rapid growth of the industry, increasingly complex technology, and its key role in Japanese economic and military development underlay the need for the enterprises to establish training programs under their own direct control to assure the flow of required labor skills.

Like the steel industry in the early 1900s, private shipyards began to transform their traditional oyakata system into work forces directly under the control of management. There were forerunners of this trend. As early as 1878 the Nagasaki shipyard management had ordered its master workmen to recruit new workers only from among their known friends over whom they would serve as foremen for training purposes as well as wage setting and work assignment. By the turn of the century, as already noted, it was apparent, however, that continued reliance upon oyakata was highly inadequate. Training remained too piecemeal, and worker turnover was still too rapid. The first known attempt to establish a directly operated company school at a private shipyard was at Onariminato in 1896. However, the major breakaway from the oyakata system came with the founding of Mitsubishi's own technical training school at Nagasaki in 1899.[26]

Mitsubishi shipbuilding had expanded very rapidly after 1890. From 1898 to 1911, Mitsubishi grew from a company of a mere 20 clerks and 800 craftsmen to more than 1,000 clerks and 10,000 trained workers. As its work force expanded, the company took the lead in establishing direct welfare benefits for its employees

[26] Nihon Kōgakukai (1925), pp. 431-432, 448 and 449-450.

in order to hold them within the company. Then it began to employ graduates of the new engineering curricula from the universities and technical high schools so that by the end of the decade the establishment of a company-operated training school at Nagasaki became the next logical step to obtain skilled workers without relying upon the uncertain external labor market. Yet, the training programs were not an abrupt changeover. Features of the traditional patron-client system long persisted in shipbuilding.

In 1899 the Nagasaki training school began with 42 students and soon grew to an enrollment of close to 200. Sons of employees, if at least 12 years old and graduates of lower elementary education, were favored in admissions. Trainees were required to remain at least three years with the company after finishing a one-year training course. Upon graduation, they were usually assigned as student workers (*shugyōsei*) to assist oyakata in the yard. For the next four years, they would also attend additional training classes; and as their practical experience grew, they themselves began to assume oyakata positions within the company. In essence, this program attempted to combine company-sponsored training with the traditional oyakata system. It was shortly before World War I that the new type of company-trained oyakata began to appear in the yards.

At the same time, still other young workers who were not selected for the training school were appointed on-the-job learners (*minaraikō*). Such apprenticeships, also for 12-year-olds, ranged over both skilled and unskilled work and usually lasted five years on the job, but they also involved some formal classroom courses in the training school. Learners, however, would become ordinary workers rather than oyakata candidates as in the case of the shugyōsei.

Despite the efforts to hold the new recruits within the company, only about one-fourth of those selected to become shugyōsei or minaraikō actually completed their formal training periods. From 1902 to 1912, for example, half of those who entered the Nagasaki yard as shugyōsei quit or withdrew. As late as 1910, only 15 percent of the Nagasaki work force had been or were minaraikō. Thus, the actual experience of converting from the traditional oyakata system to direct company control proved to be a long, drawn out process, probably showing no real impact until the 1920s when the Nagasaki yard already employed about 12,000 workers.

A major reason for the slow progress toward full control by management at Nagasaki was the company's inability to meet the labor market competition for skilled workers. Although company benefits for permanent employees had been steadily increased—such as abolishing subcontract work to oyakata, upgrading hiring standards and pay, systematizing incentive wages, and introducing various insurance schemes—the great burst of industrial activity during the First World War gave rise to acute labor shortages which encouraged workers to move about almost at will whenever it was to their financial advantage. The persistence of established oyakata-kokata connections no doubt facilitated this movement.

By the end of the war, it was clear that shipbuilding, like steel, had greatly overexpanded. (Ship production dropped about 90 percent from 1919 to 1923.) Retrenchment was further dramatized by limitations imposed by the Washington Naval Treaty in 1922 (and then later even more by the London Disarmament Treaty in 1930). For the first time in years, the modern yards offered the highest wages in the industry as small firms closed down or were curtailed under the impact of the depression. Shipyard employment dropped from about 80,000 to less than 40,000 from 1918 to 1928 and then to 30,000 by 1931. As in the case of the steel industry, rationalization soon followed, and in its wake came the conversion of the employment and training system in the shipbuilding industry to direct management control. The major companies reduced their work forces to coteries of relatively small oyakata-kokata-like groups within the yards, releasing redundant employees in large numbers. Only those groups considered permanently loyal to the firm were retained as regular workers. In essence, what Mitsubishi at Nagasaki had been attempting to accomplish since the turn of the century now rapidly took full hold in shipbuilding.

Mitsubishi's craftsmen school, which had been established at the Kobe yard in 1919, now became a major source of new recruits for permanent positions. This school, which mainly admitted sons of Mitsubishi shipyard and electric plant workers, turned out more than 1,500 graduates from 1922 to 1933, two-thirds of whom became permanent employees in Mitsubishi or Mitsubishi-related firms. Their training concentrated on the mechanics, electrical engineering, and ship engines particular to the technologies utilized by Mitsubishi.

On the other hand, around the yards there still gathered large retinues of temporary, casual, and day laborers who were employed sporadically by traditional oyakata as needed. Little systematic training was given to these workers, and as in previous years they continued to learn skills in piecemeal and informal fashion. This was in sharp contrast to the permanent employees within the yards who were going through rigorous formal programs.

When shipbuilding revived (with the help of tariffs and subsidies) in the early 1930s as part of Japan's remilitarization, the industry already had available plentiful supplies of experienced "outside" labor to draw upon in order to meet expanding work force requirements. Many of these now became employed in the yards as "half-way" or "mid-career" workers, experienced but not recruited upon school graduation and therefore slotted into the work force hierarchy at lower pay scales and status positions than their permanent employee counterparts. As the shipbuilding firms followed a new "scrap-and-build" policy and diversified into other heavy industry such as tanks, aircraft, and armaments manufacturing, this reservoir of partially trained labor furnished the workers for many of the new operations. Ship tonnage produced rose almost 10 times from 1932 to 1938; Japan was back in second place after the United States. By 1935, 64,000 workers were employed in the yards.

Like the steel industry, the shipbuilders also established Youth Schools in the mid-1930s as a means for indoctrinating and controlling the expanding force of young workers. This development as at Yahata signalled the centralization of training activities. In 1935 the Kawasaki Shipbuilding Company, for example, organized an education department to coordinate all its training programs. Another notable example of the trend at that time was the establishment of the Kawasaki Higashiyama Private School, which offered night courses to elementary school graduates newly recruited as shipyard apprentices. This school was conducted in the company dormitories with a basic course of study that lasted four years. A single basic-course class had 1,200 young recruits; while there were also classes for 180 technical middle school graduates, 60 general middle school graduates, and a small number of junior officials. The Higashiyama school was a typical case of a "quasi-secondary" school operated by private industry in the pre-World War II period.[27]

Centralization of training facilitated the military government's control over the shipyard work forces with the outbreak of the Pacific War. Employment expanded phenomenally with over 325,000 working in the yards by 1944. Of these, almost half had been recruited from the "outside." The use of standardized admissions examinations became widespread, classroom instruction was further systematized, theoretical education received increased emphasis, ideological indoctrination was strengthened, and curricula were broadened to include general instruction in such subjects as English, Japanese, history, and physical education as well as technical subjects. In some cases, such as the Uraga Dock yard, intra-enterprise training was meshed very closely with outside vocational schools to which young appren-

[27] Kawasaki Heavy Industries (1956), pp. 773-778.

tices would be assigned by the company. Increasingly, wage rates and other benefits also were automatically tied to length-of-service with a given firm, and promotion depended upon successful passing of periodical examinations based on training provided. The result of these policies was a tight and exclusive attachment of permanent work forces to their respective enterprises throughout the war years. At the same time, the old personalized system of training within the enterprise that had begun with the craftsmen school in 1919 was now surely dead.

While the post-World War II evolution of training programs in the shipyards and steel mills is not examined in this chapter, it is notable that, despite the near destruction of both industries by 1945, each was able to re-establish its enterprise-based work forces relatively quickly once recovery got under way. The large groups of trained labor already attached to each enterprise were rapidly reassembled as if they had never been dispersed especially with the prospect of permanent employment for almost all, now backed up by labor unionism. This process of drawing already-trained workers to the new yards and mills undoubtedly figured heavily in the rapid resuscitation of these industries, which became a key factor in Japan's "miraculous" economic growth after the mid-1950s. With the re-establishment of the work forces, moreover, the enterprises also revived their long-standing internal training programs, albeit now without an emphasis upon ultranationalistic indoctrination. Yahata's kyōshūsho, for example, was reorganized, upgraded in subject matter, and officially registered under the new education law as a "miscellaneous" school in the "quasi-secondary" category.

Summary

In general, what stands out in this review of human resource development in Japan's prewar steel and shipbuilding industries are the following major points:

1. Initiation of the industries and early generation of modern skills depended to a great extent upon the utilization of foreign engineers, managers, and advisers. However, as Japan acquired her own high-level talent, the foreigners were rapidly displaced, and Japanese universities and colleges themselves became the chief source for recruiting this category of skills.

2. These industries found it necessary to develop their own schools as technology became more sophisticated and scale of operation expanded. The transition, however, took an extended period of time—perhaps as long as 30 years—to shift from reliance upon informal patron-client retinues to formal within-enterprise programs. A major feature was the institutionalization of the "key" worker and permanent work force.

3. Gradual elaboration of formal training programs within large enterprises characterized Japanese heavy industry particularly in the two decades prior to World War II. This development prepared these companies to concentrate and expand skilled human resources for the large-scale armaments industries.

4. While Japan's basic industries were almost destroyed by the end of World War II, their postwar recovery depended heavily upon reassembling their own trained labor forces and re-establishing the prewar intra-enterprise training institutions. The latter have continued as key ingredients in the employment systems of the two industries to the present time—despite enormous technical change, very rapid growth, and the impact of the educational reform of the Occupation period.

VI.

Training within Government-Owned Industries: Railways and Telecommunications

ALTHOUGH many of Japan's modern industrial enterprises began under public ownership, by the 1880s the Meiji government had sold most of them to private individuals and companies. There were notable exceptions, however, to this divestiture process. Various factories, shipyards, mines, and related operations were retained under direct government control usually as part of military arsenals. In fact, as late as 1890, government-operated plants still accounted for more than four-fifths of Japan's factory employment. The growth of heavy industry after the Sino-Japanese War also mainly served the government's armament goals culminating in the opening of the publicly owned Yahata mills in 1901.

Among the critical elements for development of Japan's military strength and national unification by the new Meiji regime were the government's direct control and operation of modern systems of transportation and communications. While it was not until after the Russo-Japanese War that the major railway trunk lines were finally and permanently nationalized, the telegraph system and later telephones came under central government operation from the outset. Both enterprises took on crucial roles in the initial drive for Japan's modernization—too crucial to be left solely to private development even with government supervision, subsidy, and favor. Similarly direct efforts were made by the government authorities to train work forces precisely suitable for operating the national railways and telecommunications systems on an efficient and profitable basis. In general, in training employees for these enterprises, the government ignored the public schools and concentrated upon internal education programs. The approach to the two industries differed however.

By 1869, the Meiji government had constructed Japan's first telegraph line. Three years later the government built the first railroad. Both ran from Tokyo to Yokohama and represented huge infrastructure investments for that time. In launching these industries immediately after the Restoration, Japan entered almost completely unfamiliar technological terrain. Except for observation of railways and telegraphs in European countries and the United States, the Japanese had had no experience of their own in evolving nationwide systems of modern transport and communications. They were wholly new industrial ventures. While a limited road network, notably the *Tōkaidō*, extending from Osaka to Edo (Tokyo), and coastwise shipping had emerged during the Tokugawa era, the Shogunate government as a matter of policy had refrained from encouraging movement and contact over long distances or overseas because they feared it might upset the delicate political balance and social structure of closed, feudal Japan. The Meiji government quickly recognized that Japan's industrialization was not likely to succeed without first making substantial overhead investments in efficiently operated modern transportation and communications on a national scale.[1]

Thus, when the Meiji government resolved, as one of its first steps for national development, to construct comprehensive and extended telecommunications and railway systems as quickly as possible, to do so also required taking direct responsibility for and control of the education and training in order to assure rapid creation of the work forces needed. Perhaps for no other modern industries in Japan was the need more urgent to build skills and

---

[1] Japan National Railways, *Nihon Kokuyū Tetsudō 100 Nenshi* (Tokyo: 1969), Vol. I, pp. 3-87; Nihon Kōgakukai, *Meiji Kōgyōshi* (Tokyo: 1930), pp. 1-19.

knowledge rapidly. To achieve this, as in other modern undertakings launched in that period, heavy reliance was placed upon foreign technical assistance. At the same time, especially because of military considerations, Meiji leadership was strongly determined to achieve quick indigenization of the skills required.

Beginnings of Telecommunications

Japan first heard of the invention of the telegraph in the West even before Perry's appearance offshore. The news immediately aroused the curiosity of those Japanese who had already developed keen interests in applied Western science. Court personnel in the Satsuma and Mito daimiates translated whatever foreign documents could be obtained about telegraphy and even attempted to build small electric generators and batteries and actually succeeded in operating a local home-built telegraph. Prominent among these experimenters were Hiraga Gennai and Sakuma Shozan, well-known scientists in Japan at that time.[2] It was Admiral Perry who presented the Shogun with Japan's first Morse telegraph. The Dutch at Deshima in the meantime provided an electromagnet set. The Shogunate then ordered a sizable amount of telegraph equipment from Europe, although it was not yet evident that the government had in mind any plan for building a telegraph network.[3]

However, after the Meiji Restoration, following several years of experimenting with telegraphic equipment, a definite telecommunications plan was developed. As one of its first acts the new Meiji government decided that rapid installation of a nationwide system was essential. The Home Ministry, taking over responsibility for modern communications from the Ministry of Foreign Affairs, directed the project. Settling on British-type equipment, the government invited a team of English telegraph engineers to Japan, among whom the most notable was

[2] Nihon Kōgakukai (1930), pp. 5-10.   [3] Ibid., p. 8.

George A. Gilbert, who first instructed a number of young Japanese in telegraph operations. By the end of 1869 Japan's initial telegraph line was completed, running from Tokyo to Yokohama under government ownership. It utilized a hand-transmission instrument, with Gilbert's trainees operating the line. In the next year, Gilbert supervised construction of the government's second line, this time from Osaka to Kobe. Both lines were made available for private as well as government communications.[4]

Adopting Morse code in 1871, with its advantages of speed and distance, the Meiji government now proceeded with construction of the nationwide system. Additional foreign experts were enlisted, and responsibility was shifted to the Ministry of Industry. In 1872 fifteen foreigners, all in the government's employ, were supervising construction, manning the transmission stations, and training Japanese operatives. By 1873, the line from Tokyo to Nagasaki was completed, designed to hook up with marine cables then being laid to Vladivostok and Shanghai. Before this was completed, construction also began on the link from Tokyo to Aomori, with the building of the section to Sendai under the sole direction of a Japanese engineer for the first time. In 1874 all of the major trunk lines were completed, thus linking Japan from one end to another, from Hokkaido to Kyushu, merely four years after the first local line had begun operation. Three years later, the Ministry of Industry created a Telegraph Bureau to supervise operation of the entire system as a publicly owned enterprise.[5]

"Japanization" of the Telecommunications Industry

Rapid construction of the nationwide telegraph network was largely due to expertise provided by foreign engineers and tech-

---

[4] Arisawa Hiromi, ed., *Gendai Nihon Sangyō Kōza* (Tokyo: Iwanami Shoten, 1960), Vol. VI, p. 13.

[5] Nihon Kōgakukai (1930), pp. 28-42.

nicians, almost all of whom were British. Yet by the end of the 1870s, as the Telegraph Bureau developed its own organization, it was possible to replace most of the foreigners with native personnel, who now numbered more than 100 engineers, technicians, and operators specializing in the telegraph. By 1886, no foreigners remained. It took, thus, no longer than a decade to "Japanize" these operations.

At the same time, the Telegraph Bureau, now completely indigenous, expanded its jurisdiction from construction and operation to the manufacture of equipment, mainly of the Morse variety. It also began to produce telephones for the first time in Japan with designs imported from the United States. For almost 15 years, the government virtually monopolized the entire telecommunications manufacturing industry.

However, as in the case of other government-operated enterprises, in the mid-1880s various private companies were permitted to take over the manufacture of telephone and telegraph equipment. The entrepreneurs who founded these firms almost invariably were engineers who had received their training under the foreign experts in the Ministry of Industry during the construction of the initial nationwide telegraph system. Several were to become leaders in the electrical equipment industry in later years. Among the companies then established, for example, were the Shibaura Seisakusho, begun in 1881 (the forerunner of the present-day Toshiba Manufacturing Company); the Oki Electric Company, also in 1881; the Miyoshi Electric Company, in 1883; and the Iwabushi Electric Company in 1884.[6]

The government-owned telegraph system expanded rapidly from 1875 to 1895. Beginning with 18 stations in the national network, by the end of the Sino-Japanese War there were about 1,000 stations. In the two decades, the volume of messages grew from 80,000 to 350,000 per year. So large did the undertaking become that in 1885 the Telegraph Bureau was removed from the Ministry of Industry and became the separate Ministry of Tele-

[6] Arisawa (1960), Vol. VI, pp. 13-16.

communications, comprising six departments (railroad stations, telegraph, lighthouses, maritime, accounting, and general affairs). Five years later, this ministry also took over the postal service and combined it with the telegraph system into a single bureau in 1893, although the two were separated again in 1897. (Until 1950 in fact both telecommunications and postal services were intimately intertwined within the single ministry.)[7] By 1895, telegraph lines extended overseas to Taiwan, Korea, various areas of Mainland China, Sakhalin, and elsewhere.

While the system incurred financial deficits until standard telegraph rates were fully established in 1885, it operated thereafter at substantial profit, so much so that in the decade from 1895 to 1905 still another major expansion was undertaken. Fifteen hundred new telegraph stations were added in this period, and by the end of World War I, almost 5,000 stations in all were in operation. This number doubled again by 1945, and at present totals about 17,000 stations. The telegraph system added wireless in 1908, although wireless communications with the United States were not established until 1925.

The spread of the telephone in Japan was almost as swift as the telegraph. One year after Alexander Graham Bell's invention in 1877, the Ministry of Industry has begun to experiment with a telephone line strung between the Telegraph Bureau and the Imperial Palace. Two years later, the bureau constructed a plant to manufacture telephones and laid plans for the eventual development of a nationwide telephone service. Again, as in other fields of government enterprise, implementation of the latter was delayed because of Japan's financial crisis of the early 1880s. In 1885, however, the new Ministry of Telecommunications offered a public bond issue to raise funds to construct the national telephone network, and at the same time dispatched a number of its officials to foreign countries to study their systems.[8]

The government's plan for telephones envisioned a long-term development over several decades with the system to be built in

[7] Nihon Kōgakukai (1930), pp. 30-34.   [8] *Ibid.*, pp. 155-168.

successive stages. The first public telephone line between Tokyo and Atami was built for demonstration purposes in 1889, and, proving highly successful, immediately went into regular service with 400 subscribers. Then began construction of the first phase, which was completed in 1900, covering more than 70 communities and supported by 20,000 subscribers. The second phase was completed in 1915, with the number of subscribers expanding tenfold. By 1940, as the system steadily widened and deepened, subscribers totaled more than one million, and, while the system was severely crippled during World War II, in part destroyed by bombing, by 1950 it had recovered to its prewar level and rapidly underwent new expansion. In 1965, there were about 6.5 million subscribers and still growing. By the 1970s, there was almost one telephone for every four Japanese, outnumbering Italy and France.[9]

Although from the beginning the telephone network has been a publicly owned enterprise, in the early decades there was considerable agitation to turn the industry over to private firms. The government strongly opposed this on the grounds that private companies would form a monopoly and charge excessive rates. It argued that only a public enterprise would provide dependable service and maintenance, take immediate advantage of technical improvements, coordinate rather than compete with the telegraph expansion, construct long-distance lines, and provide both equitable access and confidential communications. By the time of the Sino-Japanese War, especially because of military needs, the issue faded away. Moreover, the government operation of the telephone system had by then proven to be a highly profitable public venture, so much so that, while additional bond issues were offered to finance expansion, it never became necessary to rely upon tax revenues.

[9] *Ibid.*, pp. 168-190; Arisawa (1960), Vol. VI, pp. 62-108; Yamazaki Toshio, *Gijitsushi* (Tokyo: Tōyō Keisai Shinpōsha, 1961), pp. 69-76; and *United Nations Statistical Yearbook* (New York: 1973), Vol. 3.

Manpower Training for Telecommunications

In line with monopolizing the industry, the government also took sole and direct responsibility for training the work force required in the telegraph and telephone operations. The programs for telecommunications in fact became the most notable examples of comprehensive intra-enterprise training developed by a government agency in Japan—a reputation that has continued to the present.

Soon after the British engineer Gilbert began to instruct Japanese in the building and operation of the telegraph, the Ministry of Industry formally established a training workshop solely for telegraph personnel. In 1871 almost 60 trainees were enrolled, and several of the best of these students were sent to England for further study. Two years later, the minister converted the workshop to a school in Tokyo with a branch in Osaka, both of which by 1876 had graduated 1,200 students in all branches of telegraphy. By this time also, telecommunications was designated a major course among the offerings at the ministry's newly established two-year technical college, and Professor W. E. Ayrton of England was placed in charge of the instruction. The most able of those who attended the training school proceeded to this technical college, which in 1877 graduated nearly 500 students. Almost all the graduates were placed in management or engineering positions in the rapidly expanding system. As noted, within a few years foreign engineers and technicians were entirely replaced by the Japanese who had received this training.[10]

After establishing the Ministry of Telecommunications, in 1887 the government further upgraded telecommunications training with the founding of the Tokyo Telecommunications School, designed mainly to prepare the future managerial and engineering staff of the telephone and telegraph networks. The new school

[10] Saegusa Hakuo et al., *Kindai Nihon Sangyō Gijitsu no Seiōka* (Tokyo: Tōyōkeizai Shinpōsha, 1960), pp. 152-157.

provided a two-year curriculum and admitted 100 students each year, requiring completion of at least middle school for entrance. There were three distinct curricula—administration, telecommunications, and engineering. Administration covered postal and communications law, money order and postal savings operations, supervisory techniques, business planning, accounting, transportation economics and law, finance, geography and English as well as telecommunications technology. In the telecommunications curriculum, students took telecommunications technology, management, theory and experimentation, geography, law, English, French, German and mathematics. Those in engineering covered electricity, electric power, cable construction, chemistry, physics, mathematics, engineering, drawing, and English.

Until 1905, the school admitted applicants from any background, but thereafter accepted only those who had already been employed for at least a year in the Ministry of Telecommunications itself—a policy that has remained in force to the present. As the size of the enrollment continually expanded, new and diversified subject matter was added. From 1904 to 1909, the school turned out 571 graduates, about equally divided among the three curricula, and virtually all became key administrative and technical personnel in the telegraph and telephone systems. It was generally recognized that in quality the school was close to the university level and served as a model for developing semmon gakkō in other fields. In 1909, the courses in administration and engineering were extended to two years. In time, most of the very top management of the telecommunications enterprise were graduates of the ministry's school rather than from the Imperial universities.

The Telecommunications School also introduced short-term courses for lower level employees in the government enterprise. For example, training for wireless operators began in 1912. The administration curriculum was divided into higher and lower divisions in 1921. In fact, the school eventually provided training for virtually every position in the entire telephone and telegraph organization. As a result, between 1909 and 1939, almost 4,000 employees had completed curricula or courses at the school.[11]

Throughout this period, the telecommunications enterprise also undertook systematic training of the operating personnel at local telegraph stations. At first only young males were hired into these posts and given about six months experience on the job combined with classroom instruction before becoming full-fledged operators able to utilize the systems of coded Japanese and English. Later their training was extended to one year. By the 1890s, the enterprise began to employ young females ranging from 14 to 22 years old, for the most part as daytime switchboard operators in the telephone system. Almost all operators were female in the early 1900s, and when the third phase of the network was completed in 1920, the system employed nearly 13,000 women. For those positions, training extended over several months, both off and on the job, and included technical operations, general education, and "personality" instruction. The central office in Tokyo maintained its own school for this training, while in Osaka the operators were sent to a local girl's school for some of the courses. Females also began to take over telegraph operator work in local stations around 1900, although this occupation remained "mixed." Training programs similar to those for telephone operators began in 1902, with added emphasis on English. In all of the cases, operators who entered the training programs had to agree to remain with the company for at least two years after finishing the course work.

In 1902 the telecommunications enterprise initiated a special training program for senior operators who had at least six months of service and could pass an examination. This program required five hours of study a day for several months in a variety of technical and administrative subjects. Graduates of a program prom-

[11] Nihon Kōgakukai (1930), pp. 126-130.

ised to remain in service for at least three years. With the second phase of building the telephone network scheduled to begin in 1909, the enterprise expanded all the operator-training programs with a series of new three-, five-, and seven-month courses. Now, girls who had completed higher elementary school were admitted without examination.

In 1921 the ministry consolidated all training programs for operating personnel in a newly established Telecommunications Training Center in Tokyo with some 30 training locations throughout the nation (combined into 12 in 1934). The center set up two separate curricula, one a basic program of nine months and the other a one-year advanced program. New female recruits, usually 14 to 25 years old, gained admittance to the basic program if they had completed higher elementary school. Already employed trainees continued to receive their regular pay. The basic program consisted of courses in telecommunications techniques, equipment, and operations, and in general education including ethics, English, mathematics, Japanese, geography, and physical education. By 1937, almost 43,000 operators had been trained at the center in this basic program.

The advanced program, designed for supervisors and senior operators, was open only to men 23 years old or more and to unmarried women who had graduated from the basic program, had at least one year of service following completion of the basic program, and had the recommendation of their supervisors. The regular wages of these trainees continued while they were in the advanced program. The subject matter covered included telecommunications techniques, rules of operation, electrical engineering, ethics, mathematics, physics, chemistry, geography, transportation, administration, correspondence, English, and physical education. By 1937, more than 3,200 had graduated from the advanced program.

In addition to the Training Center's programs, the telephone and telegraph enterprise continually sponsored supplementary and short-term courses in the offices and shops of the telecom-munications network. During the Second World War, these were greatly stepped up in order to meet expanded personnel requirements and employment of inexperienced workers. Mili-tary drill also became required of all male trainees, while females received instruction in home economics and discipline. In 1944 and 1945 alone, more than 10,000 new operators received train-ing, and 1,200 experienced operators graduated from an acceler-ated advanced program that also had been introduced. In 1944 the Training Center began a new short-term technical training program that turned out 1,500 technicians in that one year.[12]

Postwar Developments in Telecommunications Training

That the telephone and telegraph enterprise took sole and full responsibility for the training of its employees seemed a logical development within the context of government ownership of an entirely new industry launched with utmost speed on a large scale. Unlike iron and steel, shipbuilding, and other modern industries, there was no long period of experimentation and gradual accumulation of skills; nor was there a network of patron-client relationships in the labor market upon which the telecommunications enterprise could rely for its labor supplies. Education and training for this industry could not be left to any outside institutions, nor to the new public vocational and techni-cal schools. It was a classic case of directly creating an "instant," qualified work force.

With telecommunications monopolized from the outset by the government itself, the employment system in the industry, in-cluding the training process, became part and parcel of the total operation. Employment in telephone and telegraph was almost the same as the civil service; and it soon included lifetime tenure for the male employee and periodic wage progression based on

[12] *Ibid.*, pp. 284-287.

length-of-service for all regular workers. The postal service, placed under the same ministry it should be noted, soon displayed the same characteristics, no doubt reinforced by the fact that the telephone, telegraph, and postal personnel worked shoulder-to-shoulder in local stations and offices.

Since World War II, the pattern of employment and training in telecommunications has undergone little change. The Training Center with its 12 local training locations remained and indeed was strengthened. An additional feature in recent years has been special courses for numerous foreign students, especially from Southeast Asian countries, as part of Japan's reparations payments and economic and technical assistance to them.

When the Nippon Telegraph and Telephone Public Corporation was established by Occupation-sponsored law in 1949 as a national enterprise with budgetary autonomy from the Telecommunications Ministry, it also considerably upgraded the Tokyo Telecommunications School (by this time called College). A university-level curriculum, divided into sequences of business and technical courses, now admitted employees who had had at least four years of service and could pass highly competitive entrance examinations. Postgraduate courses for the school's graduates also were introduced. The corporation expanded its wide variety of courses for all employees, ranging from as long as a year's course in radio and wireless operation to as short as one or two months training in supervisory, commercial, and business subjects. For all these activities, the corporation has employed a staff of 50 full-time instructors and 120 part-time teachers drawn from various universities. The College and Training Center facilities have fully equipped classrooms, libraries, and technical training locations. Students are provided with dining rooms, club houses, medical center, and recreation facilities and programs.

As already mentioned, the training system developed within telecommunications came to embrace virtually all the corporation's employees, from the lowest ranked operators to the top management. The curricula have covered as wide a range of subject matter as any comprehensive school system, from specific technical training to broad general education. The training and education, moreover, is cumulative, allowing the employees, most hired directly after public school graduation, to progress steadily through a continual succession of programs during much of their careers in the corporation. As such, the within-enterprise programs have hardly utilized or relied upon the outside educational system except for basic general education at the elementary levels. The system of the corporation is probably one of the purest cases of "enterprise-centered" training in Japan.

The profitability of the telecommunications enterprise no doubt has made these developments possible. So great has been the emphasis upon training within the enterprise that telephone and telegraph programs gained the reputation of lavishness and exclusiveness compared to programs in other public and private organizations. Coupled with this has been a relatively high investment in welfare facilities and benefits for the telecommunications employee, who at times were required to repeat their pledge to remain with the enterprise for their working careers.

In this context it was not surprising that the employees of the corporation, threatened by loss of their jobs in the postwar chaos, were quickly organized into one of the nation's major enterprise-wide unions when the Allied Occupation encouraged labor unionization. Nor has it been surprising that the union has often strongly resisted the introduction of automated equipment that threatens to displace employees fully committed for their careers to the telephone and telegraph enterprise (in large measure as a result of the training programs the enterprise itself developed). Only the rapid expansion of the network and the development of a union-management pre-consultation system have allayed the tensions that have emerged in recent years over reassigning or reducing personnel in the employ of the corporation. For example, during the 1960s when automated equipment rapidly displaced female switchboard operators throughout the system, the union resisted reassignment of these workers, most of whom were young, until they voluntarily retired for reasons of marriage or other personal circumstances. If the employees had been males, such an approach to displacement as the result of technological change may not have been possible in the context of the telephone corporation's employment and training system. This development has been a new experience in the industry and may eventually mean the modification of the training system that has been tightly confined to the needs of the corporation alone so as to permit increased labor mobility to other industries and occupations.

Early Development of Railways

A training system almost as "enterprise-centered" as telecommunications emerged in the government-owned railway system. However, since it was not until the early 1900s that this national enterprise took final shape, the route toward exclusive within-enterprise training programs was far less direct than in the telecommunications industry. The government has not operated as a monopoly over the entire railroad industry but only in the key trunk lines.

Although Japan's first railway was not constructed until 1872, the Japanese had been aware of railroading developments in the West for several decades. As early as 1853, a Russian mission to Nagasaki displayed a model steam locomotive engine to the samurai of the Saga clan who were invited aboard a Russian vessel in Nagasaki harbor. This immediately aroused Japanese interest in learning about the construction and application of the machine. The Japanese who met Admiral Perry at Uraga a year later reacted similarly when Perry presented the Shogun with an American-built demonstration steam engine. But it was not until 1860 that any Japanese actually rode on a train, when a delegation en route to the United States went by rail across the Isthmus of Panama. Two years later, a Japanese mission to Europe traveled by train from Suez to Cairo.[13]

By the early 1860s, Japanese engaged in Western studies were in full pursuit of knowledge about rail transportation, gathering and translating documents. In 1863, seven Japanese were studying railroads and mining at London University. At the same time, several foreigners seriously eyed Japan for railway development with hopes for commercial expansion. Toward the end of the Tokugawa regime, P. F. Herald, the French consul in Japan, attempted to persuade the shogunal government to undertake construction of a railroad; while an American businessman, C. L. Westwood, actually petitioned the court for the right to build a line from Tokyo to Yokohama. The government in fact granted permission to an American diplomat to proceed, but this was not consummated as the result of the fall of the Shogun.

The new Meiji regime wasted no time, and, as in the case of the telegraph, resolved that construction and operation of a railroad were to be wholly under its own control as part of the plan to modernize Japan. There was to be no foreign ownership of this vital industry. The government quickly set about gathering information and consulting foreign railway engineers. However, lack of investment funds thwarted any decisive planning until the British Minister Harry S. Parkes made a persuasive case that existence of a railway system could have reduced the great rice losses suffered in a series of natural disasters that had occurred in Tohoku and Kyushu. Thus convinced, the Meiji government, although hesitant as a result of difficulties in securing foreign financing, successfully sought a loan of three million pounds in the London money market to initiate the government-owned system.[14]

In 1870 British engineers were invited to Japan to direct con-

[13] Ibid., pp. 10-17.
[14] Ibid., pp. 14-15 and 121-138; Saegusa et al. (1960), pp. 251-253.

struction, and promptly undertook a land survey between Tokyo and Yokohama. Responsibility for railway development was soon placed in the Ministry of Industry. The 18-mile line, completed in 1872, proved highly successful and was profitable enough for the government by 1880 to repay the foreign loan. In the meantime, also beginning in 1870, the British oversaw construction of two more government-owned lines from Osaka to Kyoto and from Osaka to Kobe, both completed in 1877.

Lacking indigenous railroad engineering talent except for the few individuals who had been trained in London, the government relied until 1878 almost exclusively upon foreigners for the. construction of the first lines. Some 114 foreign engineers were employed directly by the government up to 1872 for planning and construction. All but seven were British, and the predominant groups were locomotive mechanics, track layers, clerks, and managers; for the railroads alone, the government employed almost half of all the foreign engineers hired during this period. To the present, the Japanese national railways have largely followed British technique, material, and organization.[15]

Only in 1878 did the Japanese attempt to construct a railway on their own—from Kyoto to Ohtsu—although even on this project they utilized foreign consultants. Five years later, however, as the railroad network expanded, few foreigners remained to supervise construction. For operations also, Japanese personnel began to take charge. By 1879 Japanese had fully replaced foreigners as locomotive engineers.

It took far longer, however, for Japan to begin manufacturing railroad machinery and equipment. Rail production was not undertaken until after the Yahata steel mills went into operation in 1901. The first steam locomotive was built in 1892 at a works in Kobe under the direction of British engineers, but production fell far short of the demand for a number of years later. Thus, for

[15] Ōuchi Hyoe and Tsuchiya Takao, eds., *Meiji Zenki Zeisei Keizai Shiryō Shūsei* (Tokyo: Kaizōsha, 1931), Vol. 17, pp. 402-417.

at least a generation the Japanese railroads relied almost completely upon foreign equipment and supplies, which no doubt required close consultation with the foreign manufacturers and railroaders, particularly the British. Rails came from England, Germany, Belgium, and the United States; locomotives from England, the United States, Germany, and Switzerland.[16]

Spread of Private Railways

By 1889, the government railway had grown to 550 miles of track, and in the process construction costs per mile had been reduced by almost 80 percent. From the beginning, moreover, the lines had proved profitable. Despite this progress, as in the case of other government-owned enterprises, the financial crisis in the 1880s put a stop to further growth of the government railroads. Instead, private entrepreneurs, both indigenous and foreign, were now permitted to develop new lines—in spite of the failure of private attempts a decade or so earlier. As early as 1881 the Nihon Tetsudō Kaisha, Japan's first private railway company, was established—under the leadership of Finance Minister Matsukata and more than 460 private investors—although at first this road was operated with horse-drawn carriages rather than locomotives.

Attempting to switch from public to private ownership of industry, in 1887 the government adopted the Private Railroad Law, which encouraged private line construction and operation. As a result, four years later Japan's private track mileage was more than 1,000 miles, nearly double the government-owned lines. Twelve private companies had sprung up by this time. A private company introduced Japan's first electric train in 1893. As a power source, electricity spread rapidly in the following decade although by 1900 the private lines were also utilizing steam and experimenting with gas. With the introduction of electric trolleys

[16] Saegusa et al. (1960), pp. 254-256.

in the growing cities, the electric railroad became predominant in the private sector of the industry and has remained so to the present.[17]

Interestingly, the spread of private railways marked the end of Japan's dependence upon foreign engineers and technicians in the railroad industry. When the private companies did employ foreigners, they tended to hire Germans rather than British engineers. So promising were the private lines that the number of companies mushroomed in the 1890s, reaching 43 by 1899. A number of foreigners, it should be noted, were important shareholders in these enterprises. However, with the economic recession following the Sino-Japanese War, it became clear that the Japanese rail system had overexpanded. Several private companies began to face serious financial difficulties or went bankrupt. When the decision was made to nationalize all major trunk lines in 1906, 37 private companies remained in operation.

Partial Nationalization of the Railways

The government's decision to nationalize on a partial basis created the railway system that has continued in Japan to the present: a complementary mixture of government-owned and private railroads. The Railway Nationalization Act of 1906, was adopted only after years of debate, for with the growth of the private railways in the 1880s and 1890s, the private companies firmly opposed any further nationalization and even found strong allies for their position within the government itself. However, with the Russo-Japanese War and the rapid growth of heavy industries such as steel, the impetus for fuller nationalization strengthened. Already branches of the national railways had been established in Korea and Taiwan following the Sino-Japanese War and then in Manchuria and Karafuto after the

[17] Nihon Kōgakukai (1930), pp. 271-337.

Russo-Japanese War—primarily as a means to extend military control and exploit strategic economic resources.

In the debate over the act Prime Minister Saionji firmly insisted upon complete nationalization, referring especially to Japan's need to follow the Bismarkian policy for Prussia in order to assure the nation's industrial growth and spread of social welfare. To permit development mainly through private enterprise, Saionji argued, would run the risk of failing to integrate and rationalize Japan's transportation system and would result in higher administrative and operating costs, and therefore higher rail rates. Revenues from the railways, he urged, should flow to the government rather than to private companies (especially the foreign shareholders), on the grounds that the national interest had to come first. In this, of course, Saionji had the backing of the military, who had felt that for national defense strategy transportation was too important to be left to private management— which they believed had been fully demonstrated in both the Sino- and Russo-Japanese wars. Even among some of the private industrialists, especially those interested in expanded foreign markets, some managements also urged an integrated national system in order to secure materials and products at the lowest possible cost.[18]

The final decision, however, was to have the mixed system that has continued to the present. Within two years after passage of the railway act, the government had nationalized 17 private lines, thereby doubling the publicly owned trackage to more than 3,000 miles. This left to the private firms merely 18 percent of the mileage, and only about 10 percent of the capital investment but about one-fourth of the total revenue, one-fifth of the passenger traffic, and one-seventh of the freight carried. The reversal of the previous positions of national and private lines thereby accomplished was achieved through bond issues that al-

[18] *Ibid.*, pp. 337-368.

lowed the private railways to invest in other fields. In fact, private railway investment, which had previously absorbed 25 percent of private capital in Japan, lost its investment appeal; and the 20 private firms that remained declined in size and operated mainly in rural areas until they began to make a comeback during World War I.

Track mileage for the government lines grew slowly from slightly more than 5,000 miles in 1908 to about 6,000 in 1915. On the other hand, in the same period capital investment increased by about one-third, and the number of employees rose from less than 90,000 to about 115,000. With suburbanization, accompanying the urban growth, from 1908 to 1915 the private lines were also spreading, their mileage increasing from about 1,100 to almost 3,000, invested capital about tripling, and number of employees rising from 17,000 to 30,000.

Essentially, the government railroad enterprise took exclusive control of strategic long-haul transportation. This left local and commuter feeder transport to the private lines. When it was realized that local traffic was lagging, in 1910 the government adopted a new railroad law to subsidize the growth of the local private lines as supplements to the national lines. Encouraged by the new law and at the same time favored by economic expansion, low-interest foreign capital, and protective tariffs, the private lines steadily expanded. By 1918 the number of new private railroads reached 73 with a total additional trackage of more than 800 miles. Most, of course, were very short lines, and few proved highly profitable in these years.

In the decade from 1916 to 1925, both the public and private systems underwent notable expansion. The government lines grew by an additional 2,000 miles; the private by 1,500 miles. Capital investment more than doubled on the public roads; and passenger miles, reflecting the steady shift of the working population to suburbs for living quarters, rose almost six times on the private. By 1925 employment on the government railway reached 195,000 and on the private lines, 65,000. All of these represented steady year-by-year growth rather than spurts.

Only with the Great Depression did a slowdown occur, as a number of the private railways went bankrupt or merged. Bank loans and government subsidies rescued several. Still another reason for the tapering off of the railway expansion was the spread of automotive transportation, with the national railroads introducing bus service in 1933 for local commuter traffic. This development proved to be the beginning of a new government-controlled attempt at rationalizing the transportation system, which came to a culmination by World War II. From 1929 to 1945, the National Railways steadily expanded its lines, adding more than 4,000 miles, 2,000 locomotives, more than 2,000 passenger cars, and 55,000 freight cars. Passenger miles grew from about 13.5 billion to almost 45 billion and freight miles from more than 8 billion to above 25 billion. The war years alone accounted for more than half of this growth.

The growth of the private railways during this period was far less spectacular. Hardly any net mileage increase occurred, the number of locomotives actually declined, only a few hundred passenger cars were added, and the number of freight cars remained about the same. Losses as the result of bombing and lack of repair were registered in the closing years of World War II. On the other hand, passenger miles shot up from 2.2 billion to a peak of 13 billion by 1945, mounting very rapidly during the war years. Freight miles grew from about 330 million to a peak of 520 million in 1943. Whereas on the government railway annual passenger revenues accounted for double or triple the freight revenue, on the private, they grew ten times by the end of World War II. By 1945, the passenger revenues on the private rail lines had grown to almost one-fourth of those for the government lines.[19]

[19] Ōsato Katsuma, ed., *Honpō Shūyō Keizai Tōkei* (Tokyo: Statistics Department, The Bank of Japan, 1966), pp. 114-117.

This complementary public-private rail system has remained essentially intact to the present. Until the mid-1960s the National Railway gradually added about another 600 miles of track, while the private lines grew about 700 miles. Reflecting rapid technological advances, the government enterprise reduced its number of locomotives by almost 1,500 while adding more than 8,000 passenger cars and 18,000 freight cars. In the same period, the private lines also eliminated close to 100 locomotives, but increased passenger cars by more than 10,000 while holding freight cars at about the same level. Rail traffic grew enormously from 1945 to 1965. On the government railways, passenger mileage more than doubled and freight mileage, which had fallen drastically at the end of the war, regained its wartime peak by 1955, and increased almost 40 percent again in the following decade. The private lines almost quadrupled passenger miles in this period, and even freight miles increased close to 20 percent over the wartime high.

Training in the Railway Industry

The central government's responsibility for developing a trained labor force for the railroads began with the origins of the industry. With the first land survey between Tokyo and Yokohama, the Meiji government placed railroad development in the charge of its new Ministry of Home Affairs, although shortly thereafter, in 1871, transferred it to the newly established Ministry of Industry, which contained a railroad department (*tetsudōkyō*). As mentioned, the earliest employees received training from the foreign engineers and managers brought in by the government to supervise rail construction. Most of this training took place on the job, but as early as 1872, the railroad department sponsored formal training for telegraph operators on the Tokyo-Yokohama rail link. Training of these operators was similar to that for those who would work on the newly developing national telegraph system, and in fact became the nucleus for a comprehensive railroad school established in 1877.

This school, set up in the Osaka station, brought together a number of foreign engineers to teach mathematics, land surveying, drawing, dynamics, civil engineering, mechanical engineering, and general transportation. No longer was training exclusively on-the-job for those Japanese who would work either in railway construction or operation. The program had three grades, and students were required to pass written tests in order to move up from one grade to the next. By 1882, 25 Japanese had completed the full program, and it was this group that gradually displaced the foreign engineers in supervising railroad construction. At the same time, the ministry's new *Kōbu Daigakkō* introduced railroad engineering studies and courses, so that the special Osaka institution was no longer needed after 1882.

In 1891, the ministry established a clerical training school, in light of a then-pressing need for developing systematic procedures for handling rail shipments. Located in Kobe, the clerks' school offered programs lasting two to four months. A second school of this kind was set up at Shimbashi, Tokyo, in 1898, with six-month and one-year programs. Students received daily wages for attendance but were obliged to remain in the employ of the government railways for one to two years after graduation.[20]

By the turn of the century, school-type training had spread to the private railway companies, which, as noted, had grown extensively and were outstripping the national lines. The private Iwakura Railroad School, for example, became so attractive for railway workers that it even cut into the recruiting for the government training programs. As a result, the government forced the school to close in 1904.

Following nationalization of the trunk railroads, the government added a number of new training programs. In 1905 engineering traineeships were intitiated at the National Rail-

[20] Japan National Railways, Vol. III, pp. 272-275.

way locomotive factories, for which entry required high school or university graduation. This training was upgraded and lengthened over the next several years. In 1908, the national railroad enterprise began a training program for seamen in its employ, enrolling graduates from public maritime schools. A year later the government enterprise contracted with the Tokyo Technical College to run one-year training programs for railroad technicians. Still other programs initiated about this time were special six- to eleven-month English language training for personnel assigned to handle foreign passengers and an overseas study program for engineers and administrators.

By 1910, the same year that Yahata Steel established its own school, the National Railway began to reorganize its various training activities into a comprehensive centralized school. Within this institution were established a one-year program to train railroad administrators, an English language program, and an electrical engineering curriculum. Local railway schools, following the model of the central school, began to operate by 1911, and included six-month programs in station administration, locomotive driving, rail maintenance, locomotive production management, and the like, oriented toward handling local operations not covered in the central school. Eventually, the national railroad training schools embraced virtually every type of employee from the highest to the lowest grades.[21]

In contrast, the private railways, by this time reduced in number and financially weakened following nationalization, did not develop formalized programs. Rather, the private lines apparently relied on highly informal training, largely on-the-job, and recruited less educated employees from the open labor market. At times, moreover, the private lines lured away national railway employees to meet skill needs.

[21] *Ibid.*, Vol. V (1972), pp. 324-334, and Vol. VII (1971), pp. 347-357. See, also, Okamoto Hideaki, ed., *Sangyō Kunren 100 Nenshi* (Tokyo: Japan Industrial and Vocational Training Association, 1971), pp. 198-199.

In 1921, in the midst of the rapid railroad expansion, the National Railway extended its consolidated training system from an almost sole emphasis upon technical and skill programs to include general education. A novel feature were scholarships offered for study at both the central and local schools with the idea of attracting young recruits into the enterprise for life-time careers. It was at this time that the exclusiveness of the National Railway schools became firmly entrenched. This system was so thoroughly institutionalized over the next two decades that the National Railway school system essentially paralleled the public school system at the secondary and higher education levels and, thus, provided an alternate track.

In the mid-1920s also the National Railway management began to pursue seriously the adoption of "scientific management" techniques.[22] "Taylorism" actually had reached Japan and gained prominent adherents (and research institutes) in the private sector as early as 1911. With the prolonged depression in Japan during the 1920s, government authorities had become increasingly interested in promoting efficiency and rationality throughout industry.

Much of the initial work in "scientific management" was carried out during World War I in the Bureau of Machinery and Rolling Stock of the Railway Ministry, particularly in the area of reducing repair work and idle time due to repair delays. It is notable, however, that the National Railway engineers in charge of the program delayed adopting time-and-motion study until 1929. Rather they relied upon group discussion and group problem-solving in the shop—no doubt enhanced by the common training the National Railway workers were receiving in the enterprise schools. This work on the National Railway, led by Yamashita Okiie, soon became a prime example of Japan's industrial "ra-

[22] See Kenji Okuda, "Managerial Evolution in Japan I: 1911-1925," *Management Japan*, Vol. 5, No. 3, 1971, pp. 14-15; and "Management Evolution in Japan II, 1926-1945," *Management Japan*, Vol. 5, No. 4, 1972, pp. 17-20.

tionalization" movement in the 1920s and 1930s. Indeed, when the National Railway did adopt motion-time study, it was the first large-scale application of its kind in Japan and was important for developing pay incentive systems and safety programs throughout modern Japanese industry. In turn, this led to adoption of aptitude-testing programs for personnel on the National Railway, which were copied extensively in other enterprises.

As Okuda points out,[23] "scientific management" techniques were not applied, as in the United States, only to develop efficient and simplified work methods for employing untrained and unskilled immigrant labor. The Japanese management in contrast took advantage of the techniques by relying upon employees already trained in their own schools and expected to remain in the railway enterprise for their careers. Adoption of the techniques, it may be surmised, carried forward the training programs rather than becoming a substitute for training. Training and "scientific management" thus were considered complementary and mutually reinforcing.

In 1939, the entire training system was placed intact under the direct administration of the Transportation Ministry as a means of controlling the scarce skilled manpower needed for the expansion of the National Railway during the war period. Also, the separate National Railway schools remained virtually unchanged under the Allied Occupation although internally there were a number of organizational shifts. In 1948, the curricula were revised into three groupings of regular, advanced, and specialized courses in order to avoid duplication with the public schools in general. By 1952, the system embraced ten technician training schools, 23 clerical training schools, 28 worker training schools, and ten hospital nursing schools spread throughout the country.

While the National Railway has always relied to some degree upon outside training for its workers, the new postwar programs cut down on this dependence by about two-thirds as the new cur-

[23] *Ibid.*

ricula and courses expanded. For example, in 1945 almost half the 90,000 employees who received some type of training in that year took courses outside the system. By 1950, after the curricula had been revised, of more than 35,000 employees receiving training, only 14,000 were trained outside. The new regular curriculum that year enrolled close to 6,000, the new advanced more than 2,000, and the new specialized more than 300. At the same time, over 2,000 workers took *ad hoc* training courses and 11,000 received clerical training. What had happened in the process was a lengthening of programs, larger enrollments in the lengthened programs, and fuller coverage of employees within the National Railway school system. This pattern has continued to the present, constituting a major example in Japan of a within-enterprise institution both for technical and skill training and general education.[24]

As in the telecommunications industry, this government-operated training system has been fortified with a wide variety of welfare programs and facilities to attract and hold employees within the enterprise. The present-day welfare arrangements began about 1910 when the training system itself expanded and centralized. They include guarantees of employment upon completion of the training programs to which employees are assigned.

Also, similarly to the telephone and telegraph enterprise, the employees of the National Railway rather quickly formed their own enterprise-wide union organization after the end of World War II. No doubt a prime motivation for this was to assure continuation of the close identification of the National Railway worker with the enterprise, within which from an early age he had been recruited, trained, and advanced for a lifetime career. Later, as the National Railway further expanded and experienced rapid technological change such as electrification and dieselization, this union, which displayed militancy from the beginning,

[24] Ōi Works, Japan National Railways, *100 Nenshi* (Tokyo, 1973), pp. 231-233.

sought to exercise control over the rate of change introduced in order to protect regular employees from displacement and disadvantageous transfer.

Union resistance to technological change has been similar to that occurring in the telecommunications industry, but unlike the latter it has affected male employees almost exclusively. One group of workers, centering as one would expect on the locomotive engineers, in fact broke away from the all-inclusive National Railway enterprise union, no doubt largely motivated by the desire to preserve their own jobs, which might be sacrificed if the group remained within the larger organization. At the same time, it appears that the National Railway unions have resented the failure of the government to reward the employees with wages and benefits commensurate with the relatively high levels of training and education they received through the enterprise's fully developed separate school system. This resentment has been strengthened by the fact that the highly profitable private lines, utilizing less complex technology, performing a less strategic economic function, and employing less educated and trained personnel, have provided comparatively large wage and benefit advances to their own employees in union-management collective bargaining. In general, the recent tensions over the introduction of technological changes and now the decline of the National Railway reflect the strong sense of employee commitment to this public enterprise that no doubt derives in large measure from the elaborate training within-enterprise programs and employment system developed exclusively for these employees in the course of this industry's growth.

Summary

No doubt a major reason for the development of the centralized and coordinated training and education systems within the National Railway and Telephone and Telegraph Corporation was the fact that in Japan, unlike other industrialized nations, the rail network and telecommunications system developed in advance of much of the industrialization. This as much as any reason underpinned the decision to nationalize the telecommunications system at the outset and eventually the major railway trunk lines, leaving a supplementary feeder role to the private lines. Centralization thus existed from the beginning, originating in the government's borrowing of foreign capital and reliance upon foreign engineers, instructors, and managers and then rapidly replacing both foreign capital and personnel with indigenous resources. Similarly, this meant close control over the training of National Railway and telecommunications personnel through highly developed within-enterprise training programs and schools for all positions at both central and local levels. Exact performance had to be assured for these infrastructure enterprises to service new industry as it arose. This policy has continued in the face of ever-occurring technological and economic changes.

Like the telecommunications network, the National Railway followed the pattern of the government's administrative structure with a centralized ministry in overall control and local agents to implement policy. As such, employment in the Telephone and Telegraph Corporation and the National Railway was tantamount to civil service status, with its emphasis upon formal and graded training and education almost entirely within the bureaucratic structure, upon employment security and welfare benefits for the trainees who graduated from the government enterprise schools, and tight identification of one's career with the national corporation. This pattern has continued to the present.

VII.

Training Patterns in Traditional Private Industries: Banking, Textiles, and Mining

OF major importance in the early phases of the modern economic growth of Japan was the expansion of private-sector industries that had pre-Meiji beginnings. Their approach to human resource development contrasted with the intensive within-enterprise training of the new technologically advanced industries treated in the preceding two chapters. Such private companies, despite initial government operation in some cases, depended far less on internal programs. Moreover, considerable variations emerged among these firms. Differences in training reflected differing conditions facing each industry, particularly the level of technology and pace of technological change, educational and skill requirements for work force members, availability of labor supplies, size and complexity of organization, and historical custom.

This chapter focuses on the variety of training institutions that grew up and persisted in the banking, textiles, and mining industries. These were leading examples of traditional industrial activity that expanded greatly during the pre-World War II era. We treat them together because they carried over from the pre-industrial era and tended to be labor-intensive in character. Chapter VIII will turn to training programs in private enterprises, particularly machinery and chemical companies, which came to occupy the center of Japan's economic structure after it shifted markedly from "light" to "heavy" industry beginning in the 1930s. For each industry, a brief history of its modern development is presented before examining its pattern of training.

Rise of Modern Banking

Financial institutions in pre-Meiji Japan, while rudimentary and hardly suitable for performing the functions of gathering savings and lending capital sufficient for the needs of rapid economic development, had a history reaching back several centuries. Yet, as in the case of other industries, Japan's banking system succeeded in becoming fully modernized before World War I. Since then, Japan has claimed one of the most sophisticated and well-developed financial sectors in the world.

With the Meiji Restoration, the Japanese first engaged in considerable experimentation with forms of private banking, but continued viability of private banking in the early years depended upon a significant measure of government leadership and guidance. It took several decades, for example, before banks ventured fully into making long-term loans, so that many modern enterprises that arose in the early years had to resort to self-financing, issuing stocks to the public, and utilizing short-term borrowing. The present-day widespread practice of firms receiving renewable short-term bank loans as a major source of long-term capital financing seems to have grown out of this early experimentation.[1]

The new Meiji government was quick to realize that well-organized banks were vital for establishing a sound monetary system in order to overcome the economic chaos left by the Tokugawa regime. This was especially the case for raising tax revenues necessary to carry out government functions aimed at national unification. However, since there was little by way of national financial institutions to turn to, it was up to the govern-

[1] Hugh T. Patrick, "Japan, 1868-1914," in Rondo E. Cameron, ed., *Banking in the Early Stages of Industrialization* (New York: Oxford University Press, 1967), pp. 329-389.

ment itself to initiate Japan's systematic banking network. In the pre-Meiji era, local financial houses had long existed for special banking and exchange needs—among merchants, metalsmiths, pawnshops, moneylenders, and rotating credit associations—but none of them was suitable for the centralized operations now needed. And indeed few of them actually survived the upheaval of the Restoration. Notable exceptions were the Mitsui and Sumitomo banking houses, but neither appeared at that time to have the capacity to serve as central banks.

Faced with an urgent monetary crisis, in 1868 the Meiji leaders took the first steps in issuing nonconvertible notes (dajōkan-satsu) and establishing a government-run Commerce Bureau (shōhōshi) in Kyoto to circulate the notes, collect indirect tax revenues, and provide loans to private firms. However, while the bureau set up a number of branch offices in various cities, within a year the government concluded that the operation was a failure because of continuing deep-seated distrust among businessmen of the nonconvertible notes. In its place was then established the Trade Bureau (tsūshōshi), which was charged with the tasks of stimulating commerce, stabilizing prices, establishing money exchanges, promoting exports and imports, and organizing trading firms. Foreign trade financing was especially crucial for Japan in view of the "Unequal Treaties" imposed by the foreign powers in 1859.

Under the Trade Bureau, led by Itō Hirobumi and Inoue Kaoru, eight semi-private exchange banks (kawase kaisha) and several commercial associations were established in major cities (Tokyo, Osaka, Kyoto, Yokohama, Kobe, Niigata, Ohtsu, and Tsuruga). These groups were authorized to issue their own notes, receive savings, and grant loans; they also attempted to gather capital from wealthy merchants, farmers, moneylenders, and the government itself. Although government guarantees and loans stood behind the exchange banks, all but the one in Yokohama soon failed because government interference in their administration discouraged participation by private capital subscribers. The Trade Bureau itself soon afterwards was abolished.[2] With general economic conditions remaining highly unstable, the old established merchant houses of Mitsui and Ono (who among others were subscribers to the exchange banks) now sought permission to establish private banks with their own capital. This the government refused to allow because of the lack of an integrated legal framework for banking. The next step was for the government to try again.

In 1872, the government enacted the National Bank Act, modeled after the national bank system in the United States. Itō Hirobumi, by then a top member of the Finance Ministry, was instrumental in this development. Required to pay cash holdings to the government and in return to receive interest-bearing government securities, new national banks were legally authorized to circulate convertible bank notes redeemable in gold. The first four national banks were established under the influence and direction of Shibusawa Eichi, then an official in the Finance Ministry, in 1873 and 1874. The Ono and Mitsui companies jointly set up the First National Bank despite their continuing fears of government intervention. This bank, which eventually grew to become the largest, began with 3 million yen capital and with Shibusawa himself as manager. A year later, a group of Yokohama silk merchants, also aided by the Mitsui and Ono houses, converted the one remaining exchange bank into the Second National Bank with 250,000 yen capital. The same year, wealthy landowners and commoners (more than 350 in all) began the Fourth National Bank in Niigata, while 29 merchants and samurai established the Fifth National Bank in Kagoshima. (The Third National Bank, although granted a charter to operate in Osaka, failed to open because of protracted disputes among the wealthy merchants who were the original backers.) Despite this backing, these national banks soon also failed when it became

[2] Tōyō Keizai Shinpōsha, *Kaisha Ginkō 80 Nenshi* (Tokyo: 1955), pp. 4-34.

clear that their bank notes, designed to replace the government's inconvertible notes, which were still being issued, could not win general acceptance. Since the rate of interest paid by the government securities was considerably below prevailing market rates, profits were impossible to achieve under these conditions.

This failure led to revision of the National Bank Act in 1876, when the government issued 184 million yen of compulsory commutation bonds to the samurai as one means for abolishing the Tokugawa class system. The need for an integrated banking system was now becoming desperate, for the problem remained of how to maintain the price of the bonds and prevent demoralization and unrest among the ex-samurai. As a result, under the revision, national banks were allowed to issue nonconvertible notes and to receive interest-bearing government bonds. With inconvertibility preventing a run on specie, national banks quickly multiplied—from six in 1876 to 153 three years later, which represented the limit of expansion in terms of capital and note issue authorized by the 1876 law. Daimyo and samurai, using their commutation bonds, in the meantime had become major financiers of this expansion, probably contributing three-fourths of the total capital overall, although commoners did not play an unimportant role in actively organizing and dominating certain of the new larger institutions. A number of the new banks, it should be noted, actually were forced upon the ex-aristocrats by the government and relied mainly upon government for guidance.[3]

On the heels of the national banks came Japan's first fully private banks. Anticipating the eventual need for private banking, both Sumitomo and Mitsui had been preparing for this role. Mitsui, for example, had already sent several of the younger sons of the house to study modern banking abroad. In 1876, the

[3] Kozo Yamamura, "The Role of the Samurai in the Development of Modern Banking in Japan," *Journal of Economic History*, Vol. XXVII, No. 2, June 1967, pp. 198-220.

Mitsui Bank, the first of the private banks under the revised legislation, began with capital of 2 million yen and handled government funds. Another eight were established by 1878, 30 more by 1879, and 40 in 1880. Even after the number of national banks had reached the legal limit in 1879, private banks mushroomed too, growing to 217 by 1889. These were founded mainly by commoners, particularly in rural areas, and were especially important for financing tea and silk growing. Mitsubishi also made its debut in banking in this period.

With this huge expansion came the problem of coordinating the banking system. In 1881, upon the advice of Finance Minister Matsukata Masayoshi the Bank of Japan was established, modeled after Belgium's central bank, which after a study of various national systems was considered most suitable for Japan. Financed half by the government and half by Mitsui and other private financiers, the Bank of Japan became the center of the Japanese financial system. At the same time, the Ministry of Finance also established an accounting division for government funds held by the banks.

A further revision of the National Bank Act in 1882 forbade the national banks to issue bank notes, leading by the early 1900s to the emergence of private non-national commercial banks as the dominant institutions and eventually to the abolition of the national banks themselves, which were converted to private banks. In 1891, such private banks (now called "ordinary banks") numbered 252; by 1893, 545; by 1896, 1,005; and by 1889, 1,561. Counting branch offices, the total number of bank locations was more than double this figure.[4] At the same time, a variety of other private financial institutions or quasi-banks were springing up. By 1884, some 741 such companies had been created.

Private commercial banking therefore not only was fully established in Japan well before the end of the nineteenth century but

[4] Ōsato Katsuma, ed., *Honpō Shuyō Keizai Tōkei* (Tokyo: the Statistics Department, Bank of Japan, 1966), p. 198.

also had become the main conduit for financing Japan's new industries. Moreover, management of the finance sector by and large had become decentralized rather than, as originally visualized, centralized, coordinated, and government-dominated.

This evolution consumed at least a quarter of a century. It should be noted, however, that the national banks, while short-lived, served the purpose of launching Japan's modern banking system. With them, modern accounting developed in Japan for the first time, and modern bookkeepers trained in the national banks became available for employment in private banks and enterprises. The national banks also seemed to gain wide acceptance for the corporate form of modern business as the idea of limited liability companies as legal entities gradually replaced individual proprietorships and partnerships.

Japan's modern financial system began to round out in the 1870s with the creation of various "special banks" and savings institutions. As early as 1875, just 10 years after Britain had launched the first in the world, Japan also began its own postal savings system. This proved highly successful as a means for tapping individual capital holdings. In addition to initiating the Bank of Japan as the central bank, in 1880 Finance Minister Matsukata was the prime mover in establishing the Yokohama Specie Bank, Japan's special bank for foreign exchange transactions. After adoption of special bank legislation in 1897, over the next seven years were established the semi-governmental Hypothec Bank of Japan, 46 affiliated agricultural and industrial banks, the Hokkaido Colonial Bank, the Industrial Bank of Japan, and the Bank of Taiwan. Private savings banks began to appear in the early 1880s, while life insurance companies also started up later in that decade.

Japan's modern financial system came into being well in advance of major industrial developments. Through special efforts, the government and major merchant houses such as Mitsui and Sumitomo had secured highly able staff to oversee the operation of the system. Rather than having been created in response to the financial needs of industrialization and thereby having to scramble for experienced personnel, banks were in a position to stimulate growth of industry and became "the locus of the early promotional and entrepreneurial talent which initiated the industrial spurt." Most private banks—such as the First, Fifteenth, Mitsui, Mitsubishi, and Sumitomo—were already large when they began and have remained the cornerstone of the banking system to the present. The proliferation of private banking with the Bank of Japan as the base meant that virtually every industrializing sector of Japan had ready access to credit and finance facilities.[5]

Probably overexpansion occurred in these early years. During the panic of 1900-1901 the number of banks decreased as the result of bankruptcies and enactment by the government of tighter restrictions for establishing private banks. Nevertheless, the financial system proved to be highly stable. With Japan now on the gold standard and with the outbreak of the Russo-Japanese War, the government, the private banks, and industries such as the railroads continued to succeed in raising sufficient capital through floating bond issues particularly abroad. The financial system also readily underwrote the rapid industrial expansion of World War I.

Only in the mid-1920s—following the postwar depression, the Great Kantō Earthquake, and later the abandonment of the gold standard—did banking undergo major reorganization, as a part of the rationalization movement occurring throughout Japanese industry at that time. Between 1921 and 1932, 1,154 banks, mostly small ones, disappeared principally as the result of mergers, so that by 1932 there remained only 538 private commercial banks in Japan. The number of offices, too, fell to 4,311 in 1932 from a high of 6,320 in 1925. Out of this reorganization grew a sharp distinction, which has persisted to the present, between "city" and

[5] Patrick (1967), pp. 278-287.

"local" banks, or "large" and "small" banks. More than half the savings concentrated in the twelve largest "city" banks (Mitsui, Mitsubishi, Yasuda, Sumitomo, First, Kawasaki, 100th, Yamaguchi, 34th, Konoike, Aichi, Meiji, and Nagoya). Each of these, it should be emphasized, became an integral part of a major zaibatsu complex.[6]

The merger movement continued throughout the 1930s and the Pacific War period. By 1945 private banks numbered merely 61 (but with 3,144 offices). This system has remained intact to the present. Despite the policy of the Allied Occupation after World War II to break up the zaibatsu, in actuality the authorities left the banking system virtually undisturbed. As a result, the prewar structure, with some additional mergers and an increase in the total number of banks to 75, has continued to be divided between the large "city" banks and small "local" banks.

While these banks, along with the Bank of Japan, form the overwhelming portion of the financial system, it should be noted that by 1968 there were also 26 special commercial banks (long-term credit, foreign, and trust); 1,268 financing institutions only for small businesses, especially credit associations and credit cooperatives; 8,643 credit organizations for agriculture and fishing (mainly agricultural and fisheries cooperatives); 11 specialized government lending institutions; and 41 life insurance companies, 277 securities companies, and eight credit card companies. On the other hand, the emphasis on renewable short-term commercial loans by the banks as a substitute for long-term investment, has hampered full development of stock exchanges, even though established as early as 1878, for the raising of private capital.

As mentioned, the rise of the zaibatsu entrenched their private commercial banks as the chief institutions in Japan for long-term as well as short-term investment. With each zaibatsu developing

[6] Katō Toshihiko, *Honpō Ginkō Shiron* (Tokyo: Tokyo University Press, 1957), pp. 231-318.

its own network of commercial banks, the latter soon came to occupy a central or "organic" position in the financial operation of the zaibatsu interests and subsidiaries. In the case of the Mitsubishi and Sumitumo zaibatsu, for example, it was the conversion of their own finance departments into banks as early as 1895 that firmed up these close arrangements.

With the Bank of Japan expanding direct lending to the private commercial banks with relatively small reserve requirements, the latter could rapidly provide credit in the directions they believed most desirable for Japan's rapid industrial growth—a phenomenon that also has been especially important in rebuilding Japanese industry since World War II. Other financial institutions—such as the special banks, savings banks, life insurance companies, credit associations and cooperatives, and postal savings—were almost "afterthoughts," in serving miscellaneous needs for channeling and using investment funds that the commercial banks themselves did not fully provide.

Human Resource Development in Banking

The early and rapid institutionalization of a highly developed and integrated financial system in Japan centering on private commercial banks was due in large measure to the attraction of banking for some of the best educated and most competent individuals at that time in Japan. Despite the sputtering first attempts at establishing modern banks, the government's policy following the Meiji Restoration made it clear that bankers were to have the highest social status as well as influential political connections in the new Japan. Banks were to become the innovators for new industry, and banking was no longer to be identified with the traditional money lenders of the feudal period. The first entrants into banking after the Meiji Restoration were ex-aristocrats and samurai who had received their special stipends and commutation bonds. While commoners eventually were to become important as entrepreneurs, the former aristocrats were the first to become identified with modern banking. Such a high prestige factor undoubtedly induced wealthier merchants and farmers to follow into the banking business. The early and rapid spread of banking probably boosted the status of white collar occupations in general.

An even more practical reason for the attractiveness of banking was the profit incentive and entrepreneurship. If there were savings in Japan to be tapped and channeled into new industry, prospects for profit through private banking proved even stronger than any patriotic desire to meet government fiscal requirements. At stake there were not only profits from loans and investments but also control of rising industrial enterprises. Once private banks, especially those under the zaibatsu, came to control the scarce capital, they took the lead in launching new industrial ventures. While there were notable cases of private entrepreneurship emerging outside the zaibatsu without the initial help of bank loans, the bankers generally achieved controlling power over the industries in which they eventually invested. The likelihood of taking over enterprise for profit added to the prestige of banking occupations.[7]

The high status of banking was enhanced by the lack of competition for channeling savings into industry. The pre-Meiji money-lenders had failed in most instances to become modern financial institutions. Most savers, especially in the rural areas, were unaccustomed to investing directly in new industrial enterprises. The new entrepreneurial bankers, stimulated by government measures, became the sole middlemen for this function. For the most part, compared to other free enterprise nations, the investment role taken by commercial banks greatly overshadowed that of stock markets, which until quite recently remained relatively unimportant. This role persisted even follow-

---

[7] Yamamura (1967); Tsuchiya Kiyoshi, "Ginko," in Arisawa Hiromi, ed., *Keizai Shūtaisei Kōza* (Tokyo: Chuo Kōronsha, 1960), Vol. III, pp. 156-161.

ing the Allied Occupation reforms, which broke up the zaibatsu conglomerates and dispersed stock ownership in the general public.

Since little knowledge of and skill in the functions and techniques of modern finance existed in early Meiji Japan, learning from foreigners became a necessary first step in the development of banking personnel. The most notable banking leaders initially learned about financial institutions in other countries or from foreign bankers in Japan. Itō Hirobumi, for example, went to the United States to study the operations of the national banks and returned to Japan to author Japan's National Bank Act. Shibusawa Eichi founded the First National Bank after studying in America and receiving training from foreign bankers in Yokohama. Foreign banks in early Meiji Japan, especially the Oriental Bank of England in Yokohama, trained a number of the key individuals who later went to work in the Japanese national banks. The Mitsui Bank was set up in 1875 only after members of the head office of the Mitsui House received banking training in the United States and England.[8] From the beginning, banks depended mainly upon "outside" public and private institutions for their supply of formally trained personnel.

The first formal step within Japan for systematic training in financial operations came in 1874 when the Ministry of Finance set up its Bureau of Banking Science (*Ginkōgaku Kyoku*). This was actually the first school of commerce in Japan and was a forerunner of the Tokyo Higher School of Commerce, later to become Hitotsubashi University. Foreigners employed by the government as clerks were assigned to teach western-style book-keeping in this school; and a leading lecturer was the Englishman, Alexander Allen Shand. Most of the graduates entered the various national banks, notably the First National. The school was terminated in 1893 only as the private commercial banking

[8] Tsuchiya Takao, *Shibusawa Eiichi Den* (Tokyo: Kaizōsha, 1931), and Kume Masao, *Itō Hirobumi Den* (Tokyo: Kaizōsha, 1931).

system became fully established and staffed. The first private school relevant for banking and business, the Osaka Commercial Training School, was established in 1880. Godai Tomoatsu, the well-known Meiji entrepreneur, supervised its founding, and today it is the Osaka University of Commerce. The new banks themselves did little formal training within their organizations, although recruits were expected to remain for their careers. Apparently, the prestige of banking served to attract personnel of such high caliber that little formal inside instruction seemed necessary. Most staff members learned as they worked.

Only much later did the large banks launch their own training. In 1907 the Mitsui Bank initiated a clerical apprenticeship program which admitted only graduates of higher elementary school, by then six years of education. This program provided classes in such subjects as skilled use of the abacus, bookkeeping, and bank-note counting. Those who completed the training became full-fledged bank clerks.[9]

Soon afterwards, the Yasuda Bank (today the Fuji Bank) also began a formal program for training personnel. This training program was open only to middle school graduates or higher, although the bank did not hire many university graduates at that time. Subjects taught included bank administration, law, economics, Chinese, English, abacus, penmanship, and the like, requiring a considerable amount of formal school preparation. Duration of the training was one year, graduation depended upon passing final examinations, and examination grades were used to determine the trainee's starting salary as a regular employee. Those who completed the course were designated "key" employees and were expected to make their life-time careers within the bank. By 1920, the program had produced almost 350 graduates, who were assigned not only within the Yasuda Bank itself but also to related industrial enterprises and banks of the Yasuda zaibatsu. Apparently this was typical practice. Later, in

[9] Mitsui Bank, ed., *Mitsui Ginkō 80 Nenshi* (Tokyo: 1957), pp. 133-138.

the 1920s, Yasuda increased its hiring of university-trained graduates directly to assume many of these same positions.[10]

The Sumitomo Bank, too, developed a variety of internal training programs in the early 1900s. Its lowest-grade clerks were required to attend evening classes that dealt with banking operations, and in 1913 Sumitomo initiated a formal evening orientation program for new employees lasting 40 to 50 days. Three years later, it began to provide its new employees from middle school with three months of clerical training, six hours per day, but by 1922 this program was abandoned as the company no longer recruited many middle school graduates.[11]

By the 1920s, a number of the banks were hiring women for the lowest level clerical jobs, usually young unmarried women who had graduated from higher elementary or equivalent girls' schools. Since the males employed were coming increasingly from middle and higher schools, they no longer needed any specialized training beyond the usual orientation and instruction in routines. The First National Bank, for example, abandoned its male clerk apprenticeship program that had been in operation for a number of years and instead sent young females for evening classes at nearby commercial night schools. Early marriage and short-term careers of women no doubt explain this shift to outside institutions.

With rising levels of school preparation, male recruits to a bank were expected to learn continuously on the job, and they usually remained with the bank until retirement. Each bank, with its large number of branches and variegated operations and interests (especially if tied to a zaibatsu), had its own distinctive pattern of activities and methods, and, hence, rewards and inducements. It was highly unlikely that its employees would leave to work for another bank. If a male recruit rose steadily, moreover, he had a good chance of participating in the management of a related in-

[10] Fuji Bank, ed., *Fuji Ginkō 80 Nenshi* (Tokyo: 1960), pp. 266-268.
[11] Sumitomo Bank, ed., *Sumitomo Ginkō Shi* (Osaka: 1955), pp. 121-122.

dustrial or commercial enterprise. Indeed, banks became an important source of managerial personnel for modern industry because of the intimate knowledge of enterprises bank employees would acquire in the course of their banking careers.

In sum, because of its continuing ability to attract highly educated and competent personnel, banking has been one of the few modern industries in Japan without highly developed within-enterprise training programs. While early training efforts were initially assisted by the government, foreign banks, and private schools, these were utilized only during the period the banking system was getting under way. Many of the leading banks, indeed, established formal programs early in the twentieth century and retained them for 20 years or more; but these too were cut down or eliminated as Japan's rising educational level provided sufficiently trained personnel for the banks, and at the same time permitted a shift of the lower-level clerical occupations from males to females, or from long-term to short-term employment.

Since numerous public and private schools at the secondary and higher levels were developing full and up-to-date commercial training curricula, it was unnecessary for the banks to maintain their own elaborate training facilities as in other modern industries. Apparently, the lack of formal training programs within the banks—except for training in special operations required for computerization and occasional conferences and short courses[12]—has remained the case throughout the postwar period. Banking probably has been the most prominent case among modern Japanese industries in which training and education in the common school system articulated well with skill needs in enterprises. Moreover, because of the attractiveness of the work, banks had little difficulty in directly recruiting the brightest and ablest of the school graduates.

[12] For a description of training activities in one bank, see Thomas P. Rohlen, *For Harmony and Strength: Japanese White-Collar Organization in Anthropological Perspective* (Berkeley: University of California Press, 1974), especially pp. 192-211.

Growth of Cotton Textiles

At the other end of the spectrum from banking in human resource development within modern private enterprise was the experience in cotton textiles. As is well known, in the course of industrializing Japan followed the classic path of first developing light industries, especially cotton textile manufacturing as a major production activity. While cotton textile manufacturing today retains an important place in Japan's economic structure, it has been declining relatively since the 1930s. By that time, however, the pattern of human resource development for the industry was fully established, and it continues essentially in the same form to the present.

A traditional spinning and weaving industry had long been in existence during the Tokugawa period. Operating largely on a putting-out basis, this cottage industry was controlled by merchant-employers, who usually provided training for weavers in factories or workhouses before returning them to their homes on contract arrangements. With the opening of the Japanese ports under the treaty of 1859, this putting-out system, often as side-jobs, rapidly expanded. In silk-spinning, a method known as *zaguri*, utilizing a simple hand-operated machine technology, also became widespread.

Modern textile manufacturing in Japan may be traced back to the 1850s. It originated with some of the western clan governments as part of their attempt to achieve financial and political autonomy from the Tokugawa regime. Most prominent in this movement was the Satsuma clan, which, as previously mentioned, was considered an "outsider" in Japan's feudal system and, indeed, located in Kagoshima, was geographically remote from the Edo capital. Satsuma was noted not only for its early experiments with textile manufacturing under the leadership of the engineer Ishikawa Seiryū but also for monopolizing the sugar trade, developing plant seeds, and producing gold and other precious metals among other economic innovations. Through accumulating its own wealth, Satsuma utilized an independent army and took the lead among the Japanese in mastering the development of western-type artillery and other armaments. The clan also took a major leadership role in overthrowing the Tokugawa Shogunate and restoring the Emperor.

In the 1850s the Satsuma clan, under Lord Shimazu Nariaki, was the first to import textile machinery from the West and to construct a water-powered textile manufacturing mill. These projects were undertaken primarily to secure a supply of sail cloth for the clan's vessels. Lord Shimazu in fact dispatched 20 men to England to study operations of textile machinery and to contract with a British firm for the laying out of a plant building, operating the machinery, and training operatives. While a number of years passed before the contract was fully executed (partly because of open Satsuma-British hostilities in 1863), seven British engineers arrived in Kagoshima in 1867 with the additional machinery. Soon the mill was operating with a steam-powered engine, employing 200 workers on 10-hour shifts, and producing close to 400 pounds of cotton yarn per day. Within a year, however, the English engineers departed, even though the contract still had two years to run, because of anti-British feelings and the disruptive conditions in Satsuma just prior to the restoration. Since the British actually provided little training for the native Japanese, the Kagoshima mill limped along lacking knowledge of the operations. Nonetheless, the Japanese operatives learned by trial and error and succeeded on their own. Encouraged by the new Meiji regime, in 1870 Satsuma also built Japan's second modern textile factory, the Sakai Spinning Mill. Again, machinery was imported from England, but with the experience at Kagoshima this time the factory was built by the Japanese themselves.[13] This success demonstrated the capacity of the Japanese to operate modern textile enterprises without foreign assistance very quickly after the technology arrived from abroad.

[13] Itokawa Taichi, *Honpō Nenshi Bōseki Shi* (Osaka: Nippon Mengyō Club, 1937), Vol. I, Chapter 2.

In 1872, the Meiji government subsidized construction of Japan's first privately owned mill. Its owner, Kashima Manpei, imported American spinning machinery and employed an American engineer to direct operations. Actually, under orders from the Tokugawa government, Kashima had set out to construct the mill four or five years earlier in competition with Satsuma, but the disturbances at the time delayed the project until the Meiji government furnished the needed financial assistance.[14] Beyond this, however, private entrepreneurs hesitated to go into modern textile manufacturing at that time.

Despite these early beginnings, major impetus for the modern cotton textile industry did not occur until 1877, when the Meiji government decided to build spinning mills for purposes of import substitution. The volume of foreign-made cotton goods in Japan had been rising rapidly and under the "Unequal Treaties" had come to account for more than one-third of Japan's imports. While the Meiji government first had concentrated industrializing efforts on armaments, rail transportation, and telecommunications, it now began to construct and operate "model" factories for producing light consumer goods in order to avoid drains on scarce foreign exchange and to provide employment for dispossessed samurai and their families. Several small government-owned cotton spinning mills therefore were built in the early 1880s, including those at Aichi, Kuwabara, Tamashima, Shibutani, Himeji, and Hiroshima, each of about 2,000 spindle-size.[15]

Direct government encouragement for textiles had begun with silk rather than cotton manufacturing, after the Maebashi clan, employing a Swiss engineer, in 1870 successfully utilized Italian machinery in a mill at Tsukiji, Tokyo. The raising of silk could be readily accomplished because of the relative ease of cocoon production in Japan's natural conditions. Since the government quickly realized the potential for silk in a rapidly expanding over-

---

[14] *Ibid.*, Chapter 6.

[15] *Ibid.*, pp. 8-12; Arisawa Hiromi, ed., *Gendai Nihon Sangyō Kōza* (Tokyo: Iwanami Shoten, 1960), Vol. VII, pp. 25-30.

seas market, the Maebashi success led to concentration on silk manufacturing for export. Silk soon afterwards constituted one-third of Japan's shipments abroad.[16] Most important in the growth of silk manufacturing was the government-owned mill at Tomioka, which was built in 1872 and remained under government operation until 1893 when it was sold to Mitsui. This mill utilized French silk-reeling methods, which, combined with the indigenous skills from zaguri production, turned out to be a major success. It was the famous private entrepreneur Shibusawa Eiichi who recognized the potential for silk and convinced the government leadership to go ahead with the Tomioka mill as a pilot plant, especially to train operatives who could enter other mills to be established and to demonstrate to private investors the use of foreign technology. Indeed, Tomioka did become an important source of trained workers for the textile industry as a whole and set the pattern of training in modern cotton manufacturing as well as silk. Initially, the Tomioka mill employed ten French technicians to provide instruction, while the first workers were supplied by each prefecture from among daughters and wives of landless samurai, rich farmers, and merchant families.[17]

Despite this stimulus, traditional private textile production still thrived. By the mid-Meiji period the domestic cottage cotton industry began to produce an indigenously developed rough cloth known as *garabō*. Putting-out, in both cotton and silk, characterized most of the textile manufacturing industry in Japan even after the new Meiji government undertook to foster textile modernization and growth.[18] Although we do not go into the development of human resources in the "putting-out" sector of the

[16] Saegusa Hakuo et al., *Kindai Nihon Sangyō Gijitsu no Seiyōka* (Tokyo: Tōyō Keizai Shinpōsha, 1960), pp. 140-141.

[17] Arisawa (1960), Vol VII, pp. 36-39.

[18] Sumiya Mikio, ed., *Nihon Shokugyō Kunren Hattenshi* (Tokyo: Japan Institute of Labour, 1970), Vol. I, pp. 34-40; Okamoto Hideaki, ed., *Sangyō Kunren 100 Nenshi* (Tokyo: Japan Industrial and Vocational Training Association, 1971), pp. 77-79.

textile industry, it should be kept in mind that until the present time textile manufacturing has been a major example of Japan's structure of small, technologically less developed enterprises coexisting alongside large modern firms.

Greatly encouraged by the Tomioka success in spreading skills beginning in 1878, the government turned to establishing "model" cotton spinning factories. Very soon afterwards, the government-initiated mills, like other industries, were sold to private entrepreneurs. Between 1887 and 1896, over 50 privately owned mills were established. Despite cessation of cotton growing in Japan, by the 1880s cotton textiles in fact took the lead in Japanese manufacturing development and by 1890 accounted for 65 percent of all factory employment in Japan. By that time landless samurai and rich farmers and merchants were no longer able to provide the required labor, so that the mills reached out for peasant girls for their labor supply first in nearby areas and then in more distant regions. This was the beginning of the well-known dormitory system for female factory workers.

Unlike the experience with silk, cotton textiles, although they required less than a decade to develop, encountered a variety of technical and human obstacles. The first government purchases of cotton machinery—two sets of 10 machines with 2,000 spindles from England—proved difficult for the inexperienced Japanese to operate efficiently, resulting in cloth more expensive than that imported. The early mills suffered not only from lack of technical experience but also from too little spindlage and too few machines, accidents and fires, interferences from government bureaucrats, low quality cotton, lack of marketing facilities, and the surprising inability to attract even low-wage labor, particularly females from the villages, to work in the mills. Numerous private companies, almost all of which were essentially subsidized or underwritten by the central or prefectural governments, went into bankruptcy soon after starting up. As a result, as late as 1889 two-thirds of Japan's cotton thread consumption was being imported. Notably, a year later this dependence suddenly dropped to almost one-half.[19]

The quick change-over was due to the rise of private large-scale spinning operations, traceable to Shibusawa Eiichi's initiative in establishing the Osaka Cotton Textile Company in 1882. After traveling in England and observing modern British spinning mills, Shibusawa realized that 10,000 spindles were the minimum needed for efficient operation. Within five years after its establishment, Osaka Cotton Textiles expanded to 40,000 spindles, now utilizing steam rather than the conventional water power. This spindlage made the mill comparable to the largest in England at that time. The company also engaged several British engineers to get the mill into operation, although Japanese engineers took over rather quickly. Most notable of the latter was Yamabe Takeo, who under Shibusawa's guidance had studied at the London School of Economics in 1877 and, after spending eight months in Manchester as a mill hand, became a textile engineer and replaced the chief British manager of Osaka Cotton Textiles. In turn, he recruited young university-trained engineers within Japan and put them to work first for practical training in the established government-owned mills before bringing them into the private company. Osaka Cotton Textiles was the leader in the field. It was the first textile company to install electric lighting (only six years after Edison's invention), to replace wooden with brick buildings, and to shift from mule to ring spinning, soon standard in Japan's modern textile industry. Electric lighting permitted efficient utilization of a two-shift, day and night operation. Starting with a work force of fewer than 300, by 1891 it employed 4,000, three-fourths of whom were young females.

The success of Osaka Cotton Textiles initiated a boom in large-scale cotton manufacturing in Japan. Soon many new private companies, each of considerable size, sprang up, concen-

[19] Arisawa (1960), Vol. VII, pp. 28-30 and 40-43.

trating heavily in Osaka. Japan's total spindlage grew from 130,000 in 1888 to 1,200,000 in 1897. As the scale of mills grew, product quality rose and unit costs fell rapidly. In 1893, there were 40 modern mills in operation employing more than 25,000 workers. By this time, textile manufacturing accounted for 57 percent of Japan's total capital investment and almost 90 percent of industrial employment.[20]

Throughout this development, however, Japan continued to import virtually all of its cotton spinning machinery—almost all from a single source in England—and most large companies still relied on highly paid expert foreign advisers and technicians. On the other hand, as in most of the modern industries at that time, Japanese engineers were steadily replacing the foreigners. Most were now graduates of the Kōbu Daigakkō, who after graduation would spend time in England studying or observing the British textile industry, followed by work in the government-owned mills before joining a private company on a permanent basis.

Typical of this pattern was the Kanegafuchi Cotton Textile Company (commonly called Kanebō), which was established in 1889 and employed Japan's first recipient of a doctorate in engineering, Taniuchi Naosada. Financed by the Mitsui Bank, Kanebō was placed in the charge of Nakamigawa Hikojirō, a young graduate of Keio University who had gained financial training under foreign teachers. Nakamigawa set out to recruit and train other new Keio graduates, the best known of whom was Mutō Sanji, who studied in the United States after graduating from Keio and later rose to lead the integration of Kanebō's operations, remaining in charge for 30 years.

In 1890, the first severe depression hit the textile industry, now overdeveloped for the still relatively small domestic market especially in the face of cheaper cotton imports from India and England. The reaction was an aggressive push by the Japanese manufacturers for overseas markets, notably in Korea and China.

[20] Itokawa (1937), Vol. I, pp. 422-424.

Already formed for this and other mutual purposes as early as 1882 was Japan's first industry-wide association (*Bōseki Rengōkai*). Japan's drive for cotton exports, however, was still hampered by technological and economic problems and led to highly intense competition among the Japanese companies themselves. The technological problem, mainly inability to produce thin thread, was solved only as the scale of enterprise grew and raw cotton was imported from India. At the same time, the problem of relatively high export prices for the Japanese goods was alleviated when the government, under persistent pressure from the cotton textile industry association, eliminated the export tax on cotton goods in 1894, and two years later abolished tariffs on raw cotton. Japan's victory in the Sino-Japanese War clinched the opening of the Chinese market for Japanese textile exports.

These developments permitted large Japanese companies to compete successfully with the British and Indians in China and Korea, although the Japanese industry still lagged behind the British in levels of productivity, machine-worker ratios, and working hours. By 1897, for the first time Japan was exporting more cotton thread than it imported. The number of cotton spinning firms had grown from 45 in 1894 to 74 in 1897.

Expansion was again set back, however, by another depression in the late 1890s, which began with the silver devaluation in Shanghai followed by Japan's shift to the gold standard, bringing exports to China to a halt. As before, the Japanese cotton manufacturers reacted with demands for government protection measures to increase cotton exports, expecially government subsidies. At the same time, to achieve economies of scale a number of mergers took place. Prominent was the merger of the Miike, Kurume, and Kumamoto companies into the Kyushu Cotton Textile Company in 1899, and a year later the merger of large Kyushu Textile itself with the Nakatsu and Hakata companies. By 1903 the number of modern firms had decreased to 46.

With the turn of the century the Japanese textile industry

began to develop its own technology. In 1898 came the invention of the Toyota power loom, which was much cheaper to produce and operate than looms made abroad. But it was not until the mid-1920s that dependence upon foreign spinning equipment ended. Over these years, a notable trend was that mill size, organization, and technology became increasingly similar from company to company, thus tending to equalize competition among them.

From the 1890s on there was steady secular growth in Japan's cotton textiles. Between 1890 and 1900, production of cotton yarn grew sixfold, and by 1914 it almost tripled again. Yet, few new companies entered the field. After the Russo-Japanese War, the number of firms no longer increased. Instead, plant size grew rapidly as the number of spindles for the industry reached almost 1,426,000 and spinning machines, 8,140. The Mie Cotton Spinning Company, now the largest in the industry, alone totaled 153,000 spindles and 2,500 machines; Kanebō, 120,000 spindles. By 1913 the number of spindles totaled more than 2.4 million, and spinning machines 24,000. Production reached over 540 million pounds a year, but it was concentrated in virtually the same number of enterprises.

Despite ups and downs, the successful capture of overseas markets as well as industrial concentration dampened the previous boom-bust character of Japan's cotton spinning industry and avoided the wild price fluctuations experienced in the silk industry (which in contrast was made up of a multiplying number of small factories). In 1906 the largest cotton textile firms formed an export cartel in the Chinese market, and by 1912 this cartel had successfully superseded the Americans and British for the Asian mainland. After 1910, the Japanese also were gaining ascendancy in the Indian market in competition with the British. Cotton especially had succeeded in concentrating capital investment in large plants and in developing high productivity (now output per spinning machine was two to three times England's and America's). The high cost of importing most of the machinery led to full utilization of the capital as well as concentration. Of special advantage, of course, was employment of the low-wage female labor and the use of continuous 24-hour operations with two shifts, so that labor-processing costs were merely one-fourth the cost of the raw cotton itself.

With enforcement of eight-hour shifts under the Factory Law after 1916, the Japanese cotton industry resorted to large-scale rationalization during the First World War. This era saw Japan's major experience with time-and-motion study based on the Taylor system. Managements sought much more direct control over work standards and reduced their reliance upon senior workers for training operatives. Mills introduced more automatic machinery and set up stricter quality and maintenance controls. Machine assignments were increased. Exact cost accounting was established. As a result, capital became even more concentrated in cotton textiles, and more versatile management was sought, for example, to undertake direct investment in plants on the China mainland and to diversify production into synthetics and woolens. Mergers again increased as the smaller firms went bankrupt or were purchased by larger ones. By the end of World War I, five huge firms dominated the cotton spinning industry.

With the modern cotton textile industry dominated by a few large-scale concerns, it was quite prepared to take advantage of the increased demand for Japanese cotton goods (along with silk) generated by World War I. Significant technological progress was accomplished also, particularly advances in producing fine threads. By 1920 the number of spindles rose to more than 3.8 million, spinning machines above 50,000, and production over 786 million pounds.

Only the postwar depression put an end to this rapid expansion. Once again, the cotton industry reacted in concerted self-defense, and the cotton textile industry association demanded and received government subsidies and other aids to promote exports. However, world competition drastically changed in the 1920s as the textile industries of China and India began to emerge rapidly, and the British continued to furnish products superior to the Japanese. New protective tariffs, quotas, and boycotts throughout the world drove Japanese goods out of the Chinese, Indian, and other large markets.

With completion of the rationalization movement during the 1920s, the industry stabilized once again. But by this time the silk market was about to collapse, rayon and other man-made fibers had achieved an important place alongside cotton textiles, and Japan was on the verge of entering the militaristic period of the 1930s with its rapid shift toward heavy industry. While cotton spinning has remained a major industry until the present, with 10 large firms predominant today, it has given way to synthetics and become increasingly involved in chemical processes. The patterns of manpower resources in the industry still visible to-day, were set, however, in the years up to World War II.[21]

Human Resource Development in Cotton Textiles

Probably the best known fact about Japanese industrialization was the widespread employment of young women in the cotton spinning mills. Employment of women started with the beginning of the industry, and there is little doubt that the Japanese cotton textile companies hired proportionately more of this labor than in other countries. Much of the celebrated "paternalism" of Japanese management long focused on the treatment of the cotton mill girls.

Training female operatives in textiles began with instruction by the French engineers at the government-owned Tomioka mill established in 1872. In this early program, as mentioned, girls were "drafted" from families of samurai and wealthy farmer and merchants from various parts of Japan to serve as examples of the

[21] Arisawa (1960), Vol. VII, pp. 46-83.

"new workers" in a modernizing Japan—an approach reminiscent of the Lowell mills of the 1830s. Once trained to follow factory discipline, these model workers were to return to their local communities and instruct other young females destined to work in local mills. The Tomioka system stressed manual dexterity on the job, continual attention to the tasks of the job, acceptance of the supervisor's absolute authority, competition in work efficiency (with wages and bonuses based on individual output), use of dormitories for group living, and classroom instruction for general education on such subjects as ethics, arithmetic, and dress-making.[22]

Although few factories immediately adopted the Tomioka training pattern, Tomioka served as the model to be emulated for many years. As the textile industry spread in the 1880s and 1890s, and as the government turned over its factories to private enterprises, the employment of females as operatives grew rapidly. Textile factories invariably sought young girls from villages and peasant families, since the supply of girls from samurai, wealthy farmer, and merchant house families was quickly exhausted with the rapid growth of the industry. Given the geographical distances involved and the discipline of the two-shift system, dormitories became a necessity for successful recruiting.

From the beginning, female labor constituted an overwhelming proportion—as much as 90 percent—of the textile industry work force. Most of the women were unmarried, few were more than 20 years old, having been hired as trainees at age 13 or 14. If they did remain in the mill, usually they became full-fledged workers by age 16 and stayed on in the mills until age 21 or 22 when they were ready to marry. With such low educational levels, the dormitories served as means for additional schooling. In 1897, more than 40 percent of the female workers in the cotton industry in fact had no formal school education, while 50 percent had dropped out of lower elementary schools without graduating. Even as late as 1929, only two-thirds had completed

[22] Sumiya (1970), pp. 34-38; Okamoto (1971), pp. 77-79.

lower elementary school, while another 20 percent had dropped out without finishing.[23]

Typical of the large enterprises, Osaka Cotton Textiles recruited its workers from peasant families both in the neighboring locality and from remote villages. Almost from the beginning dormitories were built to house the girls and to provide instruction and impose discipline. Older female employees, who had had work experience in the mills, were charged with instructing the new recruits. However, no formal or systematic training programs were set up by the company. Rather than utilizing in-plant schools, reliance was placed on on-the-job experience, absolute authority of the overseers, incentive wage payments, bonuses, and group competition.[24] It was assumed that most work was simple and required little skill.

In contrast, the Hirano Cotton Spinning Company, also established in Osaka about 1887, did establish a formal elementary school for its female recruits and hired three teachers from local public schools to provide instruction. No doubt this approach was due to the leadership of Kikuchi Taizō, who became the company's chief engineer after graduation from the mechanical engineering course in the Kōbu Daigakkō and attending the Manchester Technical School. The curriculum at Hirano covered Japanese composition, reading, penmanship, dress making and ethics. Formal classes lasted two hours every morning and evening, although after an exhausting 12-hour work shift it is doubtful that the program was effective. The dormitory dining room became the class site. Few of the girls, however, apparently took advantage of the class offerings, and those who did seemed to do so only under pressure from their supervisors.[25]

The Hirano case, however, was quite exceptional, although

---

[23] Japan Ministry of Agriculture and Commerce, *Shokkō Jijō* (Tokyo: Seikatsusha, 1903), Vol. I, pp. 133-135; Yokoyama Gennosuke, *Nihon no Kasō Shakai* (Tokyo: Iwanami Shoten, 1949), pp. 179-186.

[24] Japan Ministry of Agriculture and Commerce (1903), pp. 133-135.

[25] *Ibid.*, pp. 135-137. See also Sumiya Mikio (ed.), *Shokkō oyobi Kōfu Chōsa* (Tokyo: Koseikan, 1970), pp. 122-134.

there was limited spread of formal schooling to other major mills following the Sino-Japanese War. It was not until after World War I, as part of the rationalization program, that the other large companies of the industry began systematic and formal training programs for their employees. Managements were beginning to recognize that, despite the simple skills required, longer term employees were likely to become more productive with investment in systematic training.

Despite these examples, for the most part labor conditions in the modern cotton textile industry remained chaotic and abysmal. Even with the well-advertised paternalism of textile companies, turnover among the female recruits remained high throughout the period. Typically, difficult and unpleasant working conditions, and in some cases harsh treatment, persuaded many girls to leave their job within a few months, often without notifying management. A high turnover rate among the young women persisted well into the 1930s despite management allegations of efforts to improve their lot. There is reason to suspect that in face of such turnover most managements did little to improve working conditions or to provide systematic training for the female employees.[26] For several decades the deplorable conditions in the industry were described in the famous government reports on the condition of workers in various industries of Japan, and later in 1925 in *Jōkō Aishi*, the "Tragedy of Female Workers," by Hosoi Wakizō. Young females did not flock to the mills. Not only were they reluctant to go through the process of adapting from rural to urban living and from agricultural to industrial work, but also they were well aware of the reputation that mills had achieved for mistreating workers.

Throughout the first 20 to 25 years of the industry's develop-

[26] See Gary R. Saxonhouse, "Country Girls and Communication Among Competitors in the Japanese Cotton-Spinning Industry," in Hugh Patrick, ed., with the assistance of Larry Meissner, *Japanese Industrialization and Its Social Consequences* (Berkeley: University of California Press, 1976), pp. 97-125.

ment, the unwillingness of young women to enter the mills led to intense competition for labor among the companies. The firms resorted to various devices to retain workers or to pirate them away from one another. As each new large mill started up, the company needed an instant, experienced labor force of considerable size, so it usually attempted to lure workers away from factories already in operation. Without these "older" female employees, little useful instruction could be given to the new young recruits from the rural households, given the lack of systematic training at that time. The resulting competition for experienced workers led in turn to rising wage rates and a high degree of interfirm mobility. Often, the young recruits would renege on employment agreements and return home, especially if they became ill. It was not uncommon for a company to experience 100 percent or more turnover of its workers in a year. This situation was a far cry from the model of worker commitment the government had attempted to foster in the Tomioka model.

Dormitories and contracted boardinghouses were one measure companies utilized to stem "desertions." In a sense, the dormitories and boardinghouses were also a means for detention and for preventing the girls from looking around for other employment possibilities. Shifts of 12 hours a day or night tied the girls to their jobs and exhausted their energy. Another company tactic was the use of company guards, often gangster types, who saw to it that none of the girls left the premises and, if they did, meted out physical punishment and held them up to public shame. (On the other hand, they had to "square off" against still other "goons" who were in the business of supplying workers to the highest bidder, often resorting to kidnapping to obtain their supplies.) When these practices didn't succeed in holding the girls, mills would resort to the hiring of part-time and temporary workers from the immediate city neighborhoods.

Another employer response to the labor competition was to require the young girls to commit themselves to at least three- to five-year terms of employment in a mill. Submissive country girls from remote areas were committed to the terms before they understood the adverse situations they were getting into. Most of them went to work in mills outside their home prefecture. Using recruiting agents who knew the villages, companies would paint a bright picture of the benefits of working in the mills for the girls and their families. Nagano and Hiroshima were favorite recruiting grounds for the Osaka and Tokyo mills.

As a result, the industry attracted probably the least educated and educable members of the labor force. Intense labor competition as well as disregard of employee health and safety at work and in the dormitory created a vicious circle of recruiting the least able. It also meant the lack of attention to systematic training of the female workers. While the cotton textile industry federation attempted to control this situation through self-regulation such as dividing Japan into labor territories, only when the government began to take cognizance of these conditions, culminating in the passage of the Factory Law of 1911, did a change toward improvement begin in the textile industry. Even then several decades were required to bring about better conditions.

The process of improvement developed gradually. Soon after the Russo-Japanese War, as has been noted elsewhere, the first efforts at professionalizing management practices in Japan's modern industries began. This was largely the result of the recruitment of management candidates from the new universities and more systematic and rational attention to operations. Among the most important changes was an increase in direct management control of hiring, wage payment, and worker training. For the first time, managements set up personnel departments for control and administration of employment practices, replacing labor recruiters or contractors. Firms now began to send out directly employed representatives to their respective territories to present systematically a better image of the company and to cultivate relations with the families of recruits. There was also a notable step-up in labor-saving technological changes in the mills as operations expanded. More and more the progressive managements realized that workers in textile mills suffered from extremely low morale and lack of motivation.

The new approach attempted to hold recruits in the company on the assumption that, once in continuing employment, the girls would learn to do jobs far more efficiently. To make mill employment more attractive, forward-looking managements instituted changes in pay and related practices, for example immediate daily payments instead of delayed monthly wages, direct remittance of pay to parents, individual and group attendance bonuses, housing at low charges, length-of-service wage increases, and individual merit citations. But the most widespread measures aimed at improving physical living conditions, housing, health care, work hours, and holidays. Such textile companies also instituted a variety of educational, cultural, and recreational programs within the dormitories.

However, many of these efforts to cut down worker turnover, increase the attractiveness of mill work, and heighten worker motivation in the cotton textile industry were short-lived. With the boom of World War I, extreme labor competition revived, and virtually all the earlier evils reappeared. Again the industry faced the problem of stabilizing its work force, but this could not be achieved until government regulation and the movement for rationalization of the industry took hold in the 1920s. Government enforcement of the Factory Law now required improvement in working conditions of children and females and provision for the education of working youth of school age. Establishment and control of labor exchanges under a new law adopted in 1921 also brought order to the channeling of workers into mills. Prohibition of the night shift for women and minors under the 1911 Factory Law came into force in 1929.

Formal training programs initiated in Japan's modern cotton textile industry during the 1920s were part and parcel of the more general industrial rationalization movement of that period. With cotton textiles manufacturing as Japan's most important industry, no longer could companies run the risk of employing poorly educated, low quality, and unstable workers to operate the advanced technologies and intricate organizations. Direct management control, based on systematic policies and research, became increasingly necessary. Rationalization meant the establishment of standardized job classification and promotion hierarchies, for which training could be made much more specific. The big mills began to set up the equivalent of public elementary schools for the young females in their employ. The companies usually supplied free textbooks and materials and offered curricula at both the lower elementary level, which was compulsory under the law, and at the higher elementary. This education was nontechnical, with such subjects as morals, Japanese language, arithmetic, geography, history, gymnastics, dress making, flower arranging, tea ceremony, etiquette, cooking, Japanese dancing, and housekeeping to prepare the girls for marriage.

A far more systematic approach to technical training was adopted. The Tōyō Cotton Textile Company (or Tōyōbō) was typical of the big firms in introducing induction and training programs for the young female recruits. After receiving a rigorous physical exam, the inexperienced recruit took oral tests and listened to orientation lectures covering the general factory organization, work regulations, and authority of superiors. She then received one to two weeks training in the basic motions of cotton spinning work and the application of these motions to her particular job. Simultaneously, she attended classes taught by technical supervisors or experienced female workers in techniques for improving skills, preventing accidents, and learning the names and operations of all the machines in the mill. In all of this, there were constant reminders of the need to observe strict discipline in the mill and dormitory.

Systematizing of training and education in the large mills

spread rapidly in the 1920s. In 1932 a survey of 238 factories with more than 100 employees each indicated that almost 60 percent were providing government-approved supplementary schooling for general education, while 79 percent had skill training programs like Tōyōbō's. During this period, various companies also set up government-approved Youth Training Schools and established girls' vocational schools at the middle-school level. The latter included general education classes in Japanese, arithmetic, history, geography, etiquette, flower arranging, cooking, dress making, and the like. The Youth Training Schools provided military drill for the few boys employed.

In fact, this supplementary general education was not very thorough. Usually classes were held only for an hour or two before or after work, and the compulsory courses lasted little more than a month. The completion rate, moreover, was poor; usually less than one-third of the girls finished.

These patterns of educating and training young female recruits from the rural areas have continued throughout the post-World-War-II era. Eventually the worst of the abuses in the mills were eliminated and much greater stability of work forces in the textile industry was achieved. Training techniques such as TWI and MTP found their strongest sponsors in the large cotton textile companies and reached down to the unskilled female recruits. These were especially needed in view of the very rapid introduction of the most advanced technology once the industry revived in the post-World-War-II period. Moreover, the postwar protective labor legislation was made far stronger than in the prewar period, particularly for female workers employed in cotton textiles. As educational levels rose to the middle school level and beyond, the need to provide general education for the girls lessened, although the dormitory system has prevailed down to the present with its wide range of educational, cultural, and recreational activities. Labor unions also became well established in the postwar period, assuring equitable treatment for the girls and preserving long-established welfare and educational programs. Only since about 1960, when labor shortages appeared, has there been a weakening of the dormitory system, for not only did the mills begin to recruit girls with increasing levels of education and sophistication but alternative employment opportunities in other industries and in the cities were multiplying. Starting wages were rising rapidly—backed by strong union bargaining. In some instances mills began to recruit older women and to recall former employees rather than search for young females.

As for the relatively few male employees in cotton spinning, much greater stress was placed from the beginning upon relevant technical training—mathematics, spinning techniques, drawing, and Japanese language. Men were destined to work in maintenance and repair, become foremen, or serve as technicians and semi-engineers. It was not until World War I, however, just as in the case of the female operatives, that formal training programs were begun for young male recruits in cotton textiles; these, too, included both technical and general education, offering such subjects as Japanese, mathematics, spinning and fabricating techniques, and engineering drawing. Following the past practice in the industry, senior workers provided the instruction. With the rationalization movement in the 1920s, moreover, companies such as Kanebō and Tōyōbō began their first formal programs for men in supervisory training, requiring at least a middle school background.

As noted earlier, almost from the beginning of the modern cotton textile industry, top management was formed by recruiting promising graduates in engineering and other fields from leading universities. The dramatic step in 1891 taken by Nakamigawa Hikojirō, the leader of Mitsui at that time, of virtually doubling salaries and bonuses of managers in their firms, including textiles, was highly effective in attracting top caliber graduates into management ranks. For technicians, the industry turned not only to the university engineering departments but also to the vocational and industrial middle and higher schools or semmon gakkō. While graduates of the latter were expected to become foremen, in fact they usually rose into the middle ranks of the managerial hierarchy, and many left the large companies to manage their own enterprises. Already noted was the rapid replacement of foreign engineers by Japanese in the mid-1880s, especially in the government-owned mills. The early Japanese engineers in turn played a major role in instructing still other engineers and technicians, virtually all men, informally and on the job.

There has been little change in this approach during the post-World-War-II years. However, new opportunities for the high- and middle-level personnel have expanded as the large textile companies diversified into chemical and related processes and, as a result, established their own research and development facilities. These developments have required increased reliance upon preparation in the "outside" educational system rather than within-enterprise training alone.

The Mining Industries

Whereas banking required little within-enterprise training, and cotton textiles failed for several decades to develop systematic internal or external programs, the metal mining industry almost from the start gave special attention to preparing high-level personnel for the specifics of its operations. In Japan's drive to industrialize following the Meiji Restoration, some of the earliest efforts focused on exploiting mining resources already developed in the Tokugawa era. While limited in amount, the principal deposits were nonferrous metals, especially copper, silver, gold, and zinc. (Iron ore was virtually non-existent so Japan has always imported 90 percent of requirements.)

Primitive metal mining on a limited scale had taken place from the earliest recorded times in Japan.[27] Although the daimyo held title to mineral resources, they often allowed peasants, if well-to-do, to mine their land in conjunction with small enterprises in metal-using trades. During the early premodern period, particularly from the mid-sixteenth to the early seventeenth centuries, the Tokugawa government and several of the clans had each operated large-scale gold and silver mines mainly for monetary needs. These operations financed their military forces and provided a unified money system for the nation. On the other hand, the mining of copper, which also grew rapidly in the mid-seventeenth century, was undertaken mostly for export to China and Holland.

It was not until the early Meiji era that full-blown mineral exploitation began, occasioned by the government's realization that metals (as well as coal) were key resources in modern industries. In fact, gold, silver, and copper production had all suffered declines after the mid-seventeenth century, and lack of these metals probably contributed to the weakening of the Tokugawa regime following the opening of Japan. Suddenly gold and silver were in great demand in order to import foreign goods and services. The central government took over all mines.

Foreign engineers employed by the government played a key role in the initial modernization of Japanese mining. Engineers mainly from England, France, the United States, and Germany assisted in drawing up an overall mining development plan for the Meiji government. They introduced steam-powered hoists in mining pits and truck rails in horizontal drifts. In 1878 dynamite was first used under their supervision. Most of the modernization effort initially was devoted to mining gold and silver because of Japan's urgent need for specie, but copper also made consider-

[27] For a detailed history of mining in Japan, see Nihon Kōgakukai, *Meiji Kōgyōshi Kōgyō Hen* (Tokyo: Meiji Kōgyōshi Shuppansha, 1930), pp. 3-77; and Kobata Atsushi, *Kōzan No Rekishi* (Tokyo: Shibundō, 1957).

able headway when the foreigners installed modern smelters. By 1880, metal mining production surpassed the peak of output reached more than 100 years earlier in the Tokugawa period.

Despite this progress, the government-run operations did not pay for themselves. Foreign technology was obviously necessary for development of the mines but faced difficulties adapting to Japanese geological conditions and to the peculiar properties of Japanese ores and scale of mines in Japan. Just as significant an obstacle was a continuing tendency to rely upon a highly unstable work force in the mines. As a result, private entrepreneurs increasingly became responsible for the full development of modern mining in Japan. Faced with steady losses, the government began to subcontract mining operations to private entrepreneurs who had strong political connections. Also as early as 1869, the Meiji regime repealed the government monopoly law for copper mining and invited private entrepreneurs to enter the field. The Besshi mine, one of Japan's three foremost copper deposit operations, went directly into the hands of the Sumitomo house without any stage of government operation. In 1874, the Ono house received the Ashio copper mine; while in the same year the famous entrepreneur Iwasaki bought from the government the Yoshioka copper mine, which along with Besshi was one of the other major deposits. Throughout the 1870s, therefore, metal mining had both public and private companies, although it was the government that continued to take the initiative in employing foreign engineers and introducing foreign technology.

In 1880 the government decided to divest itself fully of mine ownership as a part of its general policy for achieving financial reform although divestiture actually took place over the next 25 years. Most of the important mines were sold at relatively low prices to the emerging zaibatsu. In 1887, for example, Mitsui took over the Kamioka silver mine, which later became a principal zinc resource. The initial success of the zaibatsu—Mitsui, Mitubishi, Sumitomo, Furukawa—no doubt lay in their direct control of mining. With railroad construction spreading rapidly in the 1890s, the zaibatsu undertook an enormous expansion of mining resources. The sudden surge in demand for metals during the Sino-Japanese War assured the financial success of private enterprises. By this time, the electric generating industry had also developed, making possible a huge leap in copper production and copper exporting.

Exporting now began to dominate copper industry production, since domestic demand still remained comparatively low for the scale of operations that had developed. One result was that copper mining had to learn to adjust quickly to the highly volatile price fluctuations that copper experiences in the world market. This shift, in turn, led to an increased emphasis upon utilizing the most advanced technology as a means of controlling the flow and cost of output. Hydroelectric plants, electric hoists, electric locomotives, electric pumps, electric work drills, all made their appearance at the mine sites at that time. Copper smelting, particularly the use of oxidization, was also significantly improved.

After a sizable development up to the 1890s, silver mining in Japan began to decline. This resulted especially from the fall of the world price for silver and from the loss of the Indian market. Moreover, in 1897 Japan itself went on to the gold standard. By the beginning of the twentieth century, Japanese investment in metal mining shifted primarily to copper and gold mining, which again entered a period of hot-house growth.

The greatest impetus to metal mining came from the Russo-Japanese War. At this time, too, six large private enterprises emerged to dominate the industry: Sumitomo, Mitsui, Mitsubishi, Furukawa, Fujita, and Kuhara (later, Hitachi). As in other developing modern industries at that time, mergers and consolidations took place at a rapid pace with the six companies buying up small mines throughout Japan. Lacking sufficient capital for investment in fast-changing modern machinery and technology, the small firms could no longer compete with these giants. The

Big Six also integrated vertically with manufacturing operations, including production of copper pipe and wire, aluminum, chemicals, and eventually steel making, shipbuilding, heavy machinery, and rubber. Metal mining, however, continued as the hub of these conglomerates. The boom of World War I assured the firm hold of these giant enterprises.

Accompanying this rapid concentration and growth was a high degree of labor-management conflict. A major riot occurred at Ashio in 1907, and similar outbursts at the Besshi, Ikuno, and Horonai mines shortly afterwards. Fundamentally, this unrest arose from the instability of mine work forces throughout the merger period. One result was a terrifying increase in mine accidents; another was pollution of the natural environment, as mining companies penetrated into more and more remote farming and mountain areas.

Only the sudden depression following World War I halted the growth of metal mining. In self-protection the Big Six reacted by driving the remaining small firms, who were virtually bankrupt in any event, completely out of business and by forming an industrial cartel to divide up the market. As in cotton textiles, the cartel persuaded the government to impose tariffs on foreign copper imports and to provide production subsidies; for by the early 1920s the United States copper industry was beginning to dominate the world market and to invade the Japanese market itself. The protective measures proved effective. By the end of the 1920s, the Japanese firms gained control of 95 percent of the domestic market and successfully re-entered the export market with the recovery of the world price. Yet, stability in the industry did not remain long. As the Great Depression struck, metal mining became depressed again everywhere. Throughout the 1930s until the outbreak of World War II, Japan's copper mining industry remained in recession. The one exception to this boom and bust experience was gold. Gold mining did not suffer from the same ups and downs, since the price of gold remained constant in the world monetary system. In fact, gold was the only metal mining industry in Japan that enjoyed steady expansion throughout the decades. Production of gold leaped upward when Japan permitted its export in 1930.[28]

Throughout the 1920s and 1930s, in line with the rationalization programs in other modern industries, Japan's metal mining enterprises constantly sought ways to cut costs, mainly by substituting machinery for labor to force wages down. As a result, serious labor unrest again arose in the mining areas because of wage cuts, layoffs and dismissals, and work intensification. Metal mining was one of the few sectors in prewar Japan in which workers successfully formed lasting unions. The unions sought employment stability and blamed their poor conditions on the long-established employment system that depended on patron-client groups. The Big Six, however, generally were able to disregard union pressure in proceeding with technological change.

It is useful to contrast the development of coal mining with metal mining, for Japan had a somewhat different development in coal than metals.[29] While coal mining also was long known to the Japanese, its exploitation on a major scale did not begin until well after the mid-nineteenth century. Like metal mining, coal mining began with very small local mines. The appearance of Perry's Black Ships, however, immediately demonstrated the importance of coal as a fuel, and coal mining developed quickly thereafter. Coal was also destined for export to China and Southeast Asia as well as for fuel for Japan's new steamships and railroads. While the clan governments originally owned the coal rights, private entrepreneurs had been permitted to develop small coal mines. One of the early acts of the new Meiji regime in 1870 was to take over all coal deposits, a process completed with the abolition of the clans and establishment of the prefectures in

[28] For the development of Japanese mining before and after World War II, see Arisawa Hiromi (1960), Vol. II, pp. 319-328.

[29] See Nihon Kōgakukai (1930), pp. 619-643.

1872. As in metal mining, the Meiji government provided the major impetus for modernizing coal mining through employing foreign engineers and machinery. Under a law in 1874 large new mines at Miike and Takashima in Kyushu, among others, were soon developed using modern technology.

Despite these efforts, because coal rights remained unclear under the law, most of the private small mines continued to operate. Their technology primitive and lacking capital, about 600 such mines existed in 1884. As a group, although fiercely competing among themselves, they continually threatened to provide an oversupply of coal and depressed prices in the market. Consolidations and mergers did not characterize coal mining as they had in metals.

This "dualism" led to several efforts to reorganize the industry. In 1885, Japan's first coal mining trade association was established in Kyushu in order to regulate prices and allocate production. A similar association soon followed in Hokkaido. These associations developed under the leadership of the Mitsui and Mitsubishi zaibatsu, which as in other fields were privileged to purchase the large government-owned mines at low prices during the latter 1870s up to as late as 1892. By 1890 the government, despite its inherent control over all underground deposits, changed the Mining Law to clarify the right to mine separately from government ownership.

The real effect of this change was to encourage the entrance into the industry of highly capitalized private firms which up to then had hesitated to invest in coal mining under the law of 1870 with its unclear provisions regarding the right of property ownership. The new act also speeded up divestiture of government-owned mines into the hands of private entrepreneurs. The sizes of coal mines thereafter notably increased, but so did speculation in mining lands and mining accidents. After a series of ups and downs from the 1890s to World War I, the coal mining industry experienced notable expansion in the 1920s and 1930s. The growth of modern industry required steadily increasing supplies of coal, while militarism led to an expansion of exports for maritime and overseas needs. By this time, the zaibatsu companies also cartelized coal mining and began to develop industrial complexes near the mine sites, including machinery manufacturing, metal smelting, and chemical production. Government subsidies and tariff protection was also provided. Within this framework, coal production expanded markedly during the wartime years.

The end of World War II, of course, disrupted all mining activity in Japan.[30] In 1946 the industry was producing merely a fraction of its wartime peak. Not until the 1955-1960 period did it regain the previous high levels, the recovery due mainly to the high priority given coal mining as a fuel resource in the years after the surrender. Coal, however, has been affected by the energy revolution. Although by the early 1960s production was close to the high of 56 million tons registered in 1940 and 1941, since then it has dropped steadily and has become increasingly concentrated in large mines. In contrast, silver and copper production soared to such new heights that deposits have been almost exhausted.

Human Resources in Mining

As mentioned, training of mining engineers and administrators received top priority from the beginning of the modern period.[31] Japan's first mining school was established at the Ikuno silver mine in 1868, with admission requiring the equivalent of middle school education. A second in the same year was set up at Ani and employed a French teacher for instruction in a one-year course. By 1878 the mining department of the Kōbu Daigakkō within the Ministry of Industry—later succeeded by the en-

[30] For developments following World War II see Arisawa Hiromi (1960), Vol. III, pp. 248-255.

[31] See Nihon Kōgakukai (1930), pp. 961-969.

gineering schools of Tokyo Imperial University and the Kyoto Imperial University—became the major center for mine engineering training. Together they turned out the engineers who studied abroad, replaced the foreigners, and took over direction of the industry. M.I.T. graduate Dan Takuma, long the eminent leader of the Mitsui coal mining operations, was an example.

The Ministry of Industry school and its successors required six years of course work, followed by seven years of required employment in the mining industry. Throughout the whole period the government financially supported these students. By the early 1900s virtually all of Japan's mining engineers had graduated from these schools and programs; by 1912, 371 graduate engineers had entered top positions in the mining companies. Kyushu Imperial University, founded in 1911, soon began to add to the output of the professionally trained mining engineers. Thus, in the development of the industry virtually all of Japan's high-level manpower for mining was trained at government-sponsored institutions. Training of the highest level personnel was not left to the vagaries of private education.

By 1896, formal education of technical assistants for the mining engineers also got underway. The Osaka Kōgyō School, the first of its kind, initiated a four-year technician training course, open only to students who had completed higher elementary school. In 1899, this became a three-year program, but with middle-school graduation now required for entrance. The Osaka school turned out 147 mining technicians by the end of the Meiji period (1911).

Similar schools, both public and private, were soon established, some at mine sites, others in cities, with programs running two to four years for middle-school graduates. An example was the private school at the Sado gold mine, founded by Watanabe Wataru, then deputy director of the Ministry of Mining, which combined both work programs and classes. Some of these schools later became the mining engineering departments of various public and private universities. For example, the so-called Kōshu Technical School, which actually dated from 1888 but did not specialize in mining until somewhat later, graduated 982 mining technicians by 1911. This school probably was the most important source of technical personnel for the industry in those years. Toward the end of the Meiji era, the large companies themselves began to establish their own technical training schools. The earliest were at Niihama in 1902 and at Akaike in 1903, while Mitsui began its own in 1909 and Hitachi in 1910.

University and technical school graduates, however, constituted only a tiny fraction of the work forces employed in mining. The vast majority of the mine workers—well over 90 percent—were unskilled and uneducated, recruited only for their ability to engage in heavy physical work and their willlingness to face the hazards of mining—mostly casual rural workers, poor people from the growing city slums, hobos, gamblers, and ex-convicts.

During the Tokugawa and early Meiji eras, work in Japanese mines was mainly of the casual sort. Mines were scattered throughout the country, mostly in remote rural mountainous areas. There was little sense of worker commitment to mining jobs. As in other countries, those who worked in the mines were half-farmers, half-miners until well into the modern period. In the early years, no special attempts were made to recruit and maintain a committed labor force except when it was necessary to attach key workmen to the foreign engineers brought in to introduce modern mining techniques. Certainly employers gave little thought to attracting and training mine workers and even less to their conditions of work. Indeed, it became so difficult to attract competent labor that the first "regular" workers after the Meiji government took power were convicts. This practice began in 1876 when the privately operated Takashima Coal Mine in Nagasaki obtained government permission to employ prisoners on a continuing basis.[32] Instability and unrest thus came to char-

[32] Mikio Sumiya, *Social Impact of Industrialization in Japan* (Tokyo: Japanese National Commission for Unesco, 1963), p. 39.

acterize the work forces. There was a high degree of labor turn-over. As early as 1870, miners at Takashima conducted a violent protest when their day rates were cut, seizing the quarters of the foreign engineers and razing the machine sheds.

Before the Meiji Restoration, miners as mentioned usually had been seasonal and casual workers, drawn from farmers and peas-ants between growing and harvesting periods. Later, after Japan seized control of Korea in 1910, the mines imported Koreans to do the work. Up to the 1920s work in the coal mines became in-creasingly unattractive. As a result, the industry faced serious labor shortages in the boom during and immediately after World War I; and in protest against hazards and poor working conditions unionism among the miners spread significantly.

Only after the large private firms began to emerge in the coal industry did any semblance of a permanent work force appear. To operate such large mines as Miike or Takashima required sys-tematic searching for workers over a very wide area. Thus, few miners had their roots in the immediate neighborhoods of the mines in which they worked.

The early solution to the problem of assembling work forces in coal mining came in the form of the so-called *naya seido* or *hamba*, whereby a private mining company would engage pa-trons, or labor bosses (oyakata), to secure (and in some cases kid-nap) individuals and even whole families who would work under their full authority.[33] The naya seido were tight-knit groups, usu-ally housed together in the mining village. The patron was in full control of providing rewards and meting out penalties as well as assigning work and duties. In this system, the marginal and least educated in Japan's labor force came into the mines.

In metal mining particularly a somewhat similar but more be-nevolent system of employment emerged, tracing its beginnings to the early Tokugawa period. This was the so-called *tomoko* sys-tem, which was a simulated family structure in which the patron

[33] Ishihara Kōichi, *Nihon Gijitsu Kyōiku Shiron* (Tokyo: Sanichi Shobō, 1962) pp. 39-57.

played the role of father and the followers played subordinate members of the family. The tomoko system had a highly practical aspect as it served to create a common bond to protect its members from the hazards of mine work. The naya seido in coal mining was essentially an attempt to copy the tomoko system, but because it lacked historical development, the naya was far harsher than the tomoko system and failed in most cases to simulate a family structure. Rather, it was more out-and-out tyranny, with the patron often meting out physical punishment to keep the men in line. When subordinate workers could no longer endure the oppressiveness, they resorted to strikes and riots against the patron and his henchmen. As a reaction, the Mining Law of 1892, in recognition of the chaos besetting the industry, established Japan's first labor standards. A rash of violent strikes against patron domination, however, was to break out again in the final years of the Meiji period.

By the First World War, however, the naya seido and tomoko system were proving unworkable as the means for supplying stable work forces in the mines now populated by increasingly alienated seasonal peasants, ex-convicts, and Koreans. As the employment system weakened, companies began to recruit directly young unmarried boys from remote farm villages. Now dormitories were provided, and assurances given to families of the young boys for safety, medical care, trained supervision, welfare facilities, and severance pay. For the first time the large mining companies also established personnel departments, managed by university graduates. Probably the principal underlying reason for this shift in employment policy was due to the introduction of technological change, especially the use of winders in the mines in the 1890s. Inexperienced and poorly educated workers could no longer be depended upon to work the machinery continuously. Growing unrest among the miners and threat of unionism also contributed to this change in recruitment. But the full transformation did not take place until the 1920s. It was only then that working conditions improved, the accident rate in the coal mines fell, and unionism subsided.

As the university and technical school graduates assumed direction of the mining industry, reliance upon patron-client arrangements began to give way to more direct supervision by the engineers and technicians themselves. The need to do so became increasingly apparent with the realization that, while only unskilled labor was required for many jobs, the growing rise of machinery and sophisticated technology required systematic skill-training for at least some of the workers. The traditional patrons were unable to carry out this function.

As early as 1894, the Hokkaido Mining and Shipping company took the lead in instituting direct recruitment of its mine workers. In the following 20 years, half of the large mines adopted direct employment systems. In some cases, the big companies set up schools for miners' children and offered supplementary general education within the mines; these programs encountered difficulties because teachers were reluctant to go to remote mining areas, and the students dropped out in large numbers. In still other cases, the companies provided supplementary support to local public schools.

By the end of the Meiji era, the large mining companies had instituted a number of different training programs for their own regular miners. Most programs were of the on-the-job type, but they often included regular classroom study of as much as three years. The Ashio copper mine, although an unusual example, provided such classes in English, Japanese, Chinese, drawing, mathematics, and ethics. Miike coal mining also launched a night school for its key workers, with both technical and general education provided. In 1909, Miike established its own private elementary school for children of its regular workers and officials. Two years later, Mitsui began an engineering school at Ōmuta, the location of the Miike mines, with priority for entrance given to its own miners and their children who had completed upper elementary school. More widespread was the rise of informal apprenticeships, recruiting boys up to 16 years old who had completed lower elementary school to work with the skilled miners and with the technicians. Most of the apprenticeships aimed at providing future construction workers, mechanics, and maintenance personnel for the mines. In some cases apprentices were exchanged among the companies to diversify their training.

Following World War I direct supervision and training fully replaced the patron-client systems in the large mines. As a result, mine labor turnover declined throughout the 1920s, although it remained considerably higher than the turnover in manufacturing (which also declined in this period). In the small mines, however, the patron-client systems have probably never disappeared down to the present, although the use of physical coercion has by and large been eliminated. Shades of these old systems also re-emerged throughout the industry during World War II, when as the result of labor shortages mining employed large numbers of Koreans, Okinawans, prisoners-of-war, and, after demobilization, returning war veterans. Whatever systematic worker training did develop in the small mines had continued to be highly informal and sporadic, relying on on-the-job training and experience and instruction of superiors.

With the decline of the coal mining industry and exhaustion of metal deposits since the early 1960s, the human resource development of the industry has shifted to the problem of retraining the displaced workers (there has been a decline of more than two-thirds in the number of coal miners) and maintaining the efficiency of an increasingly aged work force. At the same time, there has been the need to attract enough young workers as replacements for the minimally required work force, now likely to increase in coal mining since emergence of the oil crisis.

Summary

The above review of three long-established industries in Japan's private sector during the pre-World War II era illustrates the varying patterns of human resource development that emerged in the course of industrial modernization. Banking employed a wide array of educated white-collar skills, providing high-level manpower needs for the management and supervision of most of the important modern enterprises and their subsidiaries and subcontractors. For this function the banking industry could depend primarily upon the outside formal education system for training key personnel and upon day-to-day experience for their upgrading. In contrast, the cotton textile industry long faced the problem of developing its own internal training programs for short-term labor forces at the lowest skill levels in order to operate increasingly sophisticated technology in the mills. This need was discovered, however, only after years of attempting to rely primarily upon the labor market to supply unskilled workers. At the same time, the modern sector of the industry utilized university and foreign training for their highest level manpower. In further contrast, while the mining industry followed a similar pattern for developing its high-level managerial and technical talents, at first it lagged behind even the cotton textile industry in establishing within-enterprise programs for mining labor. But textiles and mining during the early decades relied on paternalistic, often despotic, institutions which gathered together marginal members of the labor force in tight-knit authoritarian controlled groups. The three cases demonstrate that, while within-enterprise training programs eventually emerged to some limited extent, they did not play as prominent a role in human resource development as they did in telecommunications, railroads, steel and shipbuilding.

In all three industries, it is striking that careful emphasis was placed from the very beginning upon training and attracting personnel for the highest-level skills and talents—managerial, engineering, and technical. For the operatives, however, the assumption prevailed, and took decades to eliminate, that the open labor market and/or established family-type institutions would somehow furnish the appropriate human resources necessary to man the new modern technologies. This worked reasonably well in banking with its prestige as an occupation and the capacity of the common school systems to teach the relevant knowledge and skills for immediate employment. In cotton textiles and mining, on the other hand, not until the 1920s or 1930s was there any widespread expectation that the schools would turn out well-prepared recruits. Rather, during the very decades in which these industries modernized and expanded, when large, "instant" work forces were needed, educational requirements remained relatively minimal. Only bitter experience with labor turnover and labor unrest led the leading enterprises in these industries finally to step up their own internal training and education programs, to take direct control of personnel administration, and to seek recruits with higher educational attainment. However, compared to the full-blown programs that had developed earlier in steel, shipbuilding, telecommunications, and railways, cotton textiles and mining, despite their importance for Japan's economic growth, lagged far behind.

It is not at all clear why the cotton textile and mining industries neglected to develop their own training programs beyond the bare minimum. One reason, of course, seems to be, especially in contrast to the government-owned monopolies, the high degree of domestic and international competition among firms, so that training-within-enterprise programs were seen as a risky investment, given the ups and downs of the markets and the uniformity of technology and operation among the firms. Another likely reason was the low level of operative skills in these industries, requiring mainly finger dexterity in the case of cotton textiles and muscle in mining. With plentiful unskilled labor supplies available, such workers could be readily substituted for one another. In this context the use of dormitories and welfare programs in cotton textiles and of naya seido and tomoko systems in mining probably served more as protections against over-substitution, or complete casualness, of labor—which went too far in the other direction, given the increasingly sophisticated technology and heavy capital investment involved. If this was so, the human resource strategy in these two industries was far different, indeed at the opposite pole, from the approach in steel, shipbuilding, telecommunications, railways and banking in aiming to secure core work forces with skills specific to their respective enterprises.

VIII.

Training in Capital-Intensive Industries: Heavy Machinery, Electrical Equipment, and Chemicals

SOME of the most systematic industrial training in Japan has developed in the privately owned, technologically advanced enterprises in heavy machinery, electrical equipment, and chemicals production. Although these industries trace their origins to the late nineteenth century, major growth did not take place until the 1930s; along with steel and shipbuilding they became the center of Japan's high-speed economic growth after 1955.

Like other sectors already discussed, the main outlines of training patterns in these industries emerged before World War II. In common with others was an early and intense development of the highest manpower levels and a notable lag in training of manual workers. What was different, of course, was the dramatic shift of weight within the manufacturing sector toward these industries, beginning in the 1930s, and with it a sudden need for large work forces trained in the skills and knowledge required for increasingly complex technologies and operations. The machinery and chemical industries together accounted for less than 12 percent of all manufacturing workers in 1914 and in 1931 slightly more than 16 percent. By 1942, they employed over 50 percent. The number of workers in machinery alone advanced from about 75,000 in 1914 to almost 160,000 in 1931 and then to more than 1,680,000 by 1942.

Heavy Machine Industry in Japan: Origins and Growth

As already traced in Chapter V, the earliest use of modern machines emerged in connection with shipbuilding. Japan imported her first boring machine in 1857, 80 years after it was invented. The first lathe also arrived in 1857, 60 years after the original. The iron works built their own Western-type planers and lathes by 1860. In fact, by the time of the Meiji Restoration, most modern machinery then known in the industrialized nations of the West was also to be found in Japan.

Japan's first modern machine manufacturing plants were government operated and set up in the late Tokugawa and early Meiji eras, especially in the arsenals, shipyards, and armaments factories. As in other new industries, the government took the initiative in this industry. In 1879, the Ministry of Industry separately built the Mita Machinery Plant in order for foreigners to train Japanese workmen, and a year later a similar plant was built at Akabane. The first privately owned machine manufacturing plant did not appear until 1886 when it was built at the Ishikawajima shipyard.[1]

It was the government, however, which took major responsibility for technological innovation in the machinery industry. Although the government divested itself of shipyards and machinery manufacturing during the 1880s, it retained direct control of the machine shops and plants in the arsenals along with other military installations. As already mentioned, the government in fact continued to employ far more factory workers than did private enterprise well into the early twentieth century. In 1890, 27 government-operated plants alone accounted for more

[1] Arisawa Hiromi, ed., *Gendai Nihon Sangyō Kōza* (Tokyo: Iwanami Shoten, 1960), Vol. I, pp. 50-56; Nihon Kōgakukai, *Meiji Kōgyōshi* (Tokyo: Kōgakukai, 1930), pp. 3-15; Kajinishi Mitsuhaya, *Nihon Sangyōshihon Seiritsu Shiron* (Tokyo: Ochanomizu Shobō, 1965), pp. 215-237; and Yamaguchi Kazuo, ed., *Nihon Sangyō 100 Nenshi* (Tokyo: Nihon Keizai Shimbunsha, 1967), Vol. I, pp. 8-83.

than half of all factories using modern machinery, three-fourths of the total horsepower, and almost 90 percent of the total employment. It was the navy which produced Japan's first electric-type lathe in 1888. Four years later the Yokosuka Naval Arsenal turned out the first cast steel engines in Japan. In 1897 the Kawasaki Shipyard produced the new Miyahara-type boiler; in 1903 engineers at the Nagasaki Shipyard invented the Ikeda-type boiler; in 1904 Nagasaki undertook manufacture of Parson turbines; and in 1907 Kawasaki did the same with the Curtis turbine. In the government-owned railway field, too, Japan was building more than 80 percent of the rolling stock on her own by the early 1890s. Although it took until the 1920s for Japan to shake off completely dependence upon foreign imports for railway steam engines, manufacturing of locomotives began in Osaka in 1896. All these developments proceeded under direct government ownership or encouragement.[2]

Yet, at the same time as the government concentrated its efforts on building large-scale shipyards, iron and steel mills, and plants in arsenals, a whole host of rather small, privately owned workshops, although not factories in the modern sense, were also springing up. Proliferation of small-scale shops reflected both the dire shortage of capital, lack of skilled labor, and opportunities for private entrepreneurship. Notably, with the Meiji government's abolition of the craft guilds in 1873, many traditional craftsmen and artisans in the metal trades gradually gave up their own one-to-one master-apprentice workshops to become wage-earners in these small businesses, apparently reluctant to go to work in large, bureaucratically run government enterprises. This tendency of craftsmen to maintain their indigenous skills and independence had important implications for human resource development later, when Japan turned to building up heavy machinery and chemical manufacturing on a major scale in the 1930s.

[2] Arisawa (1960), Vol. V, Part I, Chapter I.

The slow emergence of large-scale private manufacturing meant that, despite government encouragement for development of this sector, Japan long remained dependent upon foreign imports of machinery. Exports remained insignificant, amounting to barely more than 5 percent of imports in 1902.[3] Only with the rapid growth in production of domestic pig iron and rolled steel after Yahata began did the private machine maufacturing sector suddenly explode. By 1906 pig iron output rose more than ten times and rolled steel ten times following the opening of Yahata. Now machinery for shipbuilding, ship engines, and railway equipment production received highest priority.

Following the Russo-Japanese War, the private sector began to invest increasingly in modern machinery manufacturing with the growth of the government's demand for supplementary supplies. Until then, private manufacturing had been confined to a few major establishments, such as the Ikegai Iron Works begun in 1889, the Niigata Iron Works in 1895, and the Shibaura manufacturing plant also in 1895. Paradoxically, although new private machine-tool companies proliferated after the Russo-Japanese War, the expansion was not enough to lift Japan to a level of self-sufficiency in this field. The stress on producing primarily for armaments tended to narrow the capacity of Japan's machinery industry and probably held back the diversification required for its full-scale development.[4] For example, there was little activity in textile machinery production.

Electrical manufacturing, which drew initial impetus from the construction of telegraph lines, also evolved slowly and selectively. As seen in Chapter VI, modern telecommunications were one of the first undertakings launched by the Meiji government, so there was an immediate need for readily available equipment for telegraphs and, soon afterwards, telephones. Although Japan first produced electrical equipment in the 1870s, significant ex-

[3] Nihon Kōgakukai (1930), p. 5.
[4] Arisawa (1960), Vol. V, Part I, Chapter I; and Yamaguchi (1967), pp. 195-200.

pansion of the industry waited upon the availability of electric power. By about 1880, the Japanese began to build small-scale electric power generation plants for city lighting. As a result, production of generators started in 1885 on a local basis and expanded gradually during the ensuing 20 years. In 1888 electricity as a means of home lighting was introduced on a limited basis in the large cities (only five years behind New York), and in the early 1890s electric lighting was installed in cotton spinning mills, thus allowing around-the-clock operation. It was not, however, until after the Sino-Japanese War that electric power equipment began to grow sufficiently to meet the expanding needs of widespread industrial and domestic use. This was a slow process. In 1907 Japanese engineers succeeded for the first time in supplying electricity to the cities over long-distance power lines, but it was only during World War I that long-distance electricity generation extended throughout Japan. By 1913 electric generation was providing more than half of all Japan's total power. No doubt electricity also made possible the widespread rise of small electric motors, which were especially beneficial to small as well as large-scale enterprise.[5]

In contrast to industrial machine manufacturing, which the government largely sponsored, the initial development of electric machinery was left almost entirely to private entrepreneurs. The first private company dates from 1875, when the son of a factory worker, Tanaka Hisashige, established the Tanaka Manufacturing Company, the antecedent of the well-known Shibaura Manufacturing Company. A second company, also destined to become one of Japan's leading manufacturers, was the Miyoshi Electric Machine Manufacturing Company, begun by Miyoshi Shōichi, who previously had been employed in installing electric-

[5] See Ryoshin Minami, "The Introduction of Electric Power and Its Impact on the Manufacturing Industries: With Special Reference to Smaller Scale Plants," in Hugh Patrick, with the assistance of Larry Meissner, ed., *Japanese Industrialization and the Social Consequences* (Berkeley: University of California Press, 1976), pp. 299-325.

ity in the Ministry of Industry. Engaging a professor of engineering from Tokyo University, Miyoshi set about producing a variety of electrical products, including the Matsuda brand bulbs, small dynamos, and transformers. This company branched out to merge with other firms, one of which later became the Tokyo Electric Company and, in turn, merged with the Shibaura Manufacturing Company. When Tanaka went bankrupt in the recession of 1903, his company, by then called Shibaura, was taken over by the Mitsui Bank and placed under the management of Fujiyama Raita, who turned out to be one of the most imaginative private entrepreneurs in Japan's electrical machinery industry. Other prominent companies that entered the field in the late 1890s were the Ishikawajima Shipbuilding Company, the Meiji Electrical Company, and Okumura Electrical Machine Company, all leaders to the present time. Interestingly, Ishikawajima also relied on an engineering professor of Tokyo University for its product development.[6]

By the turn of the century, only those companies with large amounts of capital and a large, steady market in industries such as mining and shipbuilding could expect to survive. Small manufacturers in the industry were no longer able to compete. Major emphasis in production had now turned to heavy producer equipment, such as dynamos, rather than consumer items. With the successful construction of long-distance electric power lines after 1907, it became economically important to diversify machine production, especially the heavier types, and to supply cable, which the Japanese companies were unable to produce satisfactorily and in quantity. To fill this gap, just prior to World War I, General Electric, Westinghouse, and Siemens entered the Japanese market. Also, about the same time a number of new large Japanese companies were established, including Kawakita Electrical Enterprises, Dengyōsha, and Hitachi Manufacturing. Supported by capital from copper mining and the steel industry,

[6] Arisawa (1960), Vol. VI, pp. 11-24.

Hitachi especially emphasized the production of new types of heavy machinery, recruiting the best engineers to be found in Japan. Hitachi also developed a group of related industries in a single complex, assuring itself of a steadily growing market, both for industrial machinery and for home appliances. Similarly diversifying, Tōshiba, Mitsubishi, Fuji, and Nihon Denki, all members of powerful established zaibatsu, became the other major companies in Japan's electrical manufacturing industry. Engineers trained at Miyoshi and Shibaura shifted to these new large companies.

Despite diversification and growth, the Japanese electrical industry, like machine tools, tended to be relatively limited. As a result, Japan continued to depend upon foreign countries for equipment such as high-voltage machines as well as raw materials. The small firms that did survive tended to become subcontractors for these giants.[7]

Like most other major industries in Japan at that time, electrical manufacturing underwent intense rationalization in the 1920s. By this time Taylor's "scientific management" had gained considerable attention among Japanese managers. Mitsubishi Electric and Shibaura Manufacturing were among the leading companies to adopt these practices, influenced by Westinghouse and General Electric, with whom they had established technical licensing agreements. After studying the Westinghouse techniques intensively, Katō Takeo of Mitsubishi became a leader in Japan in the field of time-and-motion study, while Ishida Yasushi of Tokyo Electric performed a similar role in his company. It was in this period that employee recruiting also came to depend more and more upon "scientific" aptitude, achievement, and intelligence testing. Most of the advanced companies began to utilize health examinations, interviews, school records, character references, and the like for recruiting and employment purposes. Japanese companies, such as Mitsubishi, relied to a major extent

[7] *Ibid*., pp. 37-47; Yamaguchi (1967), pp. 362-365.

upon American management consultants in developing these practices.[8]

Chemical manufacturing was perhaps the slowest of the modern industries to emerge in Japan. Since the Meiji government gave no particular priority to chemicals, for several decades the demand for chemical production remained confined to such products as phosphorous, sulfuric acid, and soda, to meet only the needs of traditional industries, such as matches, paper, and gunpowder. As a result most chemical factories remained small during most of the Meiji period. The government directly operated a few chemical plants; but sold them off between 1879 and 1889.

Private investors entered the modern fertilizer and carbide industries during the 1880s and the modern pharmaceutical industry in the 1890s on a small scale. But by and large chemicals remained a limited field of entrepreneurship. In 1882, the number of private chemical factories numbered only 91, accounting for less than 5 percent of all privately owned factories (although it should be noted that, given the preponderance of government operations, this was still more than was found in the machinery and shipbuilding industries at that time). Ten years later, although the number of chemical plants had grown to 264, or about 9 percent of all manufacturing factories, almost all were still small in size. Like textiles, they employed female and child labor for the most part.[9]

By the first decade of the twentieth century, therefore, chemical manufacturing was an industry of small handicraft shops, even though machine manufacturing during this period was expanding rapidly in scale and shifting to electric power. In terms of value of output, chemicals at first kept ahead of machinery production; but the latter went far ahead during World War I and by the time

[8] Okuda Kenji, *Rōmu Kanri no Nihonteki Tenkai* (Tokyo: Japan Productivity Center, 1972), Chap. 3; and Kenji Okuda, "Managerial Evolution in Japan," *Management Japan*, Vol. 5, No. 4, 1972, pp. 20-21.

[9] Arisawa (1960), Vol. IV, pp. 27-37.

of World War II employed four to five times more workers than the chemical industry. Considerable expansion in chemicals came in the 1930s, due in large measure to the construction of large plants operated by the zaibatsu, especially in response to the militaristic government's encouragement. After World War I the zaibatsu began to show substantial interest in chemicals; but by the 1930s these firms moved mainly into the manufacture of organic compounds (which were to become the base for plastic manufacturing following World War II). Despite this expansion, up to the Pacific War, the chemical industry remained specialized and continually relied upon importation of foreign products and technology.

The post-World War II period, in contrast, saw rapid growth in most chemical manufacturing—plastics, synthetic fabrics, fertilizers, and petro-chemical products—as well as the emergence of integrated chemical plant complexes and research and development organizations. Even then, the lack of emphasis upon chemicals in the prewar period meant that Japan lagged far behind other advanced countries in both basic and applied chemical research. As a result, the post-World War II expansion was continually hampered by shortages of advanced technology, trained manpower, and skilled management.[10]

In the development of still other heavy industrial enterprise, the growth of shops from small family firms to major enterprises was a distinctive characteristic. Most of these started up in the 20- to 30-year period after the turn of the century, usually without any initial assistance from the zaibatsu or the banks. A leading example is the Toyota Company, which began with the invention by its uneducated founder, Toyota Sakichi, of his famous automatic loom in 1902. This loom virtually revolutionized Japan's textile industry. From spinning and weaving machinery, the Toyota Company, eventually with the backing of Mitsui, by the mid-1930s moved into the manufacture of automobiles.

[10] *Ibid.*, pp. 37-46; Yamaguchi (1967), pp. 203-211.

Another major example is the Matsushita Electric Industries Company, which began during World War I as a small, one-man shop. Still the company's leader today, Matsushita Konosuke received a bare education and as a youth had a variety of odd jobs including electric trades journeyman before setting out for himself in 1915. After considerable success in manufacturing electric sockets, he began to produce a wide range of electrical appliances and by 1927 won financial backing from Sumitomo. By the mid-1930s the Matsushita company had become one of Japan's leading manufacturers in the electrical equipment field, a position it holds to the present. Notably, both the Toyota and Matsushita companies have become equally famous for recruiting young employees upon school graduation and developing formalized within-enterprise training programs for inexperienced production workers.

When the ascending militaristic government of the 1930s began to give priority to the production of armaments, steel, machinery, and chemicals, the structure of the Japanese economy began to shift markedly away from the light industries. During World War II, the government insisted on ever-increasing efficiency in the heavy industries and placed much of the responsibility to achieve this upon the newly established Japan Management Association and the Patriotic Industrial Association (*Sampō*).[11] The new plants were equipped with the most advanced technology, developed in some instances with the help of Japan's German allies, and under the pressure of wartime mobilization operated on a scale unprecedented in Japan's prewar industrial history. In the wartime period, large work forces were gathered into the heavy machinery and chemical industries, many drawn temporarily from small and medium-size firms. Efforts to stabilize the labor force in the new large companies and plants led to freezes on mobility and, in some instances, to wholesale transfers of workers from one establishment

[11] Okuda, "Management Evolution in Japan," pp. 22-23.

to another at the command of the government as the need for experienced labor grew.[12] While much of heavy industry was destroyed or allowed to run down during the war, it was clear that by 1945 the industrial base of the Japanese economy had undergone a transformation.

Resurrection of the Japanese economy from 1945 to 1955 is a well-known story. Suffice to say that the heavy machinery and chemical industries returned to their leading position in manufacturing after the mid-1950s. By 1959, machinery once again accounted for more than one-third of all factory production; chemicals, for more than 10 percent. The high-speed growth of the Japanese economy in the 1960s rested primarily on further expansion of these sectors. Hitachi, Tōshiba, and Matsushita became leading giants in the electrical machinery industry; Mitsubishi Heavy Industries, Ishikawajima-Harima, Toyota, and Nissan came to dominate heavy machinery, particularly automobiles and shipbuilding; the larger chemical firms entered joint ventures and licensing arrangements with the major companies in the U.S. and Europe, particularly in the field of petrochemicals. This success rested in large part on a long term growth in supply of formally educated engineers and technical personnel and also efforts by the large private companies in training manual workers within the enterprise.

Professional Personnel in Electrical Machinery

The electrical machinery industry illustrates the development of high-level talent in the heavy machine and chemical industries. As previously noted, the skills needed for modern machinery manufacturing first appeared in Japan with the initial production of electrical equipment in the 1870s. In 1871 the Meiji government began to recruit engineers, craftsmen, and machinery operators from England at high pay to oversee con-

[12] Arisawa (1960), Vol. I, Part II, Chap. 1.

struction of the first telegraph lines, and the Ministry of Industry with the aid of the British engineers established the Telecommunications Technical Training School. Tokyo Imperial University established electrical engineering training in 1881. Leading professors of electrical science, such as E. W. Ayrton and Clark Maxwell of England, were invited to teach, and the outstanding students were sent abroad. More than 1,200 engineers graduated from the telecommunications school by the late 1880s, and in 1897 the school became the electrical engineering department of the Tokyo Industrial School (later Tokyo Institute of Technology). By that time Japanese engineers had replaced the British as teachers in this field. Individuals who later became the leaders in Japan's electrical equipment industry were electrical engineering graduates: Sugiura Keisaburō of Tōshiba; Takao Naosaburō, Baba Norio, and Akita Seiichi of Hitachi; Tachihara Nin of Mitsubishi; and Yasukawa Daigorō of Yasukawa Electric.[13]

As an entirely new area, professionalism in electrical engineering received special emphasis almost from the beginning and set an example for emerging engineering specialties. Japan's first professional engineering association, centered on electrical engineers, was founded in 1879 with 23 members, and by 1890 had 1,200 members. In 1888, the electrical engineers formed their own separate professional association with more than 1,000 members, growing to 3,700 members by 1920. Many of the professional electrical engineers studied abroad. With this continual accumulation of high-level manpower, electrical machinery manufacture was ripe for major development by the end of the 1890s and early 1900s.[14]

Perhaps more so than for any other modern industry, formal schooling played the key role in preparing middle-level technical

[13] Ōuchi Hyōe and Tsuchiya Takao, eds., *Meiji Zenki Keizai Shiryō Shūsei* (Tokyo: Kaizōsha, 1931), Vol. 17, pp. 257-259.
[14] Saegusa Hakuo et al., *Kindai Nihon Sangyō Gijitsu no Seioka* (Tokyo: Tōyō Keizai Shinpōsha, 1960), pp. 151-161.

personnel for electrical equipment production. The Electrical Engineers Association, formed in 1879, gave impetus to this movement, in recognition of the need for well-qualified assistants for the professionals. While the Telecommunications Technical Training School and Tokyo University's electrical engineering department became the chief educational centers for top-level engineers for almost two decades, during the 1880s, the Tokyo Shokkō Gakkō was utilized for training skilled machinists and craftsmen. By 1897 this school, too, was upgraded to university-level status with the establishment of the Tokyo Industrial School. The need for full-fledged electrical engineers spread so rapidly that in 1898 a department of electrical engineering was formed at the new Kyoto Imperial University. In 1902 the privately operated Kansai School of Commerce and Engineering set up a similar department, as did the Tokyo School of Commerce and Engineering in 1903. By that time, the Tokyo Imperial University had established Japan's first electric experiment laboratory. In 1906 electrical engineering training mushroomed with the initiation of departments in the Sendai Senior Engineering School, the private Tokyo Electric Machine School, Kyoto Engineering School, and Mitsui Engineering School. This network continued to spread with new departments in the Ryojun Engineering School in 1908, the private Chuo Engineering School in 1909, the Hyōgo Prefectural Engineering School in 1909, the new Kyushu Imperial University, the Meiji Semmon Gakkō, the Kokura Prefectural Engineering School, the Hiroshima Prefectural Vocational Training School, and Waseda University, all in 1911. A year later departments were also established in the private Kōchi Engineering School and the Akita Prefectural Engineering School.

By World War I, thus, formal school training had become the principal means of preparing engineers and technicians for Japan's growing electrical machinery industry. While Japanese electrical production had concentrated until then upon a selective range of machinery, some the result of indigenous inventions, and Japan still had to depend heavily upon foreign imports, World War I marked the turning point toward eventual skill diversification as well as expansion. Without the rapid spread of formal schools, this development probably would not have been possible.[15] The high degree of engineering professionalism that emerged as a result was probably also responsible for the strong drive to adopt "scientific management" techniques in this industry.

Manual Workers in Machinery Manufacturing

In contrast to the rapid growth of education for engineers and technicians in machinery manufacturing, the training of operatives and semi-skilled workers initially was neglected. While originally formal schools were established to train machinists, they either were upgraded to the technical or engineer level or their graduates were fairly quickly promoted to managerial positions in the new large companies or themselves became independent entrepreneurs.[16] For many years, the industry relied on open-market recruits for manual workers, an unsatisfactory arrangement for fast-changing technology. Shibaura Manufacturing, for example attempted to use outside schools beginning in 1901 to train workers (about 20 to 40 a year), but because of turnover and growth the company concluded that this approach was ineffective. In 1905 Shibaura set the pace for the industry by developing its own internal training institute combining both on-the-job experience and loyalty indoctrination.[17] The Hitachi Company instituted its own formal apprentice school in 1911, offering a three-year course covering Japanese, English, ethics,

[15] Japan Ministry of Education, *Sangyō Kyōiku 80 Nenshi* (Tokyo, 1963), pp. 53-67; Ishihara Kōichi, *Nihon Gijitsu Kyōiku Shiron* (Tokyo: Sanichi Shobō, 1962), Chap. 3.

[16] Sumiya Mikio, ed., *Nihon Shokugyō Kunren Hattenshi* (Tokyo: Japan Institute of Labor, 1971), Vol. I, pp. 131-138; Okamoto Hideaki, ed., *Sangyō Kunren 100 Nenshi* (Tokyo: Japan Industrial and Vocation Training Association, 1971), pp. 70-72.

[17] Okamoto (1971), pp. 142-146.

mathematics, geography, history, drafting, science, iron-coating, boiler making, electric machinery, metal finishing, chemistry, metallurgy, and steel rolling. It also had an advanced one-year course, concentrating on electricity.[18] However, because of the constantly growing need for top-level personnel, even these schools were later upgraded to technical colleges and after World War II became components of engineering departments of new national universities.

Preoccupation with high level training in machinery manufacturing relegated the training of manual skills largely to on-the-job "watching-and-learning" (minarai) within the workplaces. As a result, patron-client systems similar to those in other industries emerged as the chief institutions for workers to learn jobs and acquire skills. Training of manual workers depended upon the knowledge, skill, and willingness of senior operatives, who as in other modern industries gained almost complete control over recruitment, job assignment, and dismissal. Top-level managers and engineers, distant from the operating level, tended to exert little authority over these senior workmen. However, instability and turnover continued to characterize the work forces, with workers moving from factory to factory, each developing his own combination of skills. These "wandering" workers characteristically banded together into patron-client groupings in the labor markets.[19]

The "watch and learn" method was highly informal, unsystematic, and casual. While helping older workers or experienced craftsmen, a young worker accumulated his knowledge, or knack, as he moved from one task to another in the small factory. Thus, just as in the shipyards, the easiest method for a large company to acquire skilled workers was to hire patron-workers' on a subcontract basis who would bring their own retinues from the small fac-

---

[18] Ibid., pp. 187-194; Sumiya (1971), Vol. II, pp. 40-47.

[19] Sumiya (1971), Vol. II, pp. 93-104; Sumiya Mikio, ed., Shokkō Oyobi Kofu Chōsa (Tokyo: Koseikan, 1970), pp. 86-87; and Japan Ministry of Agriculture and Commerce, Shokkō Jijō (Tokyo: Seikatsusha, 1948), Vol. II, pp. 36-38.

tories and workshops. These groups moved readily from one large-scale establishment to another, or their individual members moved, using the connections their patrons developed. Such mobility, of course, helped to diversify the worker's skill and experience and eventually assured his emergence as a patron with his own band of followers.[20] In contrast to today's emphasis on permanent attachment to a company, prior to World War I in Japan the most valuable skilled workers in the machinery and metal industries were those who moved around frequently, developing skills through "watching and learning."

These workers, it should be noted, were the earliest in Japan to form trade unions, beginning in 1889 among craftsmen in shipyards, arsenals, and private machine shops. The Metal Workers Union (*Tekkō Kumai*), formed in 1897, became Japan's first nationwide labor organization, although it collapsed three years later without having engaged in any real collective bargaining with management. Its major contribution lay, rather, in establishing consumer cooperatives. Probably the basic reason for the failure of unionism in the metal trades was that, in addition to government opposition through the Public Police Law of 1900, the members were mainly patrons and were more interested in achieving status vis-à-vis their employers, in providing mutual insurance and benefit schemes (including consumer and production cooperatives), and in becoming themselves independent entrepreneurs. In fact, as pointed out elsewhere, the unionism that later developed in the 1920s was as much a product of worker protest against patron mistreatment as it was of patrons vying with company management for control over work forces. At stake in these conflicts was the system and content of training and education to be provided the factory workers.[21]

[20] Sumiya, *Nihon Shokugyō Kunren Hattenshi*, Vol. I, pp. 75-92; Sumiya Mikio, *Nihon Chinrōdo Shiron* (Tokyo: Tokyo University Press, 1955), pp. 205-239.

[21] Solomon B. Levine, "Labor Markets and Collective Bargaining in Japan," in William W. Lockwood, ed. *The State and Economic Enterprise in Japan* (Princeton University Press, 1965), Chap. XIV, pp. 633-667.

When in 1910 the industry suddenly mushroomed with the establishment of several large firms including Hitachi Seiki, Mitsubishi Denki, Mitsubishi Juko, Mitsui Seiki, Shibaura Kosakukikai, and Ebara Seisakusho, there was and instant need for large numbers of skilled and semi-skilled workers. Then with the boom of World War I, it became abundantly clear to the highly educated engineers and managers who had by then risen to the top of Japan's large-scale heavy industries that the patron system was inefficient for skill training. No longer could the operation of sophisticated technology and organization depend upon haphazard teaching that took place under the patron-client system or upon workers' acquisition of appropriate experience as they moved from one enterprise to another. Thus, about that time management began to move toward direct control of the workers, including the establishment of formal schools within the company and systematized training programs both on and off the job. However, this transition took at least two decades.

"Partial" training of workers remained prevalent in the machinery industry. With the very rapid expansion of private machinery production in the period from 1910 to 1920, the need for large numbers of workers with precise skills for running complex technical operations on a sustained basis became urgent. Workers in the private sector of the industry, it should be noted, were beginning to outnumber those in the government-owned plants during this period.[22]

The supply of new workers for the expanding machinery industry had to be met by directly recruiting new young school graduates who were completely inexperienced. Not only were the "wandering" skilled workers in short supply but their skills were too disparate for rapid adaptation to the new, emerging technologies. Many, moreover, apparently preferred to retain their independent status in the labor market, to try their hand as masters of small shops, or to remain as members of a relatively

[22] Sumiya, *Nihon Shokugyō Kunren Hattenshi*, Vol. II, pp. 33-40.

tight-knit and autonomous patron-client group. These labor market conditions were highly similar to the labor markets in steel and shipbuilding, but in machinery they persisted much longer because of the lag in developing large-scale factories and the failure of government to establish adequate training facilities.

As in steel and shipbuilding, the obvious solution to this problem was for the management of large enterprises to take direct control of the work force. This shift was essentially achieved between 1910 and 1930 by coopting patrons into the managerial hierarchy through such inducements as higher pay, status, lifetime employment, and regular annual salary increases. While the patrons continued to perform training functions, they were gradually replaced by the new young workers who, continuously trained within the enterprise, eventually became the first-line supervisors. It was during this period that the major private firms began to establish formal training programs and schools for their own workers either by themselves or in cooperation with other companies.[23]

While the patron system of training faded out only gradually as senior workers retired or died, management had by the 1920s gained the initiative in determining the size of the work force required, the types of jobs to be performed, the wage rates (including incentives) to be paid, and the recruitment of new workers according to pre-established standards. This achievement was fortified by the creation of centralized personnel administration, enterprise schools, employment security, and a host of welfare benefits for the new workers. By the mid-1920s, the major firms were clearly superior to the small firms in terms of wage levels, employment tenure, and working conditions.

Machinery manufacturing has, however, remained much more "dualistic" than shipbuilding, steel, railways, telecommunications, or banking. A plethora of small shops has continued to coexist with the large firms down to the present, primarily be-

23 *Ibid.*, Vol. II, pp. 33-40 and 65-74.

cause of the high degree of technological and product diversity. As a result, the informal patron-client type of recruitment and training of workers has persisted in the small-scale sector.

The continuing existence of the small machinery shops has also permitted a wide range of subcontracting for the large companies as well as providing a readily available pool of partially skilled "half-way" workers when there were sudden needs for expanding production (as well as for releasing unneeded workers during contractions). This process was well illustrated during World War II when the large firms drew heavily upon the small shops to meet labor requirements especially under the mobilization decrees after 1940. In the unionization drive after 1945, this wholesale shift gave impetus to the demand by such "half-way" workers to remain as permanent employees of the large enterprises with guarantees of life-time tenure and periodic wage increases and benefits equal to those lured directly from school. The process was again illustrated in the 1960s when shortages of young recruits occurred during the enormous expansion of the heavy machinery industry.

Training Within Enterprise in Autos and Chemicals

Also illustrative of skill training in the heavy machinery industry is the experience in automobile manufacturing. Although automobiles first appeared in Japan in 1902 and the first attempt to build cars came in 1912 (43 were manufactured that year), Japan imported almost all its motor vehicles until the 1930s. With the introduction in the United States of Ford's Model T in 1905 and the conveyor belt system in 1913, Japan seemed to be hopelessly behind. In 1918, the Japanese government did attempt to encourage automobile production by adopting the Military Vehicle Subsidy Act, and at that time, three companies—Tokyo Gas and Electric, Ishikawajima Shipyard, and Kaisokusha—began to produce passenger cars and trucks. However, as late as 1925, they had turned out merely 357 vehicles in all. In the meantime, Ford set up a plant in Yokohama in 1925, employing 400 workers; and a year later, General Motors appeared in Osaka with 1,500 employees. The few Japanese firms in the industry became parts suppliers for G.M. and Ford.

After Japan's militaristic period began, however, the government decided to push ahead with domestic automobile manufacturing. In 1931, it adopted the Automobile Manufacturing Enterprise Law, which provided tariff protection for the production of military vehicles. At the same time, the government imposed limits on G.M. and Ford output in Japan, so that by 1939 both companies were forced to close their plants. While the Ford- and G.M.-trained workers were transferred to become the nuclei of the work forces in the Japanese-owned plants, the latter needed workers in much larger numbers and, like the other sectors of the machinery industry, resorted both to formal training-within-enterprise programs for new school graduates and to drawing experienced workers from the small and medium-sized parts companies and subcontractors.[24]

Following World War II, the rapid expansion of Japanese automobile production benefited considerably by having available a large supply of managers, engineers, and technicians who had been displaced from the defunct arsenals and destroyed industries such as aircraft and shipbuilding. Further, special attention was given to in-plant training of foremen and other supervisory personnel, particularly utilizing techniques learned from American industry such as TWI and JRT. For manual workers, increased emphasis was placed upon recruiting only new school graduates, many from high school, and training them wholly within the enterprise. This approach continued throughout the 1950s. However, since the early 1960s, growing shortages of young recruits, coupled with a high rate of technological innova-

[24] Arisawa (1960), Vol. V, Part III, Chap. 1 and 2; Yamaguchi (1967), pp. 357-361.

tion, intense foreign competition, and rising educational levels, have placed strains upon exclusive reliance on the internal training systems. One device increasingly resorted to in order to gain flexibility has been the use of subcontract work groups and temporary workers on the assembly lines and workshops within the parent factory. Other alternatives, of course, have been the adoption of automation, quality control, worker participation and job simplification.[25] As a result, the companies have curtailed their special worker-enterprise schools for new manual worker recruits and other long-term training programs.

A similar evolution occurred in the chemical industry. While the Ministry of Industry's school *(Kōbu Daigakkō)* in the early Meiji period taught chemical engineering as well as other types of engineering, the former did not receive large emphasis. Only a handful of chemical engineers were turned out by the Ministry of Industry and later by the Imperial Universities. Their training was geared to the needs of the few government-operated plants that produced sulphuric acid, cement, explosives, fertilizer, and glass. The manufacture of products such as soap, celluloid, iodine, and matches continued to follow traditional methods and, therefore, remained largely a small handicraft industry. Because the manufacture of chemicals, as well as machinery, had been secondary to steel, shipbuilding, textiles, mining, telecommunications, and armaments, very few large-scale factories had been built. The major reliance upon small shops and handicrafts continued, and these tended to employ unskilled female and child labor. In later decades, as a result, the growth of a modern chemical industry was handicapped by the lack of trained and experienced workers at all levels.

Only with the rapid growth of the chemical industry and the

[25] For a detailed analysis of these developments, see Robert E. Cole, *Work, Mobility, and Participation: A Comparative Study of American and Japanese Industry* (Berkeley: University of California Press, 1979), especially Chapters V-VII.

emergence of large plants during World War I was the need for direct training within the enterprise widely recognized. Each major enterprise, however, tended to concentrate upon a different technology and process, requiring somewhat different work hierarchies and specializations. The labor market alone could not furnish trained workers quickly enough, since workers in the small shops had no knowledge of the modern operations and many were tied closely to their own employer patrons. Direct training, closely supervised and controlled by management of the new large firm, was an inevitable consequence—a process that evolved gradually. In the post-World War I period, within-enterprise training programs and work force organizations became well entrenched. Work forces became highly compartmentalized by enterprise, and interchange of workers among these firms was rather infrequent. In chemicals, there was considerably less dependence upon subcontractors and small firms. As a result, training became far more self-contained and concentrated in the large firms than in machinery.

During the 1920s, formal in-plant training schools, aided by the establishment of Youth Schools in 1925, spread throughout the major chemical companies. Learners studied one to three hours a day, taking such subjects as ethics, history, geography, and English as well as on-the-job training. They were housed in dormitories and received cash allowances. Later the need for new recruits in the period of wartime mobilization strengthened reliance upon these in-plant training programs.[26]

After World War II, and with the enormous spurt of the chemical industries beginning in the mid-1950s, within-enterprise training was further re-enforced. Only with the shortages of young labor in the early 1960s did the firms begin to search for skilled workers among small and medium-size firms. However, the need to go "outside" has not been as severe as in machinery

[26] Sumiya, *Nihon Shokugyō Kunren Hattenshi*, Vol. II, pp. 266-283.

manufacturing because of the relatively low proportion of labor to capital required and the well-developed comprehensive training programs and work hierarchies already established in chemical plants.

Summary

This brief review of the emergence of industries that today are among the most important in Japan illustrates the broad "mix" of human resource development patterns that the Japanese have utilized in the course of industrialization. While training-with-in-enterprise programs have become major undertakings within the large private firms in heavy machinery and chemicals, rather like those developed earlier in the government-owned railways, telecommunications, steel, and shipbuilding industries, companies have relied only partially upon this approach to assure adequate supplies of skills and talents.

In the heavy industries, training within enterprises in fact emerged decades after the first stirrings of their development. The programs began only after large-scale enterprises became fully established following World War I, when it became obvious that the labor market, the formal school system, and the patron-client employment system were unable to provide the types of education and learning needed for the efficient operation of the new technologies that were being rapidly introduced from abroad on a specialized basis, firm-by-firm. Except for the highest levels of manpower, who indeed were fully and professionally trained from the earliest years of the modern period under government auspices and with foreign assistance, these industries relied for manual skills for several decades mainly upon small shops and patron workers. Establishment of training-within-enterprise programs—with the usual characteristics of hiring new school graduates, developing "key" workmen, and providing lifetime employment guarantees, annual wage increments based on length of service, welfare benefits, and early retirement—reflected the need for an immediate supply of specifically trained workers under direct control and direction of the engineers and administrators to assure the success of the large enterprises that had suddenly emerged. As in steel and shipbuilding, the high-level personnel could no longer rely upon patrons to possess adequate knowledge of the new technologies and processes. Also, since the vocational tracks of the common school system were yet to turn out appropriately trained graduates, the large enterprises were compelled to develop their own respective training programs.

This development differed from textiles, mining, and banking in that large enterprises in heavy machinery and chemicals needed workers who could learn a succession of skills. The skills needed were complex, unpredictable, and everchanging. Capable new employees had to be attracted away from other industries, from small as well as large enterprises. This was not merely a question of overcoming the inertia or oppositon of rural farm families or of improving poor reputations as in cotton textiles and mining.

Yet, these industries did not begin with the single-mindedness that in telecommunications and railways led to an immediate fostering, under government sponsorship, of relevant skills and knowledge. Such an approach was far less obviously needed in heavy machinery and chemicals, and indeed development of these industries was left largely to private entrepreneurs and to small shops. As a result, by the time large-scale growth finally occurred, there had grown up a considerable assortment of available workers, with varying skills and experiences attached to these industries. However, most of this work force was not suitable in either skills or temperament for large modern operations.

The machinery and chemical industries have long remained "dualistic" in structure. For the small shops and firms, the rising levels of general education, as well as the prewar vocational schools, were probably vital for preparing workers who could undertake subcontracting work in these industries. Small-scale companies, aided by such developments as the electric motor, continued to advance and to attract workers even after large modern firms appeared. Since 1945 both the large and small heavy machinery and chemicals firms have continued to coexist and grow. In each there has been an intensification of their respective approaches to human resource development. The large companies, in the scramble to assure the rapid growth of heavy industry in Japan, stepped up their internal training programs and strengthened their lifetime employment systems until shortages of young labor emerged. For their part, smaller firms have turned increasingly to seeking out qualified school graduates with vocational knowledge from the public and private schools. The two approaches appear unintegrated and may prevent any easy transference of skills from one sector to the other. Only recently has Japan begun to examine the efficacy of the dual training system for obtaining and allocating appropriate manpower within a context of growing labor shortages and rapid modification in size and structure of the industrial sectors. The concluding chapter turns to this problem as it applies generally to Japan.

IX.

Human Resources in Japanese Industry: Problems and Prospects

EVEN though the studies in the preceding chapters are limited to industrially advanced sectors of the Japanese economy, one may conclude that Japan's experience in generating and employing human resources for modern industries has been varied and diffuse. No single pattern emerges. Certainly, however, except for the government's initial launching of modern enterprises and its continued ownership and management of several basic industrial operations, the private sector in Japan has played the preponderant role in human resource development for modern industry. In this sense, Japanese private enterprise has paralleled the American experience.[1] In both of these market-oriented industrial economies, privately owned companies have accounted for the large majority of employment in peacetime years. Despite the similarity, Japan's approach to the development of human resources has followed sharply different contours. In this chapter we offer an overall interpretation of Japan's historical strategy for industrial skill development, set forth implications of this strategy for present-day developing nations, and point out dilemmas and pressures that Japan currently faces regarding future human resources in modern industry.

[1] For recent American experience in this regard see Charles A. Myers, *The Role of the Private Sector in Manpower Development* (Baltimore: The Johns Hopkins Press, 1971).

Interpreting Japan's Strategy

Over the more than one hundred years of industrialization in Japan, two major factors stand out with regard to skill development. On the one hand, from the outset the government itself fostered and made compulsory universal modern-type primary education. It took about a generation to establish this basic education firmly and permanently, although the attempt was aided by a comparatively high degree of carry-over of formal schooling from the pre-industrial period. Undoubtedly, this achievement not only prepared the expanding population for Japan to accept industrialization but also contributed to the creation on a national scale of political unity, social and occupational mobility, wide markets for industrial goods and services, and the like. Without this broad educational base, it is unlikely that Japan would have succeeded in developing human talents for operating modern industries at an accelerating pace.

On the other hand, despite the government's relatively early attempts to institute systematic vocation-oriented schooling beyond the elementary level, these efforts proved to be limited and ad hoc. From the beginning, the chief government effort concentrated on the most advanced educational levels, since the political leadership gave highest priority to assuring a supply of well-trained, fully informed, highly motivated, and deeply committed policy makers, managers, administrators, and professional technical personnel for the new organizations and enterprises. This centered the educational effort on a fairly small group destined to enter elitist positions. Omitted in the government's human resources strategy was a successful attempt, at least until quite recently, to establish widespread secondary education that would directly link vocational preparation with the skill needs of the growing modern industries. Indeed, while the government almost immediately did institute some of the most intensive and specific training programs in its own enterprises, such as telecommunications, and launched the multiple-track system in the formal schools to channel the young labor force into the various occupational levels, effective vocational education for modern industry, by and large, was left to a decentralized and uncoordinated system of training mainly in the private sector. As seen in Chapter IV, the spread of formal secondary education sponsored by the government beginning in the early part of this century probably served to meet the emerging skill requirements of agriculture and small and medium-size enterprises far more than large modern industry.

Although not intensively examined in this study, the role of formal public education in providing a base for developing skills for traditional sectors such as farming and small enterprise should not be underestimated. Without doubt, in these sectors there were also widespread nonformal training and learning, principally on-the-job. Small and medium-size enterprises, as Lockwood long ago pointed out, were vital for Japan's long-term growth and industrial innovation, and their contribution in these regards rested to a considerable extent on the rise and spread of both formal schooling and informal skill training.[2]

However, with the emergence of large modern industrial firms, the Japanese economy early began to exhibit a dualism that persists to the present day. Limited data make it impossible to analyze the nature of Japan's economic dualism except in the most general way.[3] One might surmise, however, that without a rising educational level the dualism might have been even more acute than it was.

Overall, as seen in Chapter III, formal and quasi-formal educa-

[2] William W. Lockwood, *The Economic Development of Japan: Growth and Structural Change* (Princeton: Princeton University Press, expanded edition, 1968), especially pp. 201-214.

[3] For one interesting analysis, see Yasukichi Yasuba, "The Evolution of Dualistic Wage Structure," in Hugh Patrick, editor, with the assistance of Larry Meissner, *Japanese Industrialization and Its Social Consequences* (Berkeley: University of California Press, 1976), pp. 249-298.

tional levels in the early decades of Japan's industrialization ran well ahead of quantitative relationships between schooling and stage of economic development observed for most of the emerging societies in recent years. It would perhaps be going too far to conclude that in comparison Japan became educationally "over-endowed" at an early stage. Both inadequate measuring techniques and the recognition that education serves non-economic as well as economic purposes do not permit a firm conclusion of that sort. However, one suspects that despite the early achievement of a widespread base of primary education, Japan did not develop or utilize the full potential of skills and abilities for modern industry that one might expect from an increasingly educated population.

Historically, large modern industries in Japan have relied upon within-enterprise training programs, rather than outside schooling, to generate high and middle level skills. These programs emerged largely through the initiatives of management, except for the highest administrative and technical personnel, who received their education in elitist universities, through overseas study, and at specialized professional academies. Although the programs varied considerably in scope and coverage from industry to industry, they demonstrated the success for the individual firm of training its own core groups of skilled manual employees who began their work careers usually with no more than elementary schooling. One wonders whether this enterprise-based training system might have had more extensive application beyond the modern firms themselves had the government pursued a more active manpower policy throughout the economy.

By and large, then, the Japanese strategy was to leave the training activity to the enterprise itself. Formal education was a base from which to take off. As noted, the programs that emerged varied significantly—from a major reliance on formal school preparation in the banking industry, to recruitment of unskilled young females with minimal education for short-term careers in cotton textiles, and to progressive career-long training within the enterprise in the heavy industries, telecommunications, and railroads. Except for banking, specific skill development took place largely within the enterprises themselves, but the level to which an employee would rise and the mix of skills he or she acquired varied greatly from industry to industry.

Thus, in contrast to centralized direction in the development of the formal school system, skill learning and application in modern industry became highly decentralized, diffuse, and compartmentalized. This decentralization has been rationalized as reflecting the Japanese cultural penchant for tight but vertically structured social organizations among primary groups, which were duplicated in modern industrial enterprises. Whether this is so is difficult to determine. As in other market economies, the decentralized approach was also a product of slow emergence of organized external labor markets for skilled workers and of competition with other institutions, notably the patron-client system, which proliferated in the non-agricultural sectors from the onset of industrialization.

The human resource problem facing the managements of new modern firms was how to obtain and organize on short notice the changing array of skills needed in their respective enterprises. In the absence of well-developed links between the new schools and new enterprises for furnishing such skills, employers at first turned to the informal channels already in existence and eventually, when those proved inadequate, to generating directly their own skill requirements through enterprise-level programs. Once training within the enterprise became institutionalized there was little incentive for extensive development of external labor markets.

Emphasis on skill training within the enterprise hinged on the technological and organizational requirements of the new large-scale enterprises that were created almost overnight and were subject to constant expansions, modifications, and improvements, especially with importation of foreign techniques that had to be adapted quickly to local conditions. Under these conditions, elitist managers intent on developing their own respective enterprises had to act directly to bring together large concentrations of potential labor skills. This, they set about achieving through their own internal approaches over which they could exercise control. Such internal efforts were already demonstrated in the earliest industrializing operations launched by the government itself—notably in telecommunications and railroads as well as in arsenals, shipyards, iron works, and textile mills (especially the Tomioka "model"). There was no time to wait for elaboration of vocational training and education in the newly established school system.

The failure of well-organized labor markets to emerge for allocating skills on a national, regional, industrial, or occupational basis in Japan probably resulted from the uncertainty and incompleteness in planning for rapid industrialization. Despite its avowed intentions to develop a modern industrial economy, Japanese leadership experienced formidable obstacles, if not failure, and became highly pragmatic in the process. The trial-and-error formation of the national banking system, sale of government-owned plants to private entrepreneurs, and piecemeal emergence of shipbuilding, steel, and machinery industries underlay this pragmatism. Within this context, centralized and detailed manpower planning, could not assume high priority at the governmental level. Even in government-owned enterprises, skill development was left to decentralized processes. Government-sponsored vocational education and training became, at best, supplemental to a plethora of specific and ad hoc informal institutions and mainly provided personnel for middle- and high-level occupations.

Except in telecommunications and railroads, major modern enterprises, it should be emphasized, were unwilling or unable to launch systematic training programs until they became fully established and assured of continued existence. Most of this development came after the turn of the century, and gradually extended through the 1920s and 1930s. By then, the uncertainties that had beset the growth of large modern industry had largely disappeared. The zaibatsu, with their capital concentrations, industrial diversification, large-scale operations, and centralized control, had become firmly established. Government economic and political policy favored their predominant role in the Japanese economy: they were assured of markets by government orders, monopolistic privileges, low taxes, tariff protections, and the like. These advantages no doubt compensated at least in part for the relatively high costs of developing elaborate enterprise-specific training programs, closely integrated with career employment, length-of-service (*nenkō*) compensation, and extensive welfare benefits for permanent members of their work forces.

Until these conditions emerged, however, the new industrial enterprises relied mainly on the numerous informal institutions that grew up in the unorganized external labor markets. Use of patron-client systems proliferated in various guises, such as territorial arrangements for female workers in cotton textiles, labor-boss control in machinery and metal working, and naya seido and hamba groups in metal and coal mining. As is characteristic of many developing countries, Japan's patron-client arrangements were carry-overs from pre-industrial social organization, but they also arose from the lack of well-organized labor market institutions linking the new schools and the new industries. As long as patron-client groupings were the predominant pattern, acquisition of modern industrial skills remained haphazard. Once modern enterprises turned directly to the problem of systematic and full skill development, they faced the necessity of finding alternatives to the already well-established patron-client systems. Direct and complete training within the large enterprise itself appeared as the only sure solution.

The elaboration of within-enterprise programs unfolded over several decades. Inexperienced in training techniques, and lacking even competent instructors in some cases, most programs emerged only gradually and, in the process, incorporated elements of the patron-client system itself. By this time, apparently, little more could be expected from the development of vocational training in the formal school system because of the latter's inability to articulate closely or keep up with the skill needs of rapidly changing modern industrial processes. Indeed, beyond minimal requirements for apprenticeship set forth in the Factory Act of 1911, government left the training problem largely to industry.

While within-enterprise training in large industry and large organization was to become a leading characteristic in industrial Japan, it needs to be stressed that this approach evolved through two to three decades of experimentation. Early examples, of course, can be traced back to the late days of the Tokugawa period, as in the first modern shipyards and iron works, even before the goal of industrialism was explicitly proclaimed for Japan. However, the most serious efforts waited until industrialization became firmly established, mainly between the Sino-Japanese War of 1894-1895 and the Russo-Japanese War of 1904-1905. Then, within-enterprise training institutions elaborated and intensified over the ensuing 30 years.

The path to within-enterprise training was strewn with obstacles. Industries such as heavy machinery, metal and coal mining, and chemicals found it difficult to abandon reliance on patron-client groups for skilled labor, since there were no alternatives immediately available to meet work force requirements in the face of sudden expansions of production, introduction of new technologies, and merging of organizations. In cotton textiles especially, the major firms had become so committed to employing unskilled low-wage female workers that management turned to improving working and living conditions rather than seek out and compete for supplies of more trainable labor. Only banking, with the attraction of its high prestige as a white collar industry, could count on directly recruiting well-educated workers from the schools.

Many of the new large firms were not well-prepared to undertake large-scale within-enterprise training programs. Changes in size and technology were taking place so rapidly that the skills could not be systematically taught and programmed even on the job. Nor were elitist managers, administrators, and technical personnel well-suited for this task, even though some began to work alongside the manual employees. Time was needed to develop experienced instructors and work leaders let alone to orient work forces to industrial processes. One temporary solution, employed in steel, shipbuilding, and heavy machinery, was to share skilled labor among the companies. Another, especially in machinery and mining, was to coopt patrons and their retinues as permanent members of an enterprise work force. A third, notably in cotton textiles and mining, was to improve working and living conditions at the mills and mine sites themselves to cut down turnover among the recruits.

Even then the changeover to direct training within enterprises awaited a train of developments and events adverse from management's viewpoint. Among these was the disorder in labor markets brought about by the boom of the First World War. Rapidly rising wages and increased work opportunities heightened voluntary labor turnover, disrupting efforts to train and hold workers in the new training program. Another factor was the rise of labor unionism, first visible at the turn of the century. Following a period of government suppression, it reemerged as a moderate but spreading movement during the First World War and then accelerated sharply during the radicalism of the 1920s. Employers perceived unionism as a dire threat to their control over and training of new work forces. Still a third influence arose from the severe business depression that hit Japan following World War I, on the heels of which came the enormous devastation of the Great Kantō Earthquake in 1923, the loss of Japan's competitive position in world markets throughout the 1920s, and the reduction of Japan's military imposed by the naval treaties of 1924 and 1931. The large zaibatsu firms, as a result, turned to intensive industrial rationalization in order to cut production costs and maintain or expand output. A part of this rationalization movement was strict control over labor recruitment and utilization, including more and more exact training in specific operations of the enterprise. Surplus labor supplies, the continuing rise and spread of basic elementary education, and wide acceptance of industrialism as a national goal facilitated these efforts.

Intensification of within-enterprise training, was not without its costs. It was during the 1920s that the large enterprises began to institute firmly lifetime or career employment systems and nenkō wages, which meant increasing fixed labor costs. Key workers recruited directly from school could now expect to remain with a firm throughout their careers, unlikely to be laid off even in slack periods. Their wages and benefits rose periodically and systematically in hierarchical progression as their life cycle needs increased; while their skills could be expected to increase with training and experience, wage rates did not necessarily correspond to individual productiveness. To assure that loyal, committed, and educated workers would be recruited, selected, and promoted, companies had to invest heavily in personnel administration, welfare benefits, and continued training. But such costs were probably not all that burdensome. Companies instituted lifetime employment only gradually and surrounded key employees with low-paid, temporary, casual, and subcontract workers. Favored by monopolistic privilege and surplus labor, higher wage rates and benefits than found in other sectors could be offered, yet not so high as they would be if labor markets had been tight. Indeed, the wage gap between large and small firms grew noticeably throughout the 1920s and 1930s even as Japan turned to heavier industrialization under militarism; and, despite considerable wage leveling during World War II and the immediate postwar period, the pay gaps reemerged with even stronger force once the boom began in the 1950s.

There is little doubt that training within enterprises enhanced productivity in the large firms and, through external economies, provided benefits for other sectors of the Japanese economy. With continual training and experience key workers became highly versatile, usually gaining knowledge and skill for many jobs within a company. Tight-knit shop-level groups of more experienced and less experienced workers assured informal transmission of skills on the job along with the formal training programs that were set up. Foremen who arose from the shop groups and other work leaders probably often were close to professional engineers in their potential functions. They and their retinues not only showed little concern for job demarcations but also were willing, if not eager, to take up any work assigned. Thus, they came to constitute a highly flexible work force useful whenever there were technological, production, and organizational changes. Assurance of life-time employment was probably a small price to pay for these advantages to the firm. With their skills, knowledge, and status specific to the enterprise, key workers were unlikely to shift, even if there were the opportunity, to other major firms and certainly not to the lower paid, unstable, small- and medium-size firm sector.

The heart of this approach at the enterprise level was to train key workers over an extended period of time. Skill training, unlike well rounded and comprehensive apprenticeships, was steadily cumulative over the years for an individual key employee. This was a vastly different training from the haphazard, ad hoc, piecemeal experience of workers in the small- and medium-size firms. It meant that a single large enterprise probably held within its employ cadres of key workers with knowledge and skills or the potential to acquire them that were probably more than sufficient to handle most tasks that would arise. Yet, there were rarely enough such key workers to furnish the skills needed in expansions, changeovers, and reorganizations. Their numbers had to be supplemented by temporary or subcontract employees.

In this context, it is perhaps little wonder that, once within-enterprise training became firmly established in the large enterprises in Japan, there was little serious attempt to foster vocational education in the formal school system or in publicly supported training institutions. Small- and medium-size firms surely benefited from what vocational education there was in the schools but were unable or unwilling to build upon this to mount their own systematic skill training programs. Only the large enterprises could undertake the training with the needed precision and reliability. Indeed, it was difficult to fit graduates beyond the elementary school into work teams; higher-level school graduates paradoxically were seen as less trainable and disciplined. One may infer, for example, that the chief reason for the government-sponsored youth schools—first in the mid-1920s and on a much broader scale a decade later—was the need for preparing young workers for the discipline of industry who otherwise would not have been recruited. Most of these recruits had not been directly hired to become key workers in major firms. Indeed, in the same vein only with considerable trepidation large enterprise turned to hiring-in experienced workers from the small- and medium-size enterprise sector following the shift to heavier industry in the 1930s. Despite their experience and skills, such workers were accepted only as "halfway" employees, downgraded in wages, benefits, and status within the work force.

The advantages to the major companies of within-enterprise training remained overwhelming even in the face of the thorough reforms and democratization of the education system and labor relations under the Allied Occupation. The ensuing rise in compulsory education levels, the opening of comprehensive secondary schools to all who wished to continue on (currently 90 percent), and the enormous expansion of higher education (now admitting at least 40 percent of the high school graduates) were significant changes, but, until fairly recently, made no notable impact on the closed employment and training systems of the large enterprises. True, the reforms in education eventually contributed to a great step up in intergenerational mobility, especially as young people increasingly left the farms and villages for urban and industrial occupations. True also, large firms had to draw on "halfway" workers in expanding their work forces to meet the needs of rapid increases in output. Nonetheless, they persisted in maintaining their internal labor systems rather than turning toward the external labor markets. By and large, they held to the established patterns of recruiting new school graduates, mostly males, to become their permanent workers.

This was not entirely a matter of employer preference. In part, continuation of this closed employment system was due to the pressures of the labor unions which spread throughout large-scale industry in the postwar period and organized largely on an enterprise basis with the intent of assuring permanent employment for the regular workers within the enterprise. In part, also the burgeoning school system was not directed toward fostering vocational education, except to meet the general increased needs of an urbanized society for professional-level personnel, and, therefore was little articulated with fast-changing industrial skill requirements. The primary objective of the educational system was to foster equality of opportunity and emphasis on democratic values in school curricula. Educational and labor reforms thus did not embrace organization of broad labor markets across regions, industries, occupations, and enterprises, even though private labor recruiters and bosses essentially were declared illegal.

Only after 1958, with the passage of the Vocational Training Act and the shortages of young recruits for industrial employment, was there serious policy consideration of an "active" manpower program for the nation as a whole. The steps toward developing this policy are traced in Chapter IV and at this date are still in construction, notably in implementing the revised Act of 1969. Even then there has been no wholesale reconstruction of the labor markets. General rather than vocational education has remained the chief route to enter lifetime careers in the large enterprises, and this no doubt served as a major motivation for the young to continue into comprehensive high schools and, in increasing numbers, on to nontechnical higher education. Vocational skill training could wait until employment was secured.[4]

The Japanese case illustrates that, in the absence of well-developed and orderly external markets for industrial workers, enterprises which are under pressures to expand rapidly and acquire advanced technology are likely to resort to and maintain their own internal programs for skill training and worker commitment as long as they can despite looming labor shortages and rising wage rates. Nonetheless, by the 1960s the internal training systems in the large companies have come under considerable pressure for change and may have now begun to deteriorate.

Implications of the Japanese Experience for Developing Economies

Japan's strategy for human resource development in the course of modern economic growth contains "lessons" for present-day developing economies. The most important of these follow:

1. Present-day developing countries should be in a far better position than was Japan a century ago to plan for the comprehensive development of skills over a much wider range of industries because of the availability of modern planning techniques and

---

[4] The relationship that has developed between the formal schools and the public employment service during the post-World War II period in comparison to other countries is well analyzed in Beatrice G. Reubens, *Bridges to Work: International Comparisons of Transition Services* (Montclair, New Jersey: Allanheld, Osmun and Co. Publishers, Inc. 1977).

technical knowledge. In Japan's early experience with industrialization and modern economic growth, industrial skill requirements were virtually unknown. There was, thus, considerable reliance upon foreign instruction in Japan and learning abroad. Even then, there was a trial-and-error approach that relied upon attempts at adopting indigenous skills and use of informal patron-client relationships outside the firm. Only in certain specific instances, such as telecommunications and railroads, were the specific skill needs clear-cut. In these cases, the Japanese government, utilizing foreign instruction at first, proceeded directly to train recruits to manage and operate these industries under its direct control. In sum, the initial Japanese approach to skill training was concentrated in a few of the most modern sectors to the neglect of industry in general.

2. On the other hand, it was clear to the Japanese leadership in the Meiji era that, however uncertain the eventual scope and level of Japan's economic and industrial development, the population in general would require basic common education to cope with and support a modern society. Thus, the government steadily moved toward universal primary education of all children—a goal essentially achieved within a 30-year period. Even though this effort may have been only weakly connected with vocational and skill needs, universal primary education no doubt served to unify a theretofore immobile population and decentralized governmental system. Along with other new institutions, universal primary education also raised aspirations and helped foster intergenerational mobility, instill disciplined study and work habits, and develop national markets for goods and services. It is doubtful that a more restrictive basic education would have served these purposes as well, although the heavy stress upon nationalism in the curriculum probably went unnecessarily far. In this regard, present-day developing countries would find the Japanese experience highly relevant.

3. From the perspective of present-day developing economies,

it may be argued that Japan erected an educational pyramid that was too narrow at the top, in that higher education produced an elite remote from the mass of the population, and may have overlooked talents and abilities highly useful for long-run economic and social development. The Japanese government, supplemented by private efforts, very quickly established such elitist institutions in order to assure a selective flow of able and dependable leadership for the new governmental, industrial, military, and educational organizations. No doubt for Japan in those days to have attempted any broader approach to higher education not only would have been exceedingly costly but also ran the risk of "overproducing" intellectuals without opportunities for employment directly useful for Japan's new modern organizations. Expansion of higher education awaited later stages of economic development.

4. Less developed countries can learn from the Japanese experience to avoid gaps in the formal educational structure. In Japan the largest gap arose at the secondary level between basic and higher education. Here, of course, was the greatest unknown for the Japanese leadership, despite attempts even before the turn of the century to provide secondary vocational schooling on a wide scale. With great uncertainties of economic development still besetting Japan and continuing lags in technological and economic knowledge at that time, it was difficult to anticipate middle-level skill needs on more than an ad hoc basis. The government essentially abandoned serious efforts to fill this gap and, thus, failed to build systematic institutions for vocational education and career training with the exception of preparing white-collar employees and technicians through specialized advanced schools. Although Japan structured elaborate formal school tracks beyond the basic elementary level, most of these tracks led nowhere in large modern industry, but were of principal benefit to the small and medium-size enterprises in the private sector. Unless a graduate found immediate employment in a large industrial or govern-

mental organization, there was little likelihood of further systematic development of his skill potential. Again, in those days, however, public vocational training on a wide scale would have been most costly and uncertain of results. In all likelihood, it would have detracted from the goals of rapid growth and industrialization in the short term.

5. In filling the gap at the middle level of skill generation, the Japanese experience with private programs may be instructive to developing economies. In the initial decades Japan relied mainly on existing private mechanisms for intermediate skill learning and employment. One of the most important was the emergence of "miscellaneous" vocational schools, which have thrived in large numbers down to the present. Another was the utilization of informal patron-client groupings in external labor markets. Still a third was the eventual development of within-enterprise training programs in the large firms and organizations. Each, in its own way, compensated for an incomplete or inadequate generation of formal vocational training tracks and follow-up through public institutions. These mechanisms were pragmatic responses to emerging demands and needs for skills, mainly in the private sector. Each represented a selective, decentralized approach to meet immediate needs. Except in the case of within-enterprise training, the skills acquired were often incomplete and not well fitted to new technologies and organizations. This partial approach probably contributed to the growing economic dualism, although it meant also that the small and medium-size industrial sectors had available large numbers of workers with growing skill levels. As in most developing economies, dualism in Japan probably could not have been avoided, but, although unnecessarily prolonged, it was reduced by a degree of integration between the advanced and less advanced sectors.

6. As already stressed, a basic reason for the development of the private institutions was the omission of conscious governmental efforts to organize external skilled labor markets in Japan.

Certainly, developing nations could do far more than Japan in this regard, even though dualism in the economy may be unavoidable. In fact, one might argue that the informal institutions that emerged in Japan became barriers to organizing systematic labor markets on a broad scale. Perhaps it could not be expected that the Japanese economy, given a background of decentralized feudalism, lack of labor mobility, and national isolation, could quickly generate well-developed labor markets for rapid industrialization. But there is little evidence that Japanese leadership gave much thought to, or was very conscious of, the concept of well-organized external labor markets. Lack of labor market planning gave room to innumerable separate and uncoordinated efforts to match jobs and workers at the enterprise level. It is not known how much skill potential was lost in this process, but with the young population being so well educated at the basic elementary level, it must have been sizable. The emergence and persistence of economic dualism, alongside rising educational levels, attests to this likelihood. One may argue that it was not so much a case of Japan's becoming "overendowed" educationally in the course of modern economic growth, but rather a case of failure systematically to generate labor market institutions for the fuller use of the latent abilities and learning capacities. In short, until recently, Japan's history of industrial manpower hardly added up to an "active" government policy.

7. It is within the above context that developing economies should gauge the seeming "success" of Japan's unusually high degree of within-enterprise training. While the large modern firms, in varying degrees, developed highly elaborated systems of internal labor markets, external labor markets remained disorganized. Under the circumstances, large organizations had no choice but to continue to concentrate upon their own internal programs. For rapid growth, there was a need for a virtually "instant" creation of work forces with complex arrays of utilizable and potential skills not available externally. Each major enter-

prise had to build and secure its own skill array, although the strategy to achieve this, as examined in Chapters V through VIII, varied among the modern industries.

The choice of this strategy basically was a product of the drive for rapid industrialization, at least in selective sectors, in the face of an undeveloped labor market organization. Developing countries should recognize that, once internal labor training systems become major institutions, they are likely to become intensified and exclusive with the result of prolonging dualism.

8. There is little doubt on the other hand that the internal labor systems in Japan offered great advantages for training regular workers in a wide range of skills specifically required by large, modern enterprises and organizations. Foremost among these advantages was the concentration of training and retraining upon a select segment or core, of the work force members who became permanently attached to a particular firm. With employment security, stability in livelihood for themselves and families, and steady progression in income and status, the workers in these training programs usually could concentrate exclusively upon learning jobs and tasks in the particular enterprise. They became highly versatile and flexible. This approach maximized identification of workers with their respective work teams, plants, and companies, and enhanced their interest in increasing output and productivity. In the process they developed little vested interest in any one occupation or job so that they were receptive to shifting from task to task and to technological and organizational change. Also, without a common occupational base, their interest in outside-led labor unionism was minimal, although, once unionism was legitimated by the Allied Occupation labor reforms following World War II, they seized upon enterprise-level unionization and collective bargaining as means to secure permanent employment in their respective companies.

For developing countries, the considerable utilization of closed internal labor markets could be attractive for generating and accumulating precisely needed skills at the right moment and in the right enterprise. But it should be recognized that modern Japanese industry resorted to the strategy out of a peculiar set of economic, political, and social circumstances that were hampering the orderly emergence of well-developed labor markets on a base broader than the enterprise itself. Closed internal labor market arrangements may be highly efficient at the outset, but they run the risk of unnecessarily increasing and prolonging economic dualism by rigidifying employment patterns and generating vested interests in these patterns.

9. Some would argue that the Japanese pattern of closed enterprise systems represents a more efficient, equitable, and humane approach to human resource development than the more open labor markets that emerged in the now advanced industrial societies of the West. In fact, it is claimed, the Japanese "model" itself will become the pattern even for economically advanced countries to emulate.[5] This argument would be convincing if indeed the enterprise-by-enterprise approach became a broad alternative to providing employment opportunities and social security protection through governmental or outside private institutions. It should be stressed, however, that despite the marked development of internal enterprise employment systems in Japan, they actually fell short of becoming universal. Not only was the majority of the labor force left out, but also it did not receive compensatory benefits either through alternative labor market mechanisms for skill development or welfare programs for economic and social security. The Japanese strategy succeeded only partially in this respect.

One might question why, in these circumstances, the "deprived" sectors of the labor force did not protest more vehemently than it did over the decades. There is no easy answer for

[5] See Ronald P. Dore, *British Factory-Japanese Factory: The Origins of National Diversity in Industrial Relations* (Berkeley: University of California Press, 1973), especially Chapters 13 and 15.

this. Among the factors at work were probably the very rapid transition from feudal agrarianism to modern industrial urbanism, which made the arousal and organization of protest difficult, the suppression and control of protest exercised by a strong centralized political leadership and bureaucracy, the socialization toward conformity induced by the universal compulsory education system and military conscription with its emphasis on nationalism and later ultranationalism, and the segmented internal employment systems themselves, which separated the modern skilled industrial workers from the remainder of the labor force. In the present era, leaders in developing nations are not likely to find a duplication of the conditions in Japan that so deeply affected the choice of human resource strategy. Large elements of the work force remained outside of systematic cumulative skill training—for example, workers in small enterprises, subcontracting companies, temporary and casual labor, women, middle-aged, and displaced workers. Present-day developing economies that rely on market mechanisms for industrialization are likely to face social unrest if groups as large as these are left behind for long.

The history of Japan's strategy poses the fundamental question of achieving balance and coverage in human resource development for manpower planners and policy makers in developing nations. Surely, the overall Japanese strategy examined in this study has been a phase in the long-term unfolding of the industrializing process. It need not be repeated elsewhere, although selected elements such as training as an integral part of a career-long employment system certainly have their uses.

Pressure for Change

To return to the basic questions posed in the introductory chapter, we conclude that in the Japanese case, as perhaps in most historical cases of national economic growth, education and skill development for modern industries was a pragmatic, piece-meal, and less-than-comprehensive process followed largely in response to uncertain and unknown economic and social forces. Formation of Japan's human resource development strategy took place over an extended period; once established, it tended to congeal in institutions that continue to persist. The skill training patterns that Japan generated in the course of industrialization became strongly embedded as integral parts of these institutions—and indeed have been rationalized by some as manifestations of unique cultural and social patterns.

In the degree to which closed enterprise systems came into being, the Japanese strategy differed from other advanced countries, providing an important and successful example of still another variation toward achieving advanced industrialization of a society. This would indicate that the universals implied by the logic of "industrialism" indeed follow different paths for implementation and emerge only after a long period of time, if ever. On the other hand, the particularism of the Japanese case of human resource development should not be overemphasized, or, for that matter, idealized. For all its touted advantages and benefits for economic and industrial growth, the approach had serious social costs and deprivations from a national point of view. It is difficult to escape the conclusion that concentration on skill development and utilization in the large enterprise sector was accompanied by something less in other sectors. Surely, if the large enterprises could generate arrays of skills from top to bottom with a minimum of vocational education in the public schools and universities, much the same might have been accomplished systematically for many other elements in the labor force.

Rapid growth and diversification of the economy and concomitant social change in Japan since the 1950s have increasingly brought into question the continued suitability of the established Japanese strategy for human resource development. However effective the heavy reliance upon internal training systems for major enterprises and organizations, it was geared to a policy of "production first" in Japan's race to come abreast of the most advanced technological and industrial societies in the world. In the large modern sector, the concentration of skill training and accumulation of skills worked admirably well for this purpose. But the price for this was economic and social dualism that has eroded only slowly as the benefits of rapid industrial growth spread throughout the nation.

Now that Japan has achieved a high level of economic activity the pressure to modify or eliminate institutions that seemingly perpetuate the inequities and inequalities of dualism has increased. In other words, especially since the late 1960s, Japan has been at a crossroads where it must choose between a continued "production first" policy or shift to greater social welfare even at the expense of growth. With the oil crisis and slowed economic growth since the early 1970s this dilemma has heightened. Within this context the closed internal employment systems and skill training patterns have come under increasing scrutiny. The growing demand for equity and equality of work opportunity is evidence of Japan's entry into a "post-industrial" phase.[6]

Despite this dilemma not only are large enterprise management and enterprise work forces in general reluctant to abandon the internal systems, but the enterprise-centered approach has become a "model" for other sectors of the industrial society. As a result, the new governmental efforts to launch an "active" policy for broadening skill training and education and organizing external labor markets have been modest and, in some respects, geared to preserving the enterprise systems. There has been no wholesale attack on the enterprise systems, but rather an expectation or hope that economic and social change will somehow

[6] For elaboration of this thesis, see John W. Bennett and Solomon B. Levine, "Industrialization and Social Deprivation: Welfare, Environment, and the Post-industrial Society in Japan," in Patrick (1976), pp. 439-492.

gradually bring about voluntary modifications with improved linkage between internal and external labor markets.

A number of factors have been undermining the internal systems and are likely to continue to do so. One is the vast rise in educational levels, so that major enterprises are no longer able to recruit new workers exclusively from elementary and middle schools to launch regular workers for their careers in enterprise-controlled training programs. This fact, coupled with the decline in population growth in the young age groups, produced labor shortages in the context of the lifetime employment system. Large enterprises have been increasingly forced to turn to experienced workers in other enterprises and sectors or to draw upon older, often retired, men and women.

Another factor is the change in values of the increasingly educated new school graduates. Although entry into a large organization with its job security and progressive benefits throughout one's career is still the major aspiration for new school graduates, they are increasingly interested in keeping their options open for satisfying alternative employment opportunities—in sharp contrast to their elders who had almost none. In part, this reflects a belief among the young that their education has prepared them for work (and leisure) beyond what any single enterprise can offer. In part, they resent the system whereby length-of-service rather than merit determines awards and benefits. They are not as willing as formerly to devote their whole existence to a single enterprise, awaiting their rewards in due time. This change in values could drastically affect the basic premise of the internal training system, which counts on career-long attachment and absence of interfirm mobility.

Still a third factor has been the rise of more efficient small and medium-size firms, growth of the service sector, spread of independent professions and occupations, and diversification of job opportunities as Japan's economic advance has progressed. Major firms have had to compete increasingly for new workers. Notably, the gap in starting wages between large- and small-scale enterprise has all but disappeared and interfirm mobility, especially among the younger workers, has been on the rise. In other words, there appears to be a growing occupation-consciousness among the Japanese in competition with enterprise-consciousness.[7] Not a small part of this trend toward diversification is the internationalization of the Japanese economy itself, not only with foreign firms entering Japan's industries and markets, but also Japanese firms locating operations abroad.

In view of these emerging changes, despite their reluctance many large Japanese enterprises are growing dubious about continuing internal training systems as intensively as in the past. Since they risk losing the benefits of internal training with the step-up of interfirm mobility, as yet they do not see the clear emergence of new training institutions as alternatives that will insure control over personnel selection, exactness in skill training and supervision, tight-knit work organization, and flexbility provided by the internal systems.

The recent government initiatives toward an "active" manpower policy seem to be aimed at eradicating the tight labor market segmentation that accompanied Japan's economic growth. But, so far, the effects have been largely in improving employment chances for the more marginal members of the labor force, now exacerbated by growing unemployment and underemployment in an era of moderate economic growth. Significant an advance as this may be, it does not get to the heart of the problem of shifting from internal to external labor market organization. While the new programs along with the expanded educational system assist in furthering intergenerational mobility, it remains to be seen what the impact will be upon intragenera-

[7] See Robert E. Cole and Ken'chi Tominaga, "Japan's Changing Occupational Structure and Its Significance," in Patrick (1976), pp. 53-96.

tional mobility, and it is likely to take as long to unravel the institutional complex that now exists as it did to develop it in the first place.

As we have pointed out, there are some who would counsel against the weakening and eventual abandonment of the closed internal employment systems in Japan's modern enterprises. This position is not without its strengths, provided, of course, that such closed employment systems could be extended fairly rapidly throughout most, if not all, of the society. This has not yet happened, although in recent years perhaps as much as 40 percent of the labor force became subject to these arrangements—not an unenviable achievement—helped in part by near full employment and high growth. To that extent the closed internal systems succeeded but with accompanying social costs in unused skill potentials, crowded and polluted urbanization, lack of public amenities, housing shortages, inadequate social security, and the like.

Recent public enactments for a more "active" manpower policy are in a sense recognition that the closed employment systems are not likely to pervade the entire Japanese economy and may recede from their present level under conditions of slower economic growth. With structural change and diversification, the workings of the economy have become increasingly complex, and with it problems have arisen in matching supplies of and demands for labor skills. The new public programs are based in part on further expected shifts in the structure of the economy in which there will be the need for increased versatility and flexibility in labor utilization on a wide scale across enterprises and sectors. They are also based on the expectation that technological processes will develop more common skill requirements from enterprise to enterprise. If these premises are correct, coupled with changing social values toward increased mobility and lessened group identification, the measures envision considerable break-down in the segmented internal labor markets and development of more organized external labor markets than have existed in Japan during the past century.

As the closed enterprise system declines, pressure for public welfare programs will increase relatively. It is well recognized that, compared to other advanced nations, Japan has lagged behind considerably in providing social security of most types and that private programs cannot be expected to fill this gap. Success in developing organized external labor markets may well lie in expanding public social security as well as public training and employment institutions themselves.

Of course, it remains to be seen how far the Japanese government will actually go in these directions. So far, the new training programs have dealt mainly with the more marginal members of the labor force. They are yet to become major institutions for career employment in industries or occupations. In the few cases where they are, the programs are still at best supplementary to the internal systems in the large enterprises.

The question also remains whether large firms with systematic training programs would utilize the new public institutions and abandon their own internal systems, which have been built up laboriously over more than half a century in many cases. The outcome remains highly uncertain for reasons already discussed.

A number of large companies have responded with new policies that stress job classification, job evaluation, and merit performance for wages and benefits and for promotion or advancement rather than simply length of service and level of formal education. Also, in various instances, managements of large enterprises have cut down or abandoned elements of training programs, particularly those oriented toward general education or welfare. Behind developments such as these is the growing recognition that labor market segmentation is increasingly incompatible with labor flexibility for the economy as a whole. In the process of Japan's rapid economic growth, the structure of the economy has undergone profound change and the dissolution of economic dualism has accelerated. While closed employment systems may have been essential in the transition—for training, accumulating, and employing skills for specific enterprises in technologically advanced industries—and no doubt will persist for some time to come (if for no other reason than as a means of maintaining employment rolls), it probably not only hampers flexible utilization and training of labor skills across organizations but also fails to utilize human talents and abilities relegated to less productive units and sectors of the economy. In the past, the mobility of labor from low productivity to high productivity industries and occupations has depended primarily upon intergenerational movement. This perhaps was economically sufficient. But with the growth and diversification of the economy, and now the entrance into a post-industrial international phase, intragenerational mobility may become far more important. This trend is likely to accelerate as old industries such as cotton textiles, shipbuilding, and mining decline, and new industries based on knowledge, sophisticated technology and service emerge.

Fundamental changes in economic structure and value systems have made it imperative that the government plan consciously to establish new training and educational institutions that would cater more and more to individual career aspirations as well as emerging manpower and employment trends. Such an "active" manpower policy may inevitably signal steady erosion of within-enterprise training systems as the major vehicle for skill development in modern enterprises. It may be expected that, as other institutions for training become more fully developed, the internal programs will become an integral portion of an overall system serving a sector, region, or the nation as a whole. Only the barest beginning toward such a transformation has occurred, and the start has been quite slow, lending credence to the proposition that Japanese industry for particular cultural reasons has an unusual reliance upon closed, internal employment systems.

However, as indicated especially in the industry-by-industry studies of Chapters V to VIII, the Japanese strategy toward developing human resources for modern industry emerged as a response to a particular set of historical conditions and forces that resulted in a predominance of segmented within-enterprise training programs in the most modern industries. Even then, considerable differences appeared from industry to industry, so that the patterns were variable. It may be expected that since the original conditions have changed markedly—among them a much higher level of overall economic activity, profound structural shifts, and steady transformation of social values—Japan is likely to make continual adaptations in training and employment patterns more consonant with emerging requirements for economy-wide complexity and flexibility. Such modifications are likely to take as much time as did the existing institutions to form and come to full development. Educationally, the population is increasingly prepared for such a new transition.

Bibliography

Allen, G. C., *A Short Economic History of Japan*, rev. ed., London, 1963.

Anderson, C. Arnold, and Mary Jean Bowman (eds.), *Education and Economic Development*, Chicago, 1965.

Anderson, Ronald S., *Japan: Three Epochs of Modern Education*, Washington, D.C., 1959.

Arai, Ikuo, "Notes on Institutions and Policies for Manpower Development in Japan," in the Japan Institute of Labour, *Industrialization and Manpower Policy in Asian Countries*, Proceedings of the 1973 Asian Regional Conference on Industrial Relations, Tokyo, 1973, pp. 143-156.

Arisawa Hiromi, *Gendai Nihon Sangyō Koza* [Discourse on Industry in Contemporary Japan], Volumes I-VII, Tokyo, 1960.

Bank of Japan, Office of Statistics, *Nihon Keizai Wo Chūshin To Suru Kokusai Hikaku Tōkei* [International Comparative Statistics with a Focus on the Japanese Economy], Tokyo, June 1977.

Becker, Gary S., *Human Capital: A Theoretical and Empirical Analysis with Special Reference to Education*, 2nd ed., New York, 1975.

Bennett, John W., and Solomon B. Levine, "Industrialization and Social Deprivation: Welfare, Environment, and the Postindustrial Society in Japan," in Hugh Patrick (ed.), with the assistance of Larry Meissner, *Japanese Industrialization and Its Social Consequences*, Berkeley, 1976, pp. 439-492.

Blaug, Mark, "The Empirical Status of Human Capital Theory: A Slightly Jaundiced Survey," *The Journal of Economic Literature*, Vol. XIV, No. 3, September 1976, pp. 827-856.

Cole, Robert E., *Japanese Blue Collar: The Changing Tradition*, Berkeley, 1971.

———, *Work, Mobility, and Participation: A Comparative Study of American and Japanese Industry*, Berkeley, 1979.

Cole, Robert E., and Ken'ichi Tominaga, "Japan's Changing Occupational Structure and Its Significance," in Hugh Patrick (ed.), with the assistance of Larry Meissner, *Japanese Industrialization and Its Social Consequences*, Berkeley, 1976, pp. 53-96.

Cole, Robert E., and Shun'ichiro Umetani, "Manpower Training and Employment in Japan," *Monthly Labor Review*, Vol. 98, No. 11, November 1974, pp. 43-45.

Dore, Ronald P. (ed.), *Aspects of Social Change in Japan*, Princeton, 1967.

————, *British Factory-Japanese Factory: The Origins of National Diversity in Industrial Relations*, Berkeley, 1973.

————, *Education in Tokugawa Japan*, Berkeley, 1965.

Fuji Bank (ed.), *Fuji Ginkō 80 Nenshi* [Eighty Year History of the Fuji Bank], Tokyo, 1960.

Fujita Wakao, *Nihon Rōdō Kyōyaku Ron* [Treatise on Japanese Labor Agreements], Tokyo, 1961.

Hall, John W., and Marius B. Jansen (eds.), *Studies in the Institutional History of Early Modern Japan*, Princeton, 1968.

Hall, John W., and Richard K. Beardsley, *Twelve Doors to Japan*, New York, 1965.

Hansen, W. Lee, *Education, Income, and Human Capital*, New York, 1970.

Harbison, Frederick H., *Human Resources as the Wealth of Nations*, New York, 1973.

Harbison, Frederick H., Joan Maruhnic, and Jane Resnick, *Quantitative Analyses of Modernization and Development*, Princeton, 1970.

Harbison, Frederick H., and Charles A. Myers, *Education, Manpower, and Economic Growth: Strategies of Human Resource Development*, New York, 1964.

————, *Manpower and Education: Country Studies in Economic Development*, New York, 1965.

Hokkaidō Tankō Kisen Co., Ltd., *Hokkaidō Tankō Kisen Kabushiki Kaisha 70 Nenshi* [Seventy Year History of the Hokkaido Coal Mining and Steamship Corporation], Tokyo, 1958.

Hollerman, Leon, *Japan's Dependence on the World Economy*, Princeton, 1967.

Ishihara Kōichi, *Nihon Gijutsu Kyōiku Shiron* [Treatise on the History of Technical Education in Japan], Tokyo, 1962.

Ishikawa Hirokatsu et al., *Yahata Seitetsu* [Yahata Steel], Tokyo, 1962.

Ishikawajima Heavy Industries Co., Ltd., *Ishikawajima Jūkōgyō Kabushiki Kaisha 100 Nenshi* [One Hundred Year History of the Ishikawajima Heavy Industries Corporation], Tokyo, 1961.

Itokawa Taichi, *Honpō Nenshi Bōseki Shi* [History of Cotton Spinning in Japan], Vol. I, Osaka, 1937.

Iwauchi, Ryoichi, "Adaptation to Technological Change," *The Developing Economies*, Vol. VII, No. 4, December 1969, pp. 428-450.

Jansen, Marius B. (ed.), *Changing Japanese Attitudes Toward Modernization*, Princeton, 1965.

Japan, Economic Planning Agency, *Kokumin Shotoku Tōkei Nenpō* [Statistical Yearbook of National Income], Tokyo, 1978.

Japan Information Service, *Japan Report*, New York.

Japan Institute of Labour, *Japan Labor Bulletin*, Tokyo.

———, *Japan Labor Statistics*, Tokyo, 1974.

———, *Wagakuni Ni Okeru Shokugyō Kunren No Shiteki Hatten Katei* [The Course of Historical Development of Vocational Training on Japan], Volumes 1, 2, 3, Tokyo, 1969, 1970, and 1972.

Japan, Ministry of Agriculture and Commerce, *Shokkō Jijō* [Conditions of Factory Workers], Volumes I, II, III, Tokyo, 1903 (reprinted 1948).

Japan, Ministry of Education, *Chihō Kyōikuhi No Chōsa Hōkoku* [Report on the Survey of Local Educational Expenditures], Tokyo, 1955.

———, *Education in Japan: A Graphic Presentation*, Tokyo, 1971.

———, *Japan's Growth and Education*, Tokyo, 1963.

———, *Gakkō Kihon Chōsa* [Basic Survey of Schools], 1960, 1965, 1970, and 1975, Tokyo.

———, *Gakusei 50 Nenshi* [Fifty Year History of the Education System], Tokyo, 1922.

———, *Kyōiku Shibō No Kokusai Hikaku* [International Comparisons of Educational Preferences], Tokyo, 1971.

———, *Sangyō Kyōiku 50 Nenshi* [Fifty Year History of Industrial Education], Tokyo, 1966.

———, Japanese National Commission for Unesco, *The Role of Education in the Social and Economic Development of Japan*, Tokyo, 1966.

————, *Wagakuni No Kyōiku No Ayumi To Kongo no Kadai* [Japan's History of Education and Future Issues], Tokyo, 1969.

Japan, Ministry of Labor, *History of Industrial Education in Japan, 1868-1900*, Tokyo, 1959.

————, *Labour Administration in Japan*, Tokyo, 1971.

————, *Rōdō Gyōseishi* [History of Labor Administration], Tokyo, 1961.

————, *Rōdō Tōkei Nenpō* [Yearbook of Labor Statistics], 1952, Tokyo.

————, *Vocational Training Administration in Japan*, Tokyo, undated.

Japan, Ministry of Welfare, *Isei 80 Nenshi* [Eighty Year History of the Medical System], Tokyo, 1955.

———— *Ishi, Shikaishi, Kakuzaishi Chōsa* [Survey of Doctors, Dentists, and Pharmacists], 1970, 1975, Tokyo.

Japan National Railways, *Nihon Kokuyū Tetsudō 100 Nenshi* [One Hundred Year History of the Japan National Railways], Vol. I, Tokyo, 1969.

Japan, Office of the Prime Minister, *Kokusei Chōsa Hōkoku* [Report on the National Census], Tokyo, 1975.

Japan, Office of the Prime Minister, Bureau of Statistics, *Japan Statistical Yearbook*, 1964, 1971, and 1976, Tokyo.

Japan Productivity Center, *Industrial Skill Training in Japan*, Tokyo, 1959.

Japan, Publishing Committee for the Japan Education Yearbook, *Nihon Kyōiku Nenkan* [Japan Education Yearbook], 1963, Tokyo.

Kaigo, Toshiomi, *Japanese Education: Its Past and Present*, Tokyo, 1968.

Kajinishi Mitsuhaya, *Nihon Sangyōshihon Seiritsu Shiron* [Historical Treatise on the Formation of Industrial Capital in Japan], Tokyo, 1965.

Kamaishi Iron Works, *Kamaishi Seitetsusho 70 Nenshi* [Seventy Year History of the Kamaishi Iron Works], Tokyo, 1956.

Katō Toshihiko, *Honpō Ginkō Shiron* [Historical Treatise on Banking in Japan], Tokyo, 1957.

Kawada, Hisashi, "Industrialization and Educational Investment in the Meiji Era," in the American Association of Colleges for Teacher Education, *Educational Investment in the Pacific Community*, Fifth Annual Conference Report on International Understanding, Washington, D.C., 1963, pp. 39-54.

Kawasaki Heavy Industries Co., Ltd., *Kawasaki Jūkōgyō Kabushiki Kaisha Shashi* [Company History of the Kawasaki Heavy Industries Corporation], Kobe, 1959.

Kerr, Clark, John T. Dunlop, Frederick H. Harbison, and Charles A. Meyers, *Industrialization and Industrial Man: The Problems of Labor and Management in Economic Growth*, Cambridge, Mass., 1960.

Kobata Atsushi, *Kōzan No Rekishi* [History of Mining], Tokyo, 1957.

Kobe Steel Corporation, *Shinkō 50 Nenshi* [Fifty Year History of Kobe Steel], Kobe, 1954.

Kume Masao, *Itō Hirobumi Den* [Biography of Itō Hirobumi], Tokyo, 1931.

Kuznets, Simon, *Postwar Economic Growth*, Cambridge, Mass., 1964.

Levine, Solomon B., *Industrial Relations in Postwar Japan*, Urbana, Ill., 1958.

———, "Our Future Industrial Society: A Global Vision," *Industrial and Labor Relations Review*, Vol. 14, No. 4, July 1961, pp. 548-555.

———, "Labor Market Segmentation in the Economic Development of Japan," in Subbiah Kannapan (ed.), *Studies of Urban Labour Market Behavior in Developing Areas*, Geneva, 1977, pp. 107-115.

———, "Labor Markets and Collective Bargaining in Japan," in William W. Lockwood (ed.), *The State and Economic Enterprise in Japan*, Princeton, 1965, Chapter XIV, pp. 633-667.

———, "Unionization of White-Collar Employees in Japan," in Adolf Strumthal (ed.), *White-Collar Trade Unions*, Urbana, Ill., 1966, pp. 205-260.

Lockwood, William W., *The Economic Development of Japan: Growth and Structural Change, 1868-1939*, Princeton, 1954. Expanded edition, 1968.

———, (ed.), *The State and Economic Enterprise in Japan*, Princeton, 1965.

Meyers, Frederick, *Training in European Enterprises*, Los Angeles, 1969.

Minami, Ryoshin, "The Introduction of Electric Power and Its Impact on the Manufacturing Industries: With Special Reference to Smaller Scale Plants," in Hugh Patrick (ed.), with the assistance of Larry

Meissner, *Japanese Industrialization and Its Social Consequences*, Berkeley, 1976, pp. 299-325.

Mitsubishi Shipbuilding Co., Ltd., *Sōgyō 100 Nen No Nagasaki Zōsensho* [One Hundred Years of Operation of the Nagasaki Shipyard], Tokyo, 1951.

Mitsui Bank (ed.), *Mitsui Ginkō 80 Nenshi* [Eighty Year History of the Mitsui Bank], Tokyo, 1957.

Myers, Charles A., *The Role of the Private Sector in Manpower Development*, Baltimore, 1971.

Myers, Charles N., *Education and National Development in Mexico*, Princeton, 1965.

Nagai, Michio, *Higher Education in Japan: Its Take-Off and Crash*, Tokyo, 1971.

Nakayama, Ichirō, *Industrialization of Japan*, Tokyo, 1963.

Nihon Kōgakukai, *Meiji Kōgyōshi* [The History of Meiji Industry], Tokyo, 1925.

————, *Meiji Kōgyōshi Kōgyō Hen* [The Industrial Sector in Meiji Industrial History], Tokyo, 1930.

Nihon Kōkan Co., Ltd., *Nihon Kōkan Kabushiki Kaisha 40 Nenshi* [Forty Year History of the Japan Steel Tube Corporation], Tokyo, 1952.

Nippon Seitetsu Co., Ltd., *Nippon Seitetsu Kabushiki Kaisha Shashi* [Company History of the Japan Steel Corporation], Tokyo, 1959.

Nippon Steel Corporation, *History of Steel in Japan*, Tokyo, 1973.

Nomiyama, Masayuki, "Employment Stablization Fund," *Japan Labor Bulletin*, Vol. 17, No. 1, January 1978, pp. 7-8.

Ohkawa, Kazushi, and Henry Rosovsky, "A Century of Japanese Growth," in William W. Lockwood (ed.), *The State and Economic Enterprise in Japan*, Princeton, 1965, pp. 47-92.

————, *Japanese Economic Growth: Trend Acceleration in the Twentieth Century*, Palo Alto, 1971.

Ōi Works, Japan National Railways, *100 Nenshi* [One Hundred Year History], Tokyo, 1973.

Okamoto, Hideaki (ed.), *Sangyō Kunren 100 Nenshi* [One Hundred Year History of Industrial Training], Tokyo, 1971.

Okamoto, Hideaki, "Vocational Training in Japan," *Japan Labor Bulletin*, Vol. 9, No. 1, June 1970, pp. 4-8.

Okochi, Kazuo, Bernard Karsh, and Solomon B. Levine (eds.), *Workers and Employees in Japan: The Japanese Employment Relations System*, Princeton, 1973.

Okuda, Kenji, "Management Evolution in Japan I: 1911-1925," *Management Japan*, Vol. 5, No. 3, 1971, pp. 14-15; and "Management Evolution in Japan II," *Management Japan*, Vol. 5, No. 4, 1972, pp. 17-20.

————, *Romū Kanri No Nihonteki Tenkai* [The Spread of Japanese-Type Labor Administration], Tokyo, 1972.

Organization for Economic Co-operation and Development, *Educational Policy and Planning: Japan*, Paris, 1973.

————, *Manpower Policy in Japan*, Paris, 1973.

Ōsato Katsuma (ed.), *Honpō Shūyō Keizai Tōkei* [Japanese Basic Economic Statistics], Tokyo, 1966.

Ōuchi Hyoe and Tsuchiya Takao (eds.), *Meiji Zenki Zaisei Keizai Shiryō Shūsei* [Documentary Collection on the Financial Economy of the Early Meiji Period], Volumes 18-20, Tokyo, 1931-1933.

Ōuchi Tsuneo, *Totei Seidō To Gijutsu Kyōiku* [Apprentice System and Technical Education], Tokyo, 1936.

Passin, Herbert, *Society and Education in Japan*, New York, 1965.

Patrick, Hugh T., "Japan, 1868-1914," in Rondo E. Cameron (ed.), *Banking in the Early Stages of Industrialization*, New York, 1967, pp. 329-389.

Patrick, Hugh (ed.), with the assistance of Larry Meissner, *Japanese Industrialization and Its Social Consequences*, Berkeley, 1976.

Reubens, Beatrice G., *Bridges to Work: International Comparisons of Transition Services*, Montclair, N.J., 1977.

Rōdō Undō Shiryō Iinkai, *Nihon Rōdō Undō Shiryō* [Documentary History of the Japanese Labor Movement], Volumes II, X, Tokyo, 1959, 1963.

Rohlen, Thomas P., *For Harmony and Strength: Japanese White-Collar Organization in Anthropological Perspective*, Berkeley, 1974.

Rosovsky, Henry (ed.), *Industrialization in Two Systems*, New York, 1966

Saegusa Hakuo et al., *Kindai Nihon Sangyō Gijutsu No Seiōka* [Westernization of Industrial Technology in Modern Japan], Tokyo, 1960

Sano Yōko, *Nihon Ni Okeru Kagakusha Oyobi Gijutsusha No Suikei*, [Estimates of the Number of Scientists and Engineers in Japan], mimeographed, Tokyo, 1978.

———, *Nihon Ni Okeru Setsuritsu Kikanbetsu Chūtō Oyobi Jun-Chūtō Kōgyō Kyōiku No Suii* [Trends of Established Middle and Quasi-middle Industrial Education Classified by Institutions in Japan], mimeo, Tokyo, 1964.

Saxonhonse, Gary R., "Country Girls and Communication among Competitors in the Japanese Cotton-Spinning Industry," in Hugh Patrick (ed.), with the assistance of Larry Meissner, *Japanese Industrialization and Its Social Consequences*, Berkeley, 1976, pp. 97-125.

Schultz, Theodore W., *The Economic Value of Education*, New York, 1963.

Shively, Donald H. (ed.), *Tradition and Modernization in Japanese Culture*, Princeton, 1971.

Simmons, John (ed.), *Investment in Education for Developing Countries: National Strategy Options*, Proceedings and Papers from a Conference on the Economics of Education, no place, October, 1973.

Sumitomo Bank (ed.), *Sumitomo Ginkō Shi* [History of the Sumitomo Bank], Osaka, 1955.

Sumitomo Steel Corporation, *Sumitomo Kinzoku Kōgyō Gojūnenshi* [Fifty Year History of the Sumitomo Metal Industries], Osaka, 1957.

Sumiya Mikio, *Nihon Chinrōdō Shiron* [Historical Treatise on Wage Labor in Japan], Tokyo, 1955.

——— (ed.), *Nihon Shokugyō Kunren Hattenshi* [History of the Development of Japanese Vocational Training], Volumes I and II, Tokyo, 1971.

——— (ed.), *Shokkō Oyobi Kōfu Chōsa* [Research on Workers and Miners], Tokyo, 1970.

———, *Social Impact of Industrialization in Japan*, Tokyo, 1963.

Swett, Francisco X., "Formal and Nonformal Education in Educational Development: Some Issues Examined," mimeographed Discussion Paper No. 53, Research Program in Economic Development, Woodrow Wilson School, Princeton University, February 1975.

Taira, Koji, *Economic Development and the Labor Market in Japan*, New York, 1970.

——, "Education and Literacy in Meiji Japan: An Interpretation," *Explorations in Economic History*, Vol. 8, No. 4, July 1971, pp. 371-394.

——, "Industrial Revolution and Factory Labor in Japan," *Cambridge Economic History of Europe*, Vol. 7, Part 2, London, 1978, pp. 166-214.

Tōyō Keizai Shinpōsha, *Kaisha Ginkō 80 Nenshi* [Eighty Year History of Bank Companies], Tokyo, 1955.

Tsuchiya Kiyoshi, "Ginkō" ["Banking"], in Arisawa Hiromi (ed.), *Keizai Shūtaisei Kōza* [Comprehensive Discourses on the Economy], Vol. III, Tokyo, 1960, pp. 156-161.

Tsuchiya Takao, *Shibusawa Eiichi Den* [Biography of Shibusawa Eiichi], Tokyo, 1931.

Umetani Noboru, *Oyatoi Gaikokujin* [Foreigners Employed from Abroad], Tokyo, 1965.

——, *The Role of Foreign Employees in the Meiji Era in Japan*, Tokyo, 1971.

Umetani, Shun'ichiro, "Prospects for Japan's Labor Market from 1975 to 1985," *Japan Labor Bulletin*, Vol. 15, No. 1, January 1976, pp. 4-8.

Ward, Robert B. (ed.), *Political Development in Modern Japan*, Princeton, 1968.

Yamaguchi Kazuo (ed.), *Nihon Sangyō 100 Nenshi* [One Hundred Year History of Japanese Industry], Vol. I, Tokyo, 1967.

Yamamura, Kozo, *Economic Policy in Postwar Japan: Growth versus Economic Democracy*, Berkeley, 1967.

——, "The Role of the Samurai in the Development of Modern Banking in Japan," *Journal of Economic History*, Vol. XXVII, No. 2, June 1967, pp. 198-220.

Yamazaki Toshio, *Gijutsushi* [History of Technology], Tokyo, 1961.

Yasuba, Yasukichi, "The Evolution of Dualistic Wage Structure," in Hugh Patrick (ed.), with the assistance of Larry Meissner, *Japanese Industrialization and Its Social Consequences*, Berkeley, 1976, pp. 249-298.

Yokoyama Gennosuke, *Nihon No Kasō Shakai* [The Lower Classes of Japan], Tokyo, 1949.

Index

Library of Congress Cataloging in Publication Data

Levine, Solomon Bernard.
  Human resources in Japanese industrial development.

  Bibliography: p.
  Includes index.
  1. Employees, Training of—Japan.
2. Occupational training—Japan. 3. Vocational
education—Japan. I. Kawada, Hisashi, 1905-1979
joint author. II. Title.
HF5549.5.T7L47   331.3′592′0952   79-19419
ISBN 0-691-03952-6